S0-BZL-587

STRESS AND COPING
ACROSS
DEVELOPMENT

STRESS AND COPING ACROSS DEVELOPMENT

Edited by
TIFFANY M. FIELD
PHILIP M. MCCABE
NEIL SCHNEIDERMAN
University of Miami Medical School

1988

LAWRENCE ERLBAUM ASSOCIATES, PUBLISHERS
Hillsdale, New Jersey   London

Copyright © 1988 by Lawrence Erlbaum Associates, Inc.
All rights reserved. No part of this book may be reproduced in
any form, by photostat, microform, retrieval system, or any other
means, without the prior written permission of the publisher.

Lawrence Erlbaum Associates, Inc., Publishers
365 Broadway
Hillsdale, New Jersey 07642

Library of Congress Cataloging-in-Publication Data
Stress and coping across development.

Based on the annual University of Miami Symposia on Stress and Coping, held Feb. 20–21, 1984.
Includes bibliographies and indexes.

1. Stress (Psychology)—Congresses.   2. Adjustment (Psychology)—Congresses.   3. Developmental psychology—Congresses.   4. Medicine and psychology—Congresses. I.   Field, Tiffany.   II. McCabe, Philip M.   III. Schneiderman, Neil.   IV. University of Miami Symposia on Stress and Coping (2nd: 1984)   [DNLM: 1. Adaptation, Psychological-congresses.
2. Human Development—congresses. 3. Stress, Psychological—congresses.   WM 172 S9127
1984]
BF575.S75S765   1987   155.9   87-24526
ISBN 0-89859-960-1

Printed in the United States of America
10   9   8   7   6   5   4   3   2   1

Contents

Preface

This is the second volume based on the annual University of Miami Symposia on Stress and Coping. These symposia are focused on current research related to developmental, physical, and mental health aspects of stress and coping. The first volume, *Stress and Coping,* provided a general discussion of the concept of stress, an overview of psychophysiological processes involved in stress and coping, and research relating behavioral stresses to the immune response, sleep disorders, depression, and cardiovascular disease. In addition, the volume covered psychosocial aspects of stress and coping involving anger, type A behavior, depression, hardiness and self-consciousness.

The present volume is focused on some representative stresses and coping mechanisms that occur during different stages of development including infancy, childhood, and adulthood. Accordingly, the volume is divided into three sections for those three stages. The first section on infancy includes chapters on maternal deprivation stress, infant feeding, and mother-infant social interactions and how the infant is stressed by these as well as the coping mechanisms available to the young infant. In the opening chapter by Doctors Schanberg and Field, animal literature is first reviewed illustrating that maternal deprivation contributes to marked behavioral and physiological "stress" responses in the offspring ranging from transient changes in body temperature, heart rate, and locomotor activity following short periods of separation to marked growth retardation, developmental delays, and immune dysfunction following more long-term separations. The authors then present data demonstrating that restriction of active tactile stimulation by the mother during maternal separation produces at least three different alterations in biochemical processes involved in the growth and development of rat pups. These included a decrease in ornithine decarboxylase activity, a fall in growth hormone secretion, and a loss of tissue sensitivity to exogenous growth hormone. These alterations were then reversed by providing tactile stimulation that grossly approximated the mother's tongue licking (brush stroking). The second group of studies documented the facilitative effects of tactile-kinesthetic stimulation on the growth and behavioral organization of preterm intensive care neonates and nonorganic failure to thrive infants. A group of intensive care preterm neonates who experienced maternal separation were provided with a tactile-kinesthetic stimulation program. The treated infants averaged 47% more weight gain, were more active, and showed more mature behavior on the neo-natal behavioral assessment scale. The combined demonstrations that tactile stimulation restores normal growth physiology for maternally-deprived rat pups and facilitates weight gain and more mature behavioral organization in separated preterm neonates suggests that similar hormonal and biochemical mechanisms might be involved in these two conditions. The authors suggest that evaluation of sympathoadrenal and adrenocortical function in understimulated and treated pre-term neonates may allow us to distinguish between "stress" and understimula-tion.

In the second chapter entitled "Patterns of infant-feeding, The mother-infant interaction and stress management," Dr. Sue Carter discusses the hypothesis that patterns of infant feeding and related early experiences provide a foundation for stress management. Existing literature suggests that breast-feeding provides an early opportunity for the human infant to obtain both an optimal source of food and some degree of environmental control as well as an opportunity to develop coping skills. The physiological systems that regulate lactation depend on behav-iorally active substances such as dopamine and possibly the endogenous opiates. These same chemicals have been implicated in organismic responses to environ-mental stressors, and lactating females may have attenuated or more efficient stress responses. Carter argues that further research is needed on the relationship between early breast-feeding experiences and later stress management.

In the final chapter of this section Doctors Gianino and Tronick present a system for describing the infant's abilities to cope with stressful interactions and the developmental changes in stability of these abilities. Very young infants are seen to develop strategies for coping with stress during their interactions with people or objects. In addition to the infants' ability to signal both positively and negatively with emotional expressions, infants are able to reject or push away a stressful object, they are able to withdraw from the stressor by turning or arching away and even by losing postural control, and they are able to decrease their perceptual receptivity to these stressful stimuli by "looking without seeing." These skills are employed whenever the flow of the interaction is disrupted by a mismatch. Effectively, in attempting to redirect an interaction which has become distressing, the infant employs his affective displays to signal the partner to change her behavior. When the partner's behavior is changed, the infant's dis-tress is typically alleviated. When interactive stresses are markedly prolonged,

exaggerated, or distorted, as in the depressed mother and still-face mother studies of these authors, the infant is unable to readjust the interaction. This results in
greater negative affect which often compels the infant to use other coping strategies such as self-comforting behavior. In addition, the authors present longitudinal data that suggest individual differences in infant coping styles that stabilize
during early infancy. These three chapters combined suggest the important role
of adequate stimulation during early infancy. Inadequate or inappropriate stimulation is seen as stressful to the infant, but the stressful mismatches in stimulation appear to provide the infant an opportunity to develop coping strategies. If
these early experiences are abnormally stressful or prolonged (as in maternal
depression or early separation) the infant may not develop adequate coping
skills.

The childhood section of this volume features chapters on type A behavior (or
coronary-prone behavior patterns) and coping behaviors in children facing medical stress and children coping with diabetes. In the first chapter of this section
Doctors McCann and Matthews discuss the antecedents of the type A or the
coronary-prone behavior pattern. They first describe how type A can be assessed
in the developing individual, discussing the reliability and validity of available
methods. They then consider the relationship of children's type A behaviors and
related psychophysiological processes to those exhibited by adults. And, finally,
they evaluate familial factors affecting the development of type A behavior.
Because type A behaviors such as competitiveness and impatience-aggression
are noted in adults experiencing coronary heart disease and because there is some
evidence for continuity of these behaviors from childhood to adulthood, the
question of the early antecedents of coronary-prone behaviors is receiving increasing attention. A greater psychophysiologic responsivity among type A
males in these authors' and others' studies suggest that the origins of type A can
be traced to very early childhood. Early familial and genetic factors might play a
critical role in the early development of type A behavior. Data from monozygotic
and dizygotic twins suggest that type A may have an inheritable component as
well as an environmental component. The latter influence has been observed in
parents' modeling of the behavior and in the parents' differential treatment of
type A-B children during stressful tasks, with type A children receiving more
pressure to perform and more positive evaluations of their performance.

Following this overview of the literature on the antecedents of type A behavior, Vega-Lahr and her colleagues present a comprehensive study of type A
behavior in preschool children. In this study type A behaviors were explored in
preschool children using questionnaires, observations, and competitive tasks.
The results suggested that the MYTH is a reliable assessment of type A behavior
in preschool children. Type A ratings of the children's mothers and fathers were
highly correlated as were fathers' ratings of their own type A behavior and that of
their children. Very few differences were noted between type A and type B
children in the freeplay situations except that the type A children were con-

sistently more active than the type B children. This relative absence of behavioral differences between the types suggests that the freeplay, unstructured classroom environment may not possess the necessary characteristics to elicit the salient components of type A behavior. In contrast, competitive situations including an inflatable punching doll, a car race, and a tower building contest elicited differences in type A and B children, with the type A children showing more competitive and impatient-aggressive behavior as well as winning the contest. Thus, as in adults, type A behavior appears to emerge more consistently in competitive situations. Knowing the effects of dyad configuration and degree of uncontrolability in both the behavioral and physiological responses (such as cardiovascular and cortisol activity) in preschool children would help clarify whether precursors of the type A pattern noted in adults can be found in early childhood.

The subsequent chapter entitled "Coping behaviors in children facing medical stress" by Doctors Melamed and Siegel argues for the use of medical settings as a prototype for the study of the development of coping behaviors in children. Theoretical support for this approach is derived from a learning theory model which emphasizes both conditioned fear and observational learning. The existing literature was reviewed and found to be inadequate in predicting vulnerability to anxiety in children facing medical procedures. The authors thus suggested that individual differences of the child be taken into account relative to the task demands as well as the social contexts. A number of parent behaviors including disciplinary styles and anxiety level and child behaviors including the child's attachment to the mother, temperament, age, cognitive and behavioral style were considered for their contributions to the child's coping with medical procedures and the stress of chronic illness. In addition, situational factors such as controllability-predictability, information on procedures and previous experience were considered for their effects on the child's coping style. A multivariate, longitudinal approach to the study of how these variables interact in determining children's individual coping style was recommended. Throughout the chapter the authors use data from their own research on children's coping with medical stress to illustrate the complexity of this problem.

The last chapter in the section on childhood by Dr. LaGrecca is entitled "Children with diabetes and their families: Coping and disease management." In this chapter a model is presented for organizing psychosocial findings on coping and disease management in children and adolescents with diabetes. The psychosocial factors included in this model are diabetes knowledge and management, treatment adherence, stress and psychological functioning. Two major trends emerged in the discussion of this model including the importance of adopting a developmental perspective and a family framework for understanding diabetes management and promoting more effective coping skills in youngsters with diabetes.

The final section on adulthood includes chapters on the physical and psychological problems most frequently studied in the context of adults' coping with stress. These include: predictors of delay behavior among women with breast symptoms, behavioral influences on immune function, the effects of hostility on hormones of heart disease, and preventing relapse following treatment for depression.

The first chapter by Dr. Singer includes a comprehensive review of the literature on breast cancer stress followed by the author's study on the effects of socio-demographic and historical variables, social network variables, psychological variables, health behavior variables, and stressful life event variables as potential predictors of delay behavior among women with breast symptoms. This study revealed that younger women with a prior history of breast symptoms did not delay, although there was a tendency for older women with prior history to delay. Another major finding was that women who knew someone who had breast cancer delayed less often. No relationships were found between psychological variables such as repression-sensitization, monitoring-blunting, and locus of control and the length of delay. Also, no relationships were found between the three health behavior variables—general health concern, knowledge of breast disease, or practice of breast self-examination and length of delay. Finally, no relationships were noted between stressful life events and delay behavior. Thus, the critical variables appeared to be the individual's past exposure to the threat of cancer, either by having a prior history of breast symptoms, or knowing someone who had breast cancer.

In the chapter by Doctors Kiecolt-Glaser and Glaser on behavioral influences on immune function, evidence was provided for the inter play between stress and health. The authors first provide a very articulate background on the functioning of the immune system followed by presentation of immunological evidence supporting the causal relationship between major and minor stressful life events and infectious disease in humans. They present data suggesting that the increase in stress regularly linked with life events is also associated with poorer immune function. Based on these data, they argue that while declines in immune function are very frequent sequelae of certain commonplace life events, factors such as the prior health of the individual (particularly in regard to immune system function) and recent exposure to pathogens are important in determining the actual organic disease outcomes. In addition, their data suggest that psychological resources which reduce stress (e.g., supportive interpersonal relationships) also concurrently attenuate adverse immunological changes.

The following chapter by Dr. Williams is entitled "Is there life after type A: Recent developments in research on coronary-prone behavior." In this chapter the literature on relationships between type A and coronary atherosclerosis (CAD) is critically reviewed and considered flawed for inadequate sample size, inadequate type A assessments, and failing to consider the effects of age. Data are presented suggesting that type A behavior, as manifested on the structured interview, is indeed associated with increased premature CAD severity—i.e., that occurring in younger patients. Williams suggests that "the fact that such well established risk factors as smoking and hyperlipidemia also behave similarly, in both epidemiologic and angiographic studies, increases our confidence that something that is being measured by the structured interview is associated with increased CAD severity."

The chapter by Dr. Dimsdale examines the increased risk of cardiovascular disease among depressed parents. Literature is reviewed suggesting that depressed patients have subtly different sympathetic nervous system activity in basal conditions. Dimsdale argues that depression itself is a type of stress response and since little is known about blood pressure or catecholamine responses in depressed patients under stress, it is important to study dynamic measures of reactivity to stressors. Thus, the chapter first deals with the measurement of cardiovascular reactivity to stressors. Epidemiological evidence is then reviewed concerning the relationship of depression and cardiovascular disease. Finally, Dimsdale reviews psychiatric research on the physiological alterations in depression.

The final chapter in the section on adulthood by Dr. Hollon examines relapse following treatment for depression and the prophylactic consequences of cognitive therapy. Three models of cognitive change during treatment are evaluated; deactivation, accommodation, and compensation. Activation-deactivation, which predicts symptomatic relief but no major change in underlying mechanisms may hold for some patients but cannot account for differential prophylaxis. Accommodation, the preferred explanatory mechanism for most cognitive intervention theorists, would predict both symptom relief and change in underlying mechanisms for therapies producing a prophylactic effect. Compensation, the third model, would predict symptom relief and specific skills acquisition, but no change in causal mechanisms for those same prophylactic therapies. These three models are examined in light of the author's recently completed cognitive-pharmacotherapy project which found clear evidence of relapse prevention following treatment with cognitive therapy.

This, then, is an overview of our second volume on stress and coping. We hope that providing representative research on different stresses and coping mechanisms at different stages of development will stimulate further exploration of stress and coping mechanisms at different stages in the life span.

Acknowledgments

Several individuals, groups and organizations helped make this symposium possible. First, we thank the participants, who gave freely of themselves and helped carry out the symposium on a modest budget. Second, we thank our postdoctoral fellows and graduate students, whose efforts attenuated the stress for all concerned. Third, we thank Ellie Schneiderman for her gracious hospitality. Fourth, we thank Ira Licht and his staff for graciously allowing us to use the aesthetically pleasing surroundings of the Lowe Art Museum for one day of our conference. Fifth, we thank, for their support and encouragement, David L. Wilson, Dean of the College of Arts and Sciences, Herbert C. Quay, Chair of the Department of Psychology, Robert S. Stempfel, Jr., Vice Chair of the Department of Pediatrics and Director of the Mailman Center for Child Development, and Stephen Weiss, Chief of Behavioral Medicine, National Heart, Lung and Blood Institute. We gratefully acknowledge financial support from the University of Miami Graduate Student Association, the College of Arts and Sciences, The Mailman Center for Child Development, the Department of Psychology, and National Heart, Lung, and Blood Training grant HL07426.

T.F.
P.M.
N.S.

INFANCY

1 Maternal Deprivation and Supplemental Stimulation

Saul M. Schanberg
Duke University Medical School

Tiffany M. Field
University of Miami Medical School

Development in mammals is profoundly affected by environmental stimuli. Those stimuli provided by the mother appear to be most critical for survival and growth. Disruption of the mother-infant relationship contributes to marked behavioral and physiological *stress* responses in the offspring ranging from transient changes in body temperature, heart rate, and locomotor activity following short periods of separation, to marked growth retardation, developmental delays, and immune dysfunction following more long-term separations (Field, 1985; Field & Reite, 1984; Harlow & Zimmerman, 1959; Hinde & Spencer-Booth, 1971; Hofer, 1984; Levine & Coe, 1985; Reite, Short, Seiler, & Pauley, 1981; Suomi, Collins, & Harlow, 1976). A number of studies demonstrate that specific sensory cues from the mother induce different physiological and behavioral responses in young animals. For example, nipple attachment in rats is promoted by specific organic substances on the ventral surface of the mother, and thermal input from the mother modulates locomotor activity in weanling-age rat pups, while compounds secreted by the mother's GI tract "orient" pups to the nest (Compton, Koch, & Arnold, 1977; Leon & Moltz, 1971,1972,1973).

More recent studies by our group suggest that mother-pup interactions also have marked effects on biochemical processes in the developing pup (Schanberg, Evoniuk, & Kuhn, 1984). These biochemical processes, like behavior, respond to specific environmental cues suggesting that mother-pup interactions are important regulators of physiological as well as behavioral functions. Sensory stimuli associated with the mother elicit coordinated physiological and biochemical responses which vary with the nature of the stimulus. Whereas some environmental stimuli are important regulators of growth and development, others subserve quite different functions, such as maintaining tissue sensitivity to specific hormones.

Although studies on human infants are less definitive, growth failure and developmental delays are characteristic problems of human infants deprived of stimulation as, for example, the premature neonate and the nonorganic failure-to-thrive infant (reactive attachment disorder). Inadequate stimulation has been implicated as a potential *stressor* and contributor to the delays in both of these groups. Previous attempts to facilitate their growth and development have yielded inconclusive data. However, recent research by our group suggests that supplemental stimulation contributes to weight gain and sleep/wake behavioral organization in these infants (Field, Schanberg, Scafidi, Bauer, Vega-Lahr, Garcia, Nystrom, & Kuhn, 1986; Goldstein & Field, 1985).

The first group of studies we discuss are those demonstrating that active tactile stimulation of preweanling rat pups by the mother provides specific sensory cues that maintain normal growth and development. The data presented demonstrate that restriction of active tactile stimulation by the mother during maternal separation produces at least three different alterations in biochemical processes involved in the growth and development of the rat pups. These alterations can be reversed by providing supplemental stimulation. The second group of studies we review document the facilitative effects of supplemental stimulation on the growth and behavioral organization of preterm intensive care neonates and nonorganic failure to thrive infants.

MATERNAL SEPARATION STRESS, TACTILE STIMULATION, AND GROWTH IN RAT PUPS

Ornithine decarboxylase (ODC), the first enzyme in the synthesis of the polyamines putrescine, spermine, and spermidine, is an important regulator of growth and differentiation that is affected by mother-pup interactions. The end products of this enzyme are intimately involved in the regulation of protein and nucleic acid synthesis (Bachrach, 1973; Raina & Janne, 1970), and activity of this enzyme is thought to be a sensitive index of environmental effects on biochemical and physiological processes in the developing animal. While ODC activity in both neonatal and adult rats responds markedly to various stresses, the pattern of tissue response is determined by the nature of the environmental stimulus, or stress. Separation of preweanling rat pups from the mother (maternal deprivation), is one stress that profoundly affects tissue polyamine systems in developing animals. Maternal deprivation causes an immediate and marked decrease in tissue ODC activity and in tissue putrescine concentration. These changes occur in all tissues that we have studied including brain, liver, heart, kidney, and spleen, and in all brain regions (Fig. 1.1, Table 1.1). ODC activity normalizes soon after rat pups are returned to the mother (Fig. 1.2). This marked effect of maternal deprivation is observed in preweanling pups, from postnatal Days 1 to 18 (Fig. 1.3). It then rapidly disappears over the next few days.

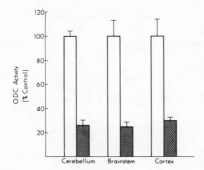

FIG. 1.1. Effect of maternal deprivation on ODC activity in different regions of 10-day-old rat brain. All values are expressed as means ± SEM. All differences are significant $P < 0.05$ or better.

TABLE 1.1
Effect of Maternal Deprivation on ODC Activity
in Organs of 8 Day Old Rats

	Control	N	Deprived	N
Brain	100 ± 10	(5)	48 ± 5[a]	(10)
Heart	100 ± 15	(15)	64 ± 8[a]	(15)
Liver	100 ± 18	(20)	31 ± 3[a]	(20)
Kidney	100 ± 4	(10)	66 ± 11[a]	(10)
Spleen	100 ± 6	(10)	58 ± 8[a]	(10)

Pups were maternally deprived and killed 2 hours later. Results are expressed as percentages of control ± sem.
[a] $p < .05$ or better relative to control.

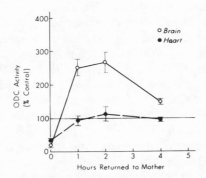

FIG. 1.2. Comparison in 10-day-old rat brain and heart of the recovery of ODC activity after a 2-hr deprivation and return to the mother. All values expressed as means ± SEM. N = 5 in each group. Brain and heart values are significantly below control ($P < 0.05$) at 2 hr. Brain values are significantly above control values at each point after return ($P < 0.05$).

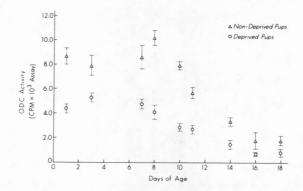

FIG. 1.3. Effect of a 2-hr maternal deprivation on preweanling rat brain ODC activity in pups of different ages. All values are expressed as means ± SEM. N = 5 in each group. All differences significant $P < 0.05$ or better.

The decline in ODC associated with maternal deprivation does not result from a change in body temperature, exposure to an unfamiliar environment, or other nonmaternal stimuli (Butler & Schanberg, 1977). Similarly, interruption of feeding does not mediate the fall in ODC, inasmuch as preweanling rat pups placed with a mother whose nipples have been ligated do not experience a similar decrease of ODC activity in all tissues. The latter demonstration is extremely important, given that feeding is one of the major components of the mother-pup interaction during the first 2 postnatal weeks, with pups feeding an average of every 10 min (Lincoln & Wakerly, 1974). Furthermore, auditory, visual, and olfactory stimulation, which play a role in mother-pup interaction at various times during the development of preweanling rats, do not influence ODC activity (Kuhn & Schanberg, unpublished observations). Apparently those stimulus modalities are not involved in the ODC response of preweanling rats to maternal deprivation. This is not surprising in that both the auditory and visual systems are not functional at birth, but mature during the first 2 to 3 weeks postpartum.

Interruption of active tactile interaction between mother and pup seems to trigger the decline in ODC activity during maternal separation. Placing pups with a mother rat that has been anesthetized (with urethane) to prevent active interaction but not feeding (Lincoln & Wakerly, 1974) changes tissue ODC activity in the same way that separating the pups from the mother alters ODC activity (Table 1.1). This finding is striking, as the decrease in ODC activity occurs despite the presence of many other sensory cues that are passively transferred by the mother (olfactory, gustatory, auditory, tactile, etc.) and actively emitted by the littermates. Furthermore, when deprived pups are given tactile stimulation grossly approximating that of maternal grooming (i.e., paint brush stroking simulating maternal licking motions) ODC activity returns to normal levels in all tissues, although other forms of sensory stimulation of equal intensity are inef-fective (Figs. 1.4 and 1.5). This finding is of particular interest because tactile stimulation appears to be an important stimulus for growth and development in a number of species, including humans (cf. Cornell & Gottfried, 1976; Field, 1980; Schaeffer, Hatcher & Barglow, 1980 for reviews).

The physiologic *signal* which triggers the decline in ODC activity following interruption of maternal-pup interaction is still unknown. The uniform decline in tissue ODC activity throughout the body suggests that some general endocrine or metabolic response to the withdrawal of maternal tactile stimulation mediates this fall. This hypothesis is strengthened by our finding that ODC decreases during maternal deprivation even when innervation of peripheral tissues is not yet functional, or when innervation is blocked pharmacologically with pro-pranolol or atropine (Butler, Suskind, & Schanberg, 1977; Schanberg, un-published observations). ODC activity is such an accurate and sensitive index of cell growth and development that its decline during maternal deprivation could represent a specific biochemical mechanism through which environmental stim-uli affect growth and development.

The change in ODC activity during maternal deprivation suggested that secre-tion of one or more of the many hormonal regulators of ODC was affected by this *stress*. In additional studies, we have shown that maternal deprivation elicits a marked and unusual neuroendocrine response. This response represents the sec-

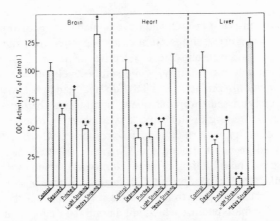

FIG. 1.4. Pups were maternally deprived for 2 hours and either left untouched or stroked heavily, stroked lightly, or pinched as described in Methods and then killed. Controls were left undisturbed with the mother for 2 hours. Results are expressed as percent control ± SEM. Control ODC activity = 0.147, 0.188 and 0.048 nmoles ornithine/g tissue/hour respectively for brain, heart and liver.* = $p < .05$ or better compared to controls.** = $p < .001$ or better compared to controls. n ≥ 15 except pinched and light stroking n ≥ 8.

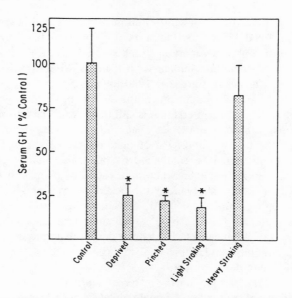

FIG. 1.5. Pups were maternally deprived and stimulated as described
in Fig. 1. Results are expressed as percent control ± SEM. Control
serum GH = 54 ng/ml.* = $p < .002$ or better compared to controls. n
≥ 15 except pinched and light stroking n ≥ 10.

ond mechanism controlling growth and development that is disrupted by maternal deprivation. When preweanling rat pups are separated from the mother, there
is an increase in corticosterone and a selective decrease in growth hormone
secretion from the anterior pituitary, while serum levels of other stress-respon-
sive hormones including prolactin and TSH do not change if nutrition and other
aspects of the environment are controlled, minimizing disruptive conditions.
This selective decrease in growth hormone is somewhat unique as *stress* almost
always elicits a complex pattern of endocrine responses which in the rat usually
involves decreased growth hormone and TSH and increased corticosterone and
prolactin secretion. The inhibition of growth hormone secretion during maternal
deprivation could affect development significantly over a prolonged period of
deprivation, as circulating growth hormone is responsible for the generation of
substances called somatomedins, which are among the major regulators of muscle and possibly organ growth.

Growth hormone is a well-known regulator of ODC activity in brain as well as
in peripheral tissues (Roger, Schanberg, & Fellows, 1974). Therefore, the
finding that growth hormone secretion decreased during maternal deprivation
provided a possible explanation for the fall in tissue ODC activity. To investigate
this possibility, we injected pups with ovine growth hormone during the separation procedure to reverse the decrease in ODC activity. Rather than restoring

TABLE 1.2
Effect of Hormones on Liver ODC Activity
in Maternally Deprived Rat Pups

Drug	Dose (μg)	ODC Activity (1% Control)			
		Control	N	Deprived	N
Vehicle		100 ± 22	(60)	11 ± 3[b]	(60)
0Growth Hormone	100	437 ± 136[a]	(20)	11 ± 2[ab]	(20)
0Placental Lactogen	100	315 ± 54[a]	(10)	10 ± 1[ab]	(10)
Dexamethasone	200	366 ± 62[a]	(10)	532 ± 51[a]	(10)
Dibutyryl cAmp	800	518 ± 172[a]	(10)	539 ± 183[a]	(10)
PGE-1	50	510 ± 66[a]	(10)	620 ± 213[a]	(10)
Insulin	10	1306 ± 422[a]	(15)	2040 ± 594[a]	(15)

Pups were maternally deprived for 2 hours, injected SC with vehicle or
hormone, and killed 4 hours later. Results expressed as percentage of
control ± sem. control ODC activity was 37 nCi/30 min/g tissue.

[a] $p < 0.05$ or better relative to vehicle treated control.
[b] $p < 0.001$ relative to paired control.

ODC activity to normal levels, as predicted, we found that tissue ODC was
completely and selectively unresponsive to growth hormone during maternal
deprivation. Growth hormone was unable to induce ODC activity in liver or
brain of deprived rats, although a number of other hormones including cyclic
AMP, insulin, and the glucocorticoid hormone dexamethasone still would induce
ODC activity normally (Tables 1.2, 1.3). This selective loss of tissue response to
growth hormone represents the third major defect in growth-regulating processes
that is disrupted by maternal deprivation.

These three effects of maternal deprivation (decrease in tissue ODC activity,
fall in growth hormone secretion, and loss of tissue sensitivity to exogenous
growth hormone) appear to be regulated by the same sensory stimulus: active

TABLE 1.3
Effect of Hormones on Brain ODC Activity
in Maternally Deprived Rat Pups

	Control	N	Deprived	N
Vehicle	100 ± 16	(10)	59 ± 5[a]	(10)
GH 100 μg	166 ± 7[a]	(10)	67 ± 9[ab]	(10)
Camp	413 ± 39[a]	(10)	352 ± 53[a]	(10)

Pups were maternally deprived for 2 hours, injected intra-
cisternally with saline, GH or cAMP, returned to the deprivation cages and killed 4 hours later. Control pups left
with the mother were injected at the same time. Results
are expressed as % control ± sem. Control ODC activity was
40 nCi/30 min/g tissue.

[a] $p < .01$ or less relative to vehicle-treated control.
[b] $p < .001$ relative to GH-injected control.

TABLE 1.4
Liver Response to GH Following Return to Mother

	ODC Activity (% Control)	N
Control	100 ± 25	(10)
Control + Growth Hormone	597 ± 132[a]	(10)
Deprived	39 ± 5[a]	(10)
Deprived + Growth Hormone	25 ± 3	(10)
Returned to Mother	203 ± 54	(10)
Returned to Mother + Growth Hormone	982 ± 186[a]	(10)

Pups were maternally deprived for 2 hours and killed or returned to the mother. Two hours after return pups were injected SC with vehicle or GH (100μg). Liver ODC activity was determined 4 hours after hormone administration. Results are expressed as percentage of control ± Sem. Control ODC activity was 40 nCi/30 min/g.
[a] $p < 0.001$ relative to control.

tactile stimulation by the mother. Therefore, placing the pups with a urethane-anesthetized mother to eliminate maternal tactile stimulation of the pups, while maintaining food intake, effects a decrease in ODC activity in organ tissue, and decreases in serum growth hormone and in liver ODC response to exogenous growth hormone (Table 1.4). In contrast, tactile stimulation (brush stroking) of maternally deprived rat pups returns all three parameters to normal (Figs. 1.4, 1.5, Tables 1.4, 1.5).

These studies of the biochemical basis of growth retardation of maternally deprived rats have significant clinical implications for the conditions called non-organic failure-to-thrive or "reactive attachment disorder" and "psychosocial dwarfism." Psychosocial dwarfism is a retardation of growth and behavioral development in children that shows a startling similarity to the animal model we

TABLE 1.5
Response of Liver ODC to GH in Pups with an Anesthetized Mother

	ODC Activity (% Control)	N
Control	100 ± 11	(20)
Control + Growth Hormone	1087 ± 144[a]	(20)
Pups with Anesthetized Mother + Vehicle	38 ± 4[a]	(20)
Pups with Anesthetized Mother + Growth Hormone	41 ± 6[ab]	(20)

Pups were placed with a urethane-anesthetized mother for 2 hours, injected SC with vehicle or growth hormone (100 μg) and killed 4 hours later. Results expressed as % control ± Sem. Control activity = 10 nCi/30 min/g.
[a] $p < .001$ relative to control.
[b] $p < .001$ relative to GH.

have just described, as it is characterized by a selective disruption of growth hormone secretion, a suppression of growth in the presence of normal nutrition, and a selective loss of tissue responsivity to growth hormone (Powell, Brasel, & Blizzard, 1967; Powell, Brasel, Raiti, & Blizzard, 1967). This condition is thought to result from a withdrawal of loving care by the mother or other caregiver, which disappears when the child is placed in a *normal* home environment (Casler, 1961). Although it is not possible to equate a rat model with human maternal behavior, the similarities in the physiological responses of human infants and rat pups to disruption of maternal-infant interactions suggest a common phenomenon and a biochemical mechanism mediating their clinical disorder. The second goal of our joint investigation was to explore the possible application of these animal studies to clinical situations which seem to share a common behavioral etiology.

EFFECTS OF SUPPLEMENTAL STIMULATION
ON PREMATURE NEONATES

A number of researchers have investigated the effects of supplemental stimulation on the development of preterm, low-birthweight infants. A large number of studies employing supplemental tactile and kinesthetic stimulation (Barnard, 1973; Barnard & Bee, 1983; Freedman, Boverman, & Freedman, 1966; Hasselmeyer, 1964; Rausch, 1981; Scott, Cole, Lucas, & Richards, 1983; Solkoff & Matuszak, 1975; Solkoff, Yaffe, Weintraub, & Blase, 1969; White & LaBarba, 1976) have demonstrated superior growth and development of the stimulated infants. In a study by Solkoff et al., (1969), for example, stroking stimulation was provided for preterm infants, and the handled infants were more active, regained their initial birthweights more rapidly, and were described as physically healthier in growth and motor development than the controls. Similarly, Solkoff and Matuszak (1975) reported that low-birthweight infants who were given supplemental stimulation had better body tone and head control, were more consolable and alert, changed states more frequently, and responded to noxious stimuli more quickly than the controls. However, there were no group differences in weight gain. In contrast, a group of higher birthweight (M = 1900 gms) preterm infants provided both tactile and kinesthetic stimulation (White & LaBarba, 1976) consumed more formula and gained weight more rapidly than a control group. Using a similar tactile/kinesthetic stimulation procedure, Rausch (1981) noted only a trend in weight gain. However, her preterm infants were smaller and of lesser gestational age than those of the White and LaBarba (1976) study, and they received fewer treatment sessions. Thus, although most of these studies reported superior development for the stimulated infants, not all of the findings have been consistent, and most of the findings are based on small samples.

One of the most inconsistent findings in these infant stimulation studies involves weight gain. Some studies reported no differences between treatment and control groups on weight gain (Barnard, 1973; Freedman et al., 1966; Hasselmeyer, 1964; Solkoff & Matuszak, 1975), while others have reported a more rapid or greater weight gain for the treatment group (Rausch, 1981; Scott et al., 1983; White & LaBarba, 1976). Activity level is another contradictory finding. Some have noted that infants receiving tactile/kinesthetic stimulation were more active than control infants (Scott et al., 1983; Solkoff & Matuszak, 1975; Solkoff et al., 1969). In contrast, Hasselmeyer (1964) reported that handled infants were less active, and Barnard (1973) found no differences in the amount of waking activity of treatment and control infants. These discrepancies may relate to variability within and between the samples studied on variables such as obstetric complications, weight and gestational age of the neonates, postnatal complications, and the amount of intensive care treatment. (See Cornell & Gottfried [1976], and Field [1980] for reviews). It is conceivable that neonates who have experienced intrauterine growth deprivation, a lower birthweight or gestational age, more severe postnatal complications, and a longer period of intensive care treatment may benefit less from supplemental stimulation for a variety of reasons. These include possible stimulation stress-related decreases in growth hormone release, higher thresholds to stimulation (Field et al., 1982; Rose, Schmidt, & Bridger, 1976), greater vulnerability to extra stimulation-related stress (Long, Alistair, Philip, & Lucey, 1980) and conditioned associations between invasive stimulation received in the ICU and noninvasive forms of tactile/kinesthetic stimulation (Bendell & McCaffree, 1984). Factors such as these, for example, may explain the significant weight gain reported by White and LaBarba (1976) and the marginal weight gain noted by Rausch (1981), the latter having assessed lesser birthweight and lower gestational age infants who had experienced longer intensive care treatment.

Another possible reason for the discrepancies in these studies relates to the type of stimulation provided. Again, using the White and LaBarba (1976) and Rausch (1981) studies as examples, the former investigators used a form of stimulation, i.e., body stroking with their hands, which might be considered more calming than the finger stroking provided by Rausch. Although mothers, in their first contacts with their newborns, are noted to engage in both palm and finger stroking, palm stroking occurs more frequently (Gewirtz, Hollenbeck, & Sebris, 1979). Finger stroking may be experienced as a *tickling* and thus more arousing form of stimulation. In addition, different measures have been used for assessing activity level and behavioral states, with most studies having employed rather gross measures of these behaviors. Finally, the discrepant findings may relate to variability in activity level/weight gain relationships. In at least two of the studies reporting greater weight gain in the stimulated infants, the infants' activity level was notably greater in the treatment versus the control infants (Scott et al., 1983; Solkoff et al., 1969). In contrast, no significant weight gain was reported in the studies in which activity level was diminished (Hasselmeyer,

1964) or similar to that of control infants (Barnard, 1973). It is conceivable that the increased activity level had derived from extra stimulation, which in turn affected weight gain. Intuitively, it seems that greater activity would lead to greater expenditure of energy and attenuated weight gain (Bernbaum, Perreira, Watkins, & Peckham, 1983; Field et al., 1982). However, some controlled manipulations of activity level in rats suggest that increased activity contributes to weight gain by increased metabolic efficiency (Mittelman & Valenstein, 1984). Exercise or increased activity is also noted to increase growth hormone release in humans which may mediate weight gain (VanWyk & Underwood. 1978).

We have recently conducted a study to investigate this complex problem of the underlying mechanisms for those growth and behavioral gains reported in neonates receiving extra tactile/kinesthetic stimulation (Field et al., 1986). In this study 20 preterm neonates (Table 1.6) were provided tactile/kinesthetic stimulation and were compared to a control group of equivalent gestational age, birthweight, and duration of intensive care. The neonates were recruited for the study at the time they entered the transitional care unit (''grower'' nursery). The treatment group was provided tactile/kinesthetic stimulation for three 15-minute periods during 3 consecutive hours per day for a 10-day period. Each stimulation session was comprised of three 5-minute phases. During the first and third phase (tactile stimulation) the neonate, in a prone position, was given body stroking for five 1-minute segments covering the head and face region, neck and shoulders,

TABLE 1.6
Means for Baseline Neonatal Measures (and Standard Deviations)

Measures[a]	Groups	
	Stimulation	Control
Gestational age (wks)	31(2.2)	31(2.8)
Birthweight (gms)	1280(249)	1268(199)
Birthlength (cms)	39(2.9)	39(3.8)
Ponderal index	2.2(.3)	2.2(.3)
Head circumference at birth (cms)	28(2.1)	27(2.1)
Apgar (1 min)	5.9(1.8)	5.8(2.2)
Apgar (5 min)	7.8(1.0	7.7(1.6)
Obstetric complications score	87(17.1)	86(13.6)
Postnatal complications score (NICU)	79(20.5)	76(18.3)
# NICU days	20(4.5)	20(4.0)
Weight at onset stimulation period	1393(114)	1385(131)
Postnatal Complications score (transitional nursery)	142(27.9)	138(30.7)

[a]None of the t tests of these measures yielded significant group differences.

TABLE 1.7
Means (and Standard Deviations) for Measures Differentiating
Tactile/Kinesthetic Stimulation Preterm Neonates from Controls

Measures	Groups Stimulation	Control	p Level
Feedings (#) per day	8.6(1.3)	9.0(1.3)	N.S.
Formula (ccs/kg/day)	171(8.5)	166(17.5)	N.S.
Calories/kg/day	114(5.7)	112(12.2)	N.S.
Calories/day	169(11.2)	165(27.1)	N.S.
Daily weight gain (grams)	25(6.0)	17(6.7)	.0005
% Time awake	16(15.5)	7(10.7)	.04
% Time movement	32(5.6)	25(6.2)	.04
Braselton scores			
Habituation	6.1(.6)	4.9(.5)	.02
Orientation	4.8(.9)	4.0(1.0)	.02
Motor	4.7(.7)	4.2(.7)	.03
Range of State	4.6(.8)	3.9(1.0)	.03

the back, legs and arms. The middle phase (kinesthetic stimulation) involved gentle flexing of the infants' limbs in a supine position.

In addition to the recording of daily clinical data including formula intake and weight gain, the neonates were given the Brazelton Neonatal Behavior Assessment Scale, and their sleep/wake behavior was monitored at the end of the 10-day treatment period. Sleep-wake behavior observations were conducted over a 45-minute period by a trained observer using a 10-second time sample unit methodology coding sleep states including no-REM sleep, active sleep without REM, REM sleep, drowsy, alert inactivity, alert activity and crying (Thoman, 1975). In addition to coding behavioral states, the observer recorded single limb movements, multiple limb movements, gross body movements, facial expressions, smiling, mouthing, twitching, startles and head-turning.

Data analyses revealed the following (Table 1.7):

1. The treated infants averaged 47% more weight gain per day than the control infants even though the groups did not differ on number of feedings per day or average formula intake (volume or calories) prior to or during the treatment period. The mean daily weight gain for the treatment and control groups during the stimulation period is shown in Fig. 1.6. A significant repeated measures effect indicated that the linear increase in daily weight was significant, and a treatment/control group by days interaction effect revealed a greater increase in daily weight for the treatment group. A histogram of the distribution of treatment and control infants based on their daily weight gain is illustrated in Fig. 1.7.

2. The treatment infants were awake (drowsy or alert inactivity) and active a greater percentage of time during the sleep/wake behavioral observations.

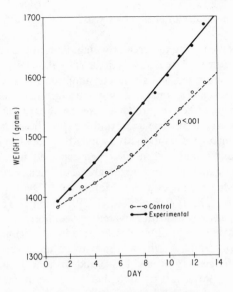

FIG. 1.6. Mean weight per day.

3. The treatment infants, as assessed by the Brazelton scale, showed more mature habituation, orientation, motor, and range of state behavior.

4. The treatment infants were hostpitalized 6 days less than the control infants after the onset of the treatment period, yielding an average hospital cost savings of $3000 per infant.

These data suggest that very small, preterm neonates experiencing maternal separation can benefit from tactile/kinesthetic stimulation administered during their stay in the transitional care nursery. This form of stimulation appears to contribute to greater weight gain, motor activity, alertness and performance on the Brazelton scale. The greater weight gain, motor activity, and alertness in these neonates are consistent with supplemental stimulation data on preterm

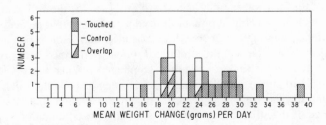

FIG. 1.7. Frequency distribution of neonates by mean weight change per day. Overlap signifies one subject from each group.

neonates who did not require intensive care (Solkoff & Matuszak, 1975; White & LaBarba, 1976).

The mechanisms mediating the greater weight gain of the stimulated neonates cannot be determined from these data. As in the animal model, food intake was not a significant factor inasmuch as caloric consumption did not differ in the two groups. Furthermore, caloric intake was not a significant factor when tactile stimulation of rat pups effectively reversed maternal deprivation associated decreases in growth hormone release and ornithine decarboxylase activity (Schanberg et al., 1984). Increased motor activity may be related to the greater weight gain of the treatment infants, as it has been reported that increased activity contributes to weight gain via increased metabolic efficiency in rats (Mittleman & Valenstein, 1984; Musacchia, Deavers, Meininger & Davies, 1980) and in humans (Torun, Schutz, Viteri, & Bradfield, 1979; Young & Torun, 1981). Also, increased activity is associated with elevated growth hormone release in humans (VanWyk & Underwood, 1978). Furthermore, inadequate stimulation appeared to contribute to the diminished activity and growth failure noted in our maternally deprived rat pups (Schanberg et al., 1984) and in nonorganic failure to thrive infants (Powell et al., 1967). It is possible that these conditions may share similar underlying physiological mechanisms. Continuous recording of sleep/wake behavior and activity level, neuroendocrine measures and metabolic efficiency assessments would provide more definitive data on the relationships between stimulation, motor activity and weight gain.

The treatment neonates also showed better performance on the Brazelton scale, specifically in the areas of habituation, orientation, motor, and range of state behaviors. The greater alertness and motor activity of the treatment infants in general may have contributed to their more organized behavior on the Brazelton assessment. Better performance in these areas may facilitate early parent-infant interactions which in turn may affect the later development of preterm infants (Field, Dempsey, & Shuman, 1983). Finally, a 6-day shorter hospital stay (yielding cost savings of approximately $3000 per treatment infant) suggests that this would be a cost effective intervention for small preterm neonates during maternal separation.

The positive effects of this stimulation appear to persist for at least the first 8 months of development. In a preliminary analysis of the 8-month developmental follow-up data for a subsample of this group (N = 25) the following emerged (Table 1.8): (1) the treatment infants showed a greater weight percentile than the control infants, although their length and head circumference percentiles were not significantly greater; (2) the stimulated infants performed better on the Bayley mental and motor scales; (3) fewer stimulated infants were noted to have neurological soft signs; and (4) compliance or attendance at the follow-up clinic was greater for the treatment group. The greater weight and developmental performance of the stimulated infants at 8 months poststimulation suggests that this neonatal stimulation may have persistent effects on growth and development of preterm infants.

TABLE 1.8
Means for Eight-Month Follow-Up Data

Measures	Groups Stimulation	Control	p Level
Weight percentile	48	33	.05
Length percentile	35	31	N.S.
Head circumference percentile	44	40	N.S.
Bayley mental scale score	101	89	.05
Bayley motor scale score	105	90	.05
# Infants with neurological soft signs	1	6	.05
# Infants missing visits	1	5	.05

WEIGHT GAIN AND RESPONSIVITY TO STIMULATION IN NONORGANIC FAILURE-TO-THRIVE INFANTS

Another clinical situation showing considerable overlap with our animal model is the syndrome, "nonorganic failure-to-thrive," generally defined as growth retardation with no clear organic etiology, and frequently attributed to inadequate maternal stimulation (Powell et al., 1967). One of the reasons nonorganic failure-to-thrive has been labeled the "maternal deprivation syndrome" or "reactive attachment disorder" is that the infant's growth retardation is often reversed during hospitalization when the infant is (reputedly) provided more adequate stimulation than that routinely received in the home environment. Pathological disturbances in sleeping, eating, elimination, auto-erotic and self-harming behaviors frequently noted in these infants (Bithoney & Rathbun, 1983; Pollitt & Eichler, 1976; Powell et al., 1967) typically disappear during hospitalization, especially the problems of food intake and weight gain. This association had led some investigators to hypothesize the existence of a "physiologic pathway whereby emotional deprivation affects the neuroendocrine system regulating growth" (Powell et al., 1967).

At least one study has documented relationships between behavioral change and growth gains in NOFT (Rosenn, Loeb, & Jura, 1980). In this study, Rosenn et al. compared normal, organic, and nonorganic failure-to-thrive infants and noted that the nonorganic infants initially preferred distal social stimulation and play with inanimate objects as opposed to proximal stimulation such as touching, cuddling, and face-to-face interaction. After a week of hospitalization they shifted to a preference for proximal stimulation. Interestingly, in those infants who gained weight during the first week or two of hospitalization, the most substantial weight gain occurred within 1-to-2-days after the shift to a preference for proximal tactile stimulation. Paradoxically, this effect was not associated with increased caloric consumption. Because the assessments of the infants' responsivity to stimulation were conducted several times daily over the course of the infants' hospitalization, the stimulation associated with the assessments may have served as a form of intervention facilitating weight gain. However, the relationships between stimulation, responsivity to stimulation, activity level, sleep behavior, and weight gain in these infants remain obscure.

In an attempt to understand the relationships between weight gain and responsivity to stimulation in nonorganic failure-to-thrive infants, we monitored the hospital course of nonorganic failure-to-thrive, organic failure-to-thrive, and control infants (Goldstein & Field, 1985). Daily weight gain was recorded, and the infants' responsivity to distal and proximal stimulation was assessed at the beginning, middle, and end of the infants' hospitalization using the Behavioral Assessment Scale (Rosenn et al., 1980). Data analyses revealed that responsivity to touching at the initial assessment was negatively correlated with weight gain at the final assessment, but responsivity to touching stimulation at the middle assessment was related to weight gain at the final assessment. Thus, it appeared that positive responses to tactile stimulation at the initial assessment were related to weight loss, while positive responses to the same tactile stimulation at the middle assessment were related to weight gain. These unexpected findings coupled with a bimodal distribution of weight gain (with 70% of the infants gaining weight and 30% losing weight across hospitalization) lead to a comparison between infants who gained and infants who lost weight. An increase in responsivity to touching and other forms of stimulation occurred only for the infants who gained weight.

Paradoxically, the infants who lost weight had come from better home environments than those that gained weight. It is conceivable that the infants who lost weight may have had undetected organic problems that worsened from inadequate treatment. Alternatively, the losers may have experienced hospital stimulation as less adequate than maternal stimulation (a stimulation deprivation experience), while the gainers may have experienced hospital stimulation as more adequate than home stimulation. Unfortunately, in the absence of growth hormone and cortisol data, these complex relationships are difficult to understand. However, at the very least, these data, in contrast to those of Rosenn et al. (1980), who showed general improvement in responsivity to stimulation and weight gain across hospitalization, suggest that the stimulation associated with the daily, multiple assessments provided by Rosenn et al. (1980) may have contributed to the weight gain and increased responsivity of their nonorganic failure-to-thrive infants. In fact, these findings suggest that growth and developmental change may require more stimulation than the routine care provided in our hospital setting and the minimal stimulation associated with our infrequent assessment procedure.

We are currently piloting the use of tactile/kinesthetic stimulation (as described earlier) with these hospitalized nonorganic failure-to-thrive infants. To date, three nonorganic failure-to-thrive infants have been provided this stimulation. Although the data are only suggestive, the average daily weight gain of the stimulated infants was greater than the control infants of the Goldstein & Field (1985) study (39 vs. 16 grams), and their hospital stay was 6 days shorter (10 days versus 16 days) than the control infants. Thus, it would appear that this tactile/kinesthetic stimulation may also have positive effects on the growth rates of nonorganic failure to thrive infants.

DISCUSSION

In summary, data from animal studies (Coe, Mendoza, Smotherman, & Levine, 1978; Hofer, 1984), as well as research on an animal model developed by our group (Schanberg et al., 1984) suggest that the early interruption of mother-infant interaction has significant, specific biochemical and physiological consequences in mammalian species. We have shown that ornithine decarboxylase (ODC), a sensitive index of tissue growth and differentiation, is decreased markedly in most vital organs of rat pups that have been separated from the mother (maternally deprived pups). This decrease is triggered specifically by the loss of tactile stimulation from the mother, not by the absence of sensory cues from littermates, passive stimuli from the mother, or nutritional deprivation (Butler et al., 1977; Schanberg et al., 1984). The decrease in ODC is accompanied by a decrease in growth hormone (GH) secretion as well as a loss of tissue sensitivity to exogenous growth hormone (Kuhn, Evoniuk, & Schanberg, 1979; Schanberg & Kuhn, 1985). Only a specific type and pattern of tactile stimulation (brush strokes mimicking the mother's licking pattern), was adequate for reinstating the normal function of these processes (Evoniuk, Kuhn, & Schanberg, 1979).

These findings of impaired growth physiology in maternally deprived rat pups are consistent with clinical findings of impaired growth hormone secretion and tissue responsivity to growth hormone in nonorganic failure-to-thrive children (maternal deprivation syndrome, reactive attachment disorder, and psychosocial dwarfism). It has been reported that even when nonorganic failure-to-thrive children are well fed, they fail to secrete growth hormone normally in response to administration of insulin or arginine, have lowered serum levels of the growth hormone-dependent peptide somatomedin C and are resistant to exogenous growth hormone (D'Ercole, Underwood, & VanWyk, 1977; Frasier & Rallison, 1972; Powell et al., 1967; Rayner & Rudd, 1973). Similarly, we have shown that separated rat pups fail to release GH normally following pharmacologic challenge with 5-hydroxytryptophan (Schanberg & Kuhn, 1985). As with the rat pup paradigm, drug-induced GH release often returns to normal in nonorganic failure-to-thrive or psychosocial dwarfism children when they are provided more adequate stimulation during hospitalization (Powell, Brasel, & Blizzard, 1967; Powell, Hopwood & Barratt, 1973).

The combined demonstrations that patterned tactile stimulation restores normal growth physiology in maternally deprived rat pups and facilitates weight gain and more mature behavioral organization in preterm neonates suggests that similar hormonal and biochemical mechanisms might be involved in these two conditions. While tactile stimulation may be essential for normal growth in preterm neonates, the specific form of stimulation that facilitates growth in older nonorganic failure-to-thrive infants has not been established. Our animal studies show that tactile stimulation alone is sufficient to restore the biochemical changes associated with maternal deprivation in 8-day-old rat pups that cannot hear, see, or make accurate olfactory discriminations. However, in older rat pups that can see and hear, tactile stimulation only partially mediates the biochemical responses to mother-pup separation (Schanberg & Kuhn, 1985).

As reviewed above, significant disturbance of growth hormone secretion is the major endocrine finding in nonorganic failure to thrive children and in our animal model of maternal deprivation. In these children, evoked GH secretion and serum somatomedin C levels are suppressed, and in maternally deprived rat pups, basal GH secretion and 5-hydroxytryptophan-evoked GH secretion are suppressed (D'Ercole et al., 1972; Kuhn, Butler, & Schanberg, 1978; Powell, Brasel, Raiti, & Blizzard, 1967). The absence of evoked GH secretion that improves simply with hospitalization could prove to be diagnostic for the nonorganic failure-to-thrive syndrome.

The two clinical populations we are studying, preterm neonates and nonorganic failure-to-thrive, may share a common problem of understimulation, and may show an associated impaired GH secretion. It is well known that serum GH levels are quite high in premature neonates, as compared to term neonates, and that they remain high for up to 2 months after birth (Cornblath, Parker, Reisner, Forbes, & Doughaday, 1965; Reitano, Grasso, Distefano, & Messina, 1971). Although our hypothesis suggests that these levels will increase with stimulation, an alternative possibility is that elevated basal levels in preterm neonates may reflect *stress,* and supplemental stimulation may actually lower basal GH levels. A final possibility is suggested by the work of Stubbe and Wolfe (1971), who reported that stress decreases GH in infants (see also Table 1.9 preliminary data on preterm neonates' growth hormone decreases following the stress of Brazelton assessments). This response contrasts with the frequently documented increase in GH secretion elicited by stress in older children and adults. Although decreased GH secretion with stress in infants has not been studied systematically, if this does occur, observed decreases in GH secretion during our stimulation would have to be interpreted quite differently.

Evaluation of sympathoadrenal and adrenocortical functions would allow us to distinguish between stress or stress-reduction mediated decreases in GH secretion associated with stimulation. A number of studies have shown that *stressed* premature infants have high levels of catecholamines and cortisol, and that improvement in physiologic status is correlated with a decrease in these parameters (Fiselier, Monnens, Moerman, Munster, Jansen, & Peer, 1983; Gunnar, Malone, & Fish, 1985; Lagercrantz & Bistoletti, 1977; Lagercrantz, Bistoletti,

TABLE 1.9

Preliminary Data on Preterm Neonates' Baseline Growth
Hormone and Growth Hormone Samples Taken Within 2
Hours Following Brazelton Assessments

| | Plasma Level of GH (ng/ml) | | |
Newborn	Baseline Samples	Brazelton	Δ
1	26.0 (27,25)	19.0	-7.0
2	20.0 (20,20)	12.0	-8.0
3	29.5 (31,28)	14.0	-15.5
4	19.5 (18,21)	9.0	-10.5
5	19.0 (17,21)	9.0	-9.0
6	25.0 (31,19)	19.0	-6.0
7	13.5 (12,15)	13.0	-0.5
8	19.5 (25,14)	19.0	-0.5
			-7.1
			S.E.±1.8
			$p < .02$

& Nylund, 1981; Nakai & Yamada, 1983). However, these studies focused on severe stresses such as respiratory distress, venipuncture, and circumcision.

There are virtually no studies on the effects of supplemental stimulation on endocrine status in preterm neonates. Coe, Levine, and their colleagues have reported that infant monkeys show a marked secretion of cortisol when separated from their mothers (Coe et al., 1978; Coe & Levine, 1981; Coe, Mendoza, Davidson, Smith, Dallman, & Levine, 1978; Coe, Wiener, & Levine, 1983). This adrenocortical response to mother-infant separation is also accompanied by a marked sympathoadrenal activation (Breese et al., 1973). Interestingly, in nonorganic failure-to-thrive children, the only other significant endocrine finding was a suppression, not a stimulation, of hypothalamohypophyseal-adrenal function as measured by basal 17-OHCS and 17-OHCS response to metyrapone (Powell et al., 1967). Therefore, evaluation of sympathoadrenal and adrenocortical function in understimulated and treated preterm neonates and NOFT infants may allow us to distinguish between *stress* and understimulation, as well as provide critical new information concerning the physiologic responses of infants to supplemental stimulation.

REFERENCES

Bachrach, U. (1973). *Function of naturally occurring polyamines.* New York: Academic Press.

Barnard, K. E. (1973). The effect of stimulation on the sleep behavior of the premature infant. *Communicating Nursing Research, 6,* 12–40.

Barnard, K. E., & Bee, H. L. (1983). The impact of temporally patterned stimulation on the development of preterm infants. *Child Development, 54*, 1156–1167.

Bendell, D., & McAffree, M. (1984). *Aversive procedures in the neonate.* Unpublished manuscript. University of Oklahoma Health Sciences Center.

Bernbaum, J., Perreira, G. R., Watkins, J. B., & Peckham, E. J. (1983). Nonnutritive sucking during gavage feeding enhances growth and maturation in premature infants. *Pediatrics, 71*, 41–45.

Bithoney, W. G., & Rathbun, J. M. (1983). Failure to thrive. In M. D. Levine, W. B. Carey, A. C. Crocker, & R. T. Gross (Eds.), *Developmental-behavioral pediatrics* (pp. 557–572). Philadelphia: W. B. Saunders.

Breese, G. R., Smith, R. D., Mueller, R. A., Howard, J. L., Prange, A. J., Lipton, M. A., Young, L. D., McKinney, W. T., & Lewis, J. K. (1973). Induction of adrenal catecholamine synthesizing enzymes following mother-infant separation. *Nature, 246*, 94–96.

Butler, S. R., & Schanberg, S. M. (1977). Effect of maternal deprivation on polyamine metabolism in pre-weanling rat brain and heart. *Life Science, 21*, 877–884.

Butler, S. R., Suskind, M. R., & Schanberg, S. M. (1977). Maternal behavior as a regulator of polyamine biosynthesis in brain and heart of the developing rat pup. *Science, 199*, 445–446.

Casler, L. (1961). Maternal deprivation a critical review of the literature. *Monographs for Research in Child Development, 26*, No. 2. New York: Child Development Publications.

Coe, C. L., & Levine, S. (1981). Normal responses to mother-infant separation in non-human primates. In D. F. Kline & J. G. Rabkin (Eds.), *Anxiety: New research and changing concepts* (pp. 155–177). New York: Raven Press.

Coe, C. L., Mendoza, S. P., Davidson, J. M., Smith, E. R., Dallman, M. F., & Levine, S. (1978). Hormonal response to stress in the squirrel monkey (Saimiri sciureus). *Neuroendocrinology, 26*, 367–377.

Coe, C. L., Mendoza, S. P., Smotherman, W. P., & Levine, S. (1978). Mother-infant attachment in the squirrel monkey: adrenal response to separation. *Behavior Biology, 22*, 256–263.

Coe, C. L., Wiener, S. G., & Levine, S. (1983). Psychoendocrine responses of mother and infant monkeys to disturbance and separation. In L. A. Rosenblum & H. Moltz (Eds.), *Symbiosis in parent-offspring interactions* (pp. 189–214). New York: Plenum Press.

Compton, R. P., Koch, M. D., & Arnold, W. J. (1977). Effect of maternal odor on the cardiac rate of maternally separated infant rats. *Physiological Behavior, 18*, 769–773.

Cornblath, M., Parker, M. L., Reisner, S. H., Forbes, A. E., & Doughaday, W. H. (1965). Secretion and metabolism of growth hormone in premature and full-term infants. *Journal of Clinical Endocrinology, 25*, 209–218.

Cornell, E. M., & Gottfried, A. W. (1976). Intervention with premature human infants. *Child Development, 47*, 32–39.

D'Ercole, A. J., Underwood, L. E., & VanWyk, J. J. (1977). Serum somatomedin-C in hypopituitarism and in other disorders of growth. *Journal of Pediatrics, 90*, 375–381.

Evoniuk, G. E., Kuhn, C. M., & Schanberg, S. M. (1979). The effect of tactile stimulation on serum growth hormone and tissue ornithine decarboxylase activity during maternal deprivation in rat pups. *Communications in Psychopharmacology, 3*, 363–370.

Field, T. (1980). Supplemental stimulation of preterm neonates. *Early Human Development, 4*(3), 301–314.

Field, T. (1985). Affective responses to separation. In T. B. Brazelton & M. W. Yogman (Eds.), *Affective development in infancy.* Norwood, NJ: Ablex.

Field, T., Dempsey, J., & Shuman, H. H. (1983). Five-year follow-up of preterm respiratory distress syndrome and postterm postmaturity syndrome infants. In T. Field & A. Sostek (Eds.), *Infants born at risk: Physiological, perceptual and cognitive processes.* New York: Grune & Stratton.

Field, T., Ignatoff, E., Stringer, S., Brennan, J., Greenberg, R., Widmayer, S., & Anderson, G. (1982). Nonnutritive sucking during tube feedings: Effects on preterm neonates in an ICU. *Pediatrics, 70,* 381–384.

Field, T., & Reite, M. (1984). Children's responses to separation from mother during the birth of another child. *Child Development, 55,* 1308–1316.

Field, T., Schanberg, S. M., Scafidi, F., Bauer, C. R., Vega-Lahr, N., Garcia, R., Nystrom, J., & Kuhn, C. M. (1986). Tactile/kinesthetic stimulation effects on preterm neonates. *Pediatrics, 77,* 654–658.

Fiselier, T., Monnens, L., Moerman, E., Munster, P. van, Jansen, M., & Peer, P. (1983). Influence of the stress of venepuncture on basal levels of plasma renin activity in infants and children. *International Journal of Pediatric Nephrology, 4,* 181–185.

Frasier, S. D., & Rallison, M. L. (1972). Growth retardation and emotional deprivation: Relative resistance to treatment with human growth hormone. *Journal of Pediatrics, 80,* 603–609.

Freedman, D. G., Boverman, H., & Freedman, N. (1966). *Effects of kinesthetic stimulation on weight gain and smiling in premature infants.* Paper presented at the meeting of the American Orthopsychiatric Association, San Francisco.

Gewirtz, J. L., Hollenbeck, A. R., & Sebris, S. L. (April, 1979). *Mother-infant contact following vaginal delivery.* Paper presented at the biennial meeting of the Society for Research in Child Development, San Francisco.

Goldstein, S., & Field, T. (1985). Affective behavior and weight changes among hospitalized failure-to-thrive infants. *Infant Mental Health Journal, 6,* 187–194.

Gunnar, M. R., Malone, S., & Fish, R. D. (1985). Psychobiology of Stress and Coping in the Human Neonate: Studies of Adrenocortical Activity in Response to Stress. In T. Field, P. M. McCabe, & N. Schneiderman (Eds.), *Stress and Coping.* Hillsdale, NJ: Lawrence Erlbaum Associates.

Harlow, H. F., & Zimmerman, R. R. (1959). Affectional responses in the infant monkey, *Science, 130,* 421–432.

Hasselmeyer, E. G. (1964). The premature neonate's response to handling. *American Nurses' Association, 11,* 15–24.

Hinde, R. A., & Spencer-Booth, Y. (1971). Effects of brief separation from mother on rhesus monkeys. *Science, 173,* 111–118.

Hofer, M. A. (1984). Relationships as regulators. A psychobiologic perspective on bereavement. *Psychosomatic Medicine, 46,* 183–197.

Kuhn, C. M., Butler, S. R., & Schanberg, S. M. (1978). Selective depression of serum growth hormone during maternal deprivation in rat pups. *Science, 201,* 1034–1036.

Kuhn, C. M., Evoniuk, G. E., & Schanberg, S. M. (1979). Loss of tissue sensitivity to growth hormone during maternal deprivation in rats. *Life Science, 25,* 2089–2097.

Lagercrantz, H., & Bistoletti, P. (1977). Catecholamine release in the newborn infant at birth. *Pediatric Research, 11,* 889–893.

Lagercrantz, H., Bistoletti, P., & Nylund, L. (1981). Sympathoadrenal activity in the fetus during delivery and at birth. In L. Stern, B. Salle, & B. Friis-Hansen (Eds.), *Intensive care in the newborn III.* New York: Masson Publications.

Leon, M., & Moltz, H. (1971). Maternal pheromone: Discrimination by preweanling albino rats. *Physiological Behavior, 7,* 265–267.

Leon, M., & Moltz, H. (1972). The development of the pheromonal bond in the albino rat. *Physiological Behavior, 8,* 683–686.

Leon, M., & Moltz, H. (1973). Endocrine control of maternal pheromone in the postpartum female rat. *Physiological Behavior, 10,* 65–67.

Levine, S., & Coe, C. L. (1985). The use and abuse of cortisol as a measure of stress. In T. Field, P. McCabe, & N. Schneiderman (Eds.), *Stress and Coping.* Hillsdale, NJ: Lawrence Erlbaum Associates.

Lincoln, L. W., & Wakerly, J. B. (1974). Electrophysiological evidence for the activation supraoptic neurones during the release of oxytocin. *Journal of Physiology, 242,* 533–554.

Long, J. G., Alistair, G. S., Philip, M. B., & Lucey, J. F. (1980). Excessive handling as a cause of hypoxemia. *Pediatrics, 65,* 203–207.

Mittleman, G., & Valenstein, E. S. (1984). Ingestive behavior evoked by hypotholamic stimulation and schedule-induced polydipsia are related. *Science, 27,* 415–417.

Mussachia, X. J., Deavers, D. R., Meininger, G. A., & Davies, T. P. (1980). A model for hypokinesia: Effects on muscle atrophy in the rat. *Journal of Applied Psychology, 48,* 479–485.

Nakai, T., & Yamada, R. (1983). Urinary catecholamine excretion by various age groups with special reference to clinical value of measuring catecholamines in newborns. *Pediatric Research, 17,* 456–460.

Pollitt, R., & Eichler, A. (1976). Behavioral disturbances among failure to thrive children. *American Journal of Diseases of Children, 130,* 24–29.

Powell, G. F., Brasel, J. A., & Blizzard, R. M. (1967). Emotional deprivation and growth retardation simulating idiopathic hypopituitarism. Clinical evaluation of the syndrome. *New England Journal of Medicine, 276,* 1271–78.

Powell, G. F., Brasel, J. A., Raiti, S., & Blizzard, R. M. (1967). Emotional deprivation and growth retardation simulating idiopathic hypopituitarism. II. Endocrinologic evaluation of the syndrome. *New England Journal of Medicine, 276,* 1279–1283.

Powell, G. F., Hopwood, N. J., & Barratt, E. S. (1973). Growth hormone studies before and during catch-up growth in a child with emotional deprivation and short stature. *Journal of Clinical Endocrinology and Metabolism, 37,* 674–679.

Raina, A., & Janne, J. (1970). Polyamines and the accumulation of RNA in mammalian systems. *Federation Proceedings, 29,* 1568–1574.

Rausch, P. B. (1981). Effects of tactile and kinesthetic stimulation on premature infants. *Journal of Obstetric, Gynecological and Neonatal Nursing, 10,* 34–37.

Rayner, P. H. W., & Rudd, B. T. (1973). Emotional deprivation in three siblings associated with functional growth hormone deficiency. *Australian Paediatrics Journal, 9,* 79–84.

Reitano, G., Grasso, S., Distefano, G., & Messina, A. (1971). The serum insulin and growth hormone response to arginine and to arginine with glucose in the premature infant. *Journal of Clinical Endocrinology,* 58–66.

Reite, M., Short, R., Seiler, C., & Pauley, J. D. (1981). Attachment, loss and depression. *Journal of Child Psychology and Psychiatry, 22,* 141–169.

Roger, L. J., Schanberg, S. M., & Fellows, R. E. (1974). Growth and lactogenic hormone stimulation of ornithine decarboxylase in neonatal rat brain. *Endocrinology, 95,* 904–911.

Rose, S. A., Schmidt, K., & Bridger, W. M. (1976). Cardiac and behavioral responsivity to tactile stimulation in premature and full-term infants. *Developmental Psychology, 12,* 311–320.

Rosenn, D. W., Loeb, L. S., & Jura, M. B. (1980). Differentiation of organic from non-organic failure to thrive syndrome in infancy. *Pediatrics, 66,* 698–704.

Schaeffer, H., Hatcher, R. P., & Barglow, P. D. (1980). Prematurity and infant stimulation: A review of research. *Child Psychiatry and Human Development, 10.* 199–212.

Schanberg, S. M., Evoniuk, G., & Kuhn, C. M. (1984). Tactile and nutritional aspects of maternal care: Specific regulators of neuroendocrine function and cellular development. *Proceedings of the Society for Experimental Biology and Medicine , 175,* 135–146.

Schanberg, S., & Kuhn, C. (1985). *Suppression of growth hormone release by S-HPT in maternally deprived rat pups. Unpublished manuscript, Duke University.*

Scott, S., Cole, T., Lucas, P., & Richards, M. (1983). *Weight gain and movement patterns of very low birthweight babies nursed on lambswool. The Lancet,* October 1014–1016.

Solkoff, N., & Matuszak, D. (1975). Tactile stimulation and behavioral development among low-birthweight infants. *Child Psychiatry and Human Development, 6,* 33–37.

Solkoff, N., Yaffe, S., Weintraub, D., & Blase, B. (1969). Effects of handling on the subsequent development of premature infants. Developmental Psychology, 4, 6, 765–768.

Stubbe, P., & Wolf, H. (1971). The effect of stress on growth hormone, glucose and glycerol levels in newborn infants. *Hormones and Metabolic Research, 3,* 175–179.

Suomi, S. J., Collins, H. L., & Harlow, H. F. (1976). Effects of maternal and peer separations on young monkeys. *Journal Child Psychology and Psychiatry, 17,* 101–112.

Thoman, E. B. (1975). Sleep and wake behaviors in neonates: Consistencies and consequences. *Merrill-Palmer Quarterly, 21,* 295–314.

Torun, B., Schutz, Y., Viteri, F., & Bradfield, R. B. (1979). Growth, body composition and heart rate/VO_2 relationship changes during the nutritional recovery of children with two different physical activity levels. *Bibliotheca Nutritoet Dieta, 27,* 55–56.

VanWyk, J. J., & Underwood, L. E. (1978). Growth hormone, somatomedins and growth failure. *Hospital Practice, 68,* 57–67.

White, J. L., & La Barba, R. C. (1976). The effects of tactile and kinesthetic stimulation on neonatal development in the premature infant. *Psychosomatic Medicine, 9,* 569–577B.

Young, V. R., & Torun, B. (1981). Physical activity: Impact on protein and amino acid metabolism and implications for nutritional requirements. *Nutrition in Health and Disease and International Development.* Symposia from the XII International Congress of Nutrition, New York: Alan R. Liss.

2 Patterns of Infant Feeding, the Mother-Infant Interaction and Stress Management

C. Sue Carter
University of Maryland

Feeding behavior and the concomitant mother-infant interactions form core experiences in an infant's early life. This paper discusses the hypothesis that patterns of infant feeding and related early experiences provide a foundation for stress management. Breastfeeding, by the nature of the process, virtually guarantees appropriate mother-infant interactions. It is possible that breast-feeding may provide both infants (Table 2.1) and their mothers (Table 2.2) with other behavioral and physiological advantages that are only now becoming apparent.

Among child care specialists and educated parents it is generally accepted that breastfeeding is both *good* and natural. In spite of this acceptance there remains controversy, at least within the American medical community, regarding the importance of breastfeeding. When breastfed infants are compared to bottle-fed

TABLE 2.1
Functions of Nursing:
The Infant's Perspective

Nutrition
Immunities
Growth modulation
Protection
Temperature regulation
Birth spacing
Access to mother
Emotional development
Intellectual development?
Stress management

TABLE 2.2
Functions of Nursing:
The Mother's Perspective

Reproduction and genetic immortality
Contraception and birth spacing
Temperature and weight regulation
Stress management
Emotional satisfaction

infants under otherwise optimal environmental circumstances, most, but not all studies indicate significant advantages for the breastfed populations. It is rare for populations of formula-fed infants to outperform those that are breastfed (Kovar, Seidula, Marks, & Fraser, 1984).

There is growing evidence that frequent and/or nocturnal breastfeeding may have powerful physiological consequences for the mother, providing both enhanced milk production and ovulatory suppression. Based on these and other observations, hypotheses are discussed regarding the functional significance of various patterns of breastfeeding for both the mother and the infant.

NUTRITION, IMMUNITIES AND BREAST FEEDING

Viable alternatives to breastfeeding are recent and the history of formula feeding has been reviewed by Jelliffe and Jelliffe (1978), Lawrence (1980) and Minchin (1985). Nutritionists agree that human breast milk is a superior form of food for human infants. Milk composition is species specific and human milk may contain a variety of unrecognized but important components. Formulas have been developed which attempt to incorporate the essential nutritional elements found in human milk. Most of the widely used infant formulas are based on cow's milk and there is increasing concern that ingestion of cow's milk-based products or other inadequacies of formulas may present unforeseen health risks to the human newborn (Minchin, 1985). For example, it has been shown that the ingestion of whole cow's milk within the 1st year of life is associated with gastrointestinal bleeding, iron deficiency anemia, and food allergies (Foucard, 1985; Oski, 1985).

In addition, to the possible hazards of substances in formulas, the bottle-fed infant may also suffer from the absence of protective factors present in human breast secretions. The mucosal barrier of the digestive system of the human newborn matures after birth and is initially very vulnerable to penetration by disease causing substances (Hanson et al., 1985). Substances capable of causing potentially dangerous diseases such as gastrointestinal allergy, necrotizing enterocolitis, sepsis, and hepatitis can invade the body through the digestive tract. However, as stated by Walker (1985):

> Fortunately, 'nature' has provided a means for passively protecting the 'vulnerable' newborn against the dangers of a deficient intestinal defense system, namely human milk. It is now increasingly apparent that human milk contains not only antibodies and viable leukocytes but many other substances that can interfere with bacterial colonization and prevent antigen penetration. (p.167)

There are many anti-infective properties associated with human milk (Jelliffe & Jelliffe, 1978; Lawrence, 1980). Among the cellular components of human colostrum and milk are macrophages and lymphocytes. Macrophages and related phagocytic cells in breast milk may ingest and alter antigens. Both T- and B-lymphocytes are present in human milk and colostrum and are particularly concentrated on the first days following delivery. Immunoglobulins. including secretory IgA, are produced by the lymphocytes. Secretory IgA is resistent to digestion and may provide local intestinal protection against infections which could otherwise invade the body through the intestinal mucosa. Human infants do not initially secrete IgA and IgA levels in cow's milk are low; therefore, the breastfed infant may benefit from the protection of IgA and related immunoglobulins. Among the other protective compounds found in human milk are the bifidus factor, lactoferrin, lysozyme, and interferon. These and other agents in human breast secretions play roles in the development of the bacterial flora of the intestine and protect the infant against pathogenic bacteria and other harmful agents. There is also evidence from animal research suggesting that bacteria present in the mouth of the suckling infant may enter the mother's breast and can rapidly stimulate immunological responses on her part; substances produced by the mother in turn may be passed back to the infant confering immunity (Jelliffe & Jelliffe, 1978).

The health benefits associated with breastfeeding are most apparent in populations for which general sanitation, nutrition, and medical care are inadequate (Jason, Nieburg, & Marks, 1984). However, even in studies conducted under more optimal conditions there are reports that rates of illness are lower in breastfed infants. For example, Chandra (1979) studied prospectively the incidence of illness in Canadian children from families with a history of allergies. In formula-fed infants versus breastfed infants respiratory infections were twice as common, diarrhea occurred three times more commonly and ear infections (otitis) were more than nine times as likely to occur. In another study of a comparable population Chandra (1979) also observed much higher levels of eczema, recurrent wheezing, and other in vitro correlates of allergy in formula-fed versus breastfed infants. Fergusson, Horwood, Shannon et al. (1978) differentiated among various categories of infant feeding practices including totally breastfed, partially breastfed with supplements, and bottle-fed from birth. Medical consultations for gastrointestinal illnesses in the first 4 months of life were highest in bottle-fed babies (16.4%) and lowest in breastfed infants (4.5%).

Growth modulators are found in human milk and colostrum. Human milk is the most potent known source of epidermal growth factor and this substance is not found in cow's milk. Epidermal growth factor may play an important role in the development of the intestinal mucosa and could contribute to the development of the digestive system. Nerve growth factor, which influences the development of sensory and sympathetic nerves, is found in high concentrations in human milk. Taurine, an amino acid which has been implicated in rapid cellular growth and neural development, is concentrated at high levels in human milk. At least 70 different enzymes have been identified in human milk and presumably others remain to be identified (Gaull, Wright, & Isaacs, 1985). In addition, human milk is a dynamic substance constantly modified to meet the changing nutritional demands of the infant. The composition of milk fluctuates as a function of the length of pregnancy, stage of lactation, and time of day. There are even differences in milk obtained in the early versus later part of a single feeding or from the right versus left breast (Hamosh, Bitman, Wood, Hamosh, & Menta, 1985). Commercial attempts to precisely duplicate human milk have not been and are unlikely to be successful.

THE BIOLOGY OF LACTATION

In order to understand the significance of behavioral events in the mother-infant interaction it is important to have a knowledge of the physiology underlying the induction and maintenance of milk production (reviewed Jelliffe & Jelliffe, 1978; Lawrence, 1980; Neville & Neifert, 1983). The hormonal events of pregnancy, including placental hormones, prime the breasts and endocrine system. The initial secretory products of the breast (colostrum) differ in composition from milk. Actual milk production begins within approximately 2 to 3 days postpartum.

In general milk production depends on the presence of breast stimulation, most typically provided by suckling by an infant (Short, 1984; Fig. 2.1). Neural pathways from the nipple stimulate the brain (hypothalamus), resulting (at least in animal-studies) in an increased release in beta-endorphins (endogenous opiates) and a decline in the synthesis of a brain hormone/neurotransmitter known as dopamine (Short, personal communication). A decline in dopamine signals the anterior pituitary to increase the secretion of prolactin. (Dopamine is considered to be a prolactin-inhibiting factor). Prolactin enters the blood stream and acts on hormone primed breast tissue to maintain milk production. In general

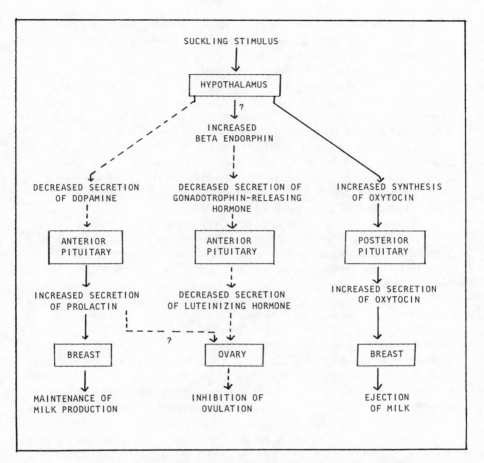

FIG. 2.1. Hormonal effects of breast feeding are set in motion by the stimulus of suckling. Here some of the hormones made by the hypothalamus and the pituitary gland are identified. When the effect of a hormone is to stimulate or increase a process, the effect is represented by a solid arrow. The inhibition of a hormone or a process is represented by a broken arrow. Since the secretion of prolactin by the pituitary is normally inhibited by the secretion of dopamine by the hypothalamus, lowering the level of dopamine increases the secretion of prolactin. Oxytocin is synthesized by the hypothalamus and passed down nerve fibers to the posterior pituitary gland from which it is released into the circulatory system of the body, aiding the ejection of milk. (From Short, 1984).

milk production will continue as long as frequent suckling stimuli are provided.

Stimuli from the infant are also capable of regulating the ejection of breast milk (known as "milk let-down"). Hypothalamic stimulation, provided by suckling, the sight or smell of the infant, the infant's cry or even thinking about the infant may trigger neural events leading to the increased synthesis of and release of oxytocin from the posterior pituitary into the general circulation. Blood-borne oxytocin in turn reaches the breast tissue where it acts on the myoepithelial cells to cause contraction and milk ejection (Neville & Neifert, 1983).

Both milk production and ejection can be influenced by stimuli in addition to those provided by the infant. The milk let-down reflex is particularly susceptible to inhibition in the presence of stress. Distraction, anxiety, or fear may inhibit milk let-down, possibly in part due to physiological effects on the breast. Stress induced vasoconstriction, mediated by the sympathetic nervous system, apparently inhibits the access of oxytocin to the myoepithelium of the breast.

Stress or anxiety may also reduce milk production. Dopamine levels must decrease to permit prolactin release. Stress or related phenomena may directly prevent dopamine levels from declining and, thus, can prevent prolactin levels from increasing.

Various events associated with modern birthing and child care customs may contribute to the inhibition of lactation. The effects of maternal disturbance on milk availability were documented by Newton and Newton (1967, 1968) who found that undisturbed infants received approximately 168 grams of milk per feeding. When mothers were distracted or stressed by receiving a saline injection the amount of milk obtained was only 99 grams. In contrast, if the mother received an oxytocin injection the apparent effects of the injection procedure were prevented (presumably by the added oxytocin) and 153 grams of milk were obtained by the infants. Based on anecdotal evidence from nursing women it appears that anything that limits suckling or increases maternal anxiety may potentially inhibit lactation. However, controlled studies of the role of emotional factors in lactation are rare (Neville & Neifert 1983).

Women who are lactating probably are not totally at the mercy of their environment, and may have an enhanced ability to deal with stress and anxiety. Wiesenfeld, Malatesta, Whitman, Grannose, & Vile (1985) found physiological indications that breastfeeding mothers are more relaxed than women who are bottle feeding. Both skin conductance and heart rate patterns showed higher levels of sympathetic arousal in nonlactating women. Adler, Cook, Davidson, West, and Bancroft (1986) also found indications of more positive moods in nursing versus bottle-feeding mothers. In rats it has been reported that lactation suppresses pituitary and adrenocortical activity and aggression in response to the stress of ether, surgical trauma, and electric shock (Smotherman, Weiner, Mendoza, & Levine, 1976, Stern, Goldman, & Levine, 1973, Thoman, Conner, & Levine, 1970).

NURSING PATTERNS, MILK PRODUCTION AND THE MOTHER-INFANT INTERACTION.

Many educated women, at least in Westernized cultures, now elect to breastfeed. In one large survey taken in the United States it was found that the incidence of breastfeeding while in the hospital more than doubled from less than 25% in 1971 to about 55% in 1980 (Martinez, Dodd, & Samartgedes, 1981). However, by 3- to 6-months postpartum less than half of the mothers that chose to breast-feed were in fact still nursing their children. Among those women that elected to breastfeed many stopped earlier than planned. The most commonly given reason for discontinuing breastfeeding is "insufficient milk" (Ellis & Hewat, 1984, Gussler & Briesemeister, 1980). It has been suggested (Salariya, Easton, & Cater, 1980) that insufficient milk may be given as a reason for stopping breast-feeding by three basic groups of women: (1) those who lack information, (2) those who do not desire to breastfeed and/or who are inhibited physiologically by anxiety, social pressure, etc. and (3) those who are lactating, but need a socially acceptable reason for stopping the feeding.

To insure adequate lactation nursing bouts must be frequent and closely spaced. Carvalho, Robertson, Friedman, & Klaus (1983) found that by day 15 postpartum the infants of women who were instructed to nurse their babies frequently (approximately 10 times per day versus 7.3 times per day in a control group) were receiving more milk (725 versus 502 milliliter/ 24 hours) and had gained more weight (561 versus 347 grams) than infants from the control group. In another study (Salariya et al., 1980) it was observed that mothers who were instructed to nurse at 2 hour intervals had an earlier onset of milk production (by at least 24 hours) than did women who were breastfeeding at 4 hour intervals. Some of the women in this study were also asked to nurse their infants immediately after delivery (within 10 minutes versus 4 to 6 hours). Women from this early initiation of nursing group continued to breastfeed their babies for a longer period of time (i.e., weaned the infants later) than those in the later onset group.

Infrequent or widely spaced nursing bouts are associated with the development of real or perceived cases of "insufficient milk." Insufficient milk, may arise from a conflict between the biological demands of lactation and culturally determined patterns of child care. For example, in the Kung bushmen (hunter-gathers from Africa) nursing bouts are very frequent (as often as 4 times per hour) and closely spaced (averaging about 13 minutes between bouts) and con-tinue at night (Konner & Worthman, 1980). In our own culture, even "on-demand" feeding is usually much less frequent than this.

It has been argued that man evolved in a hunter-gather society and that our physiology maintains features selected for by these evolutionary pressures (Kon-ner, 1972). Bowlby (1969) and Blurton Jones (1972) have suggested, based on the anthropological literature, that humans are adapted to have relatively continuous contact with their young infants. Further evidence in favor of the continuous contact hypothesis comes from the nutritional characteristics of human milk (low protein and fat). In addition, human infants are notoriously vocal if separated from the mother and/or a food source for prolonged periods of time; in mammalian species that cache, rather than carry, their young for extended periods these traits are not common (Murray, 1979).

In a complex urban society, the mother-infant dyad may be physically separated for a variety of reasons and nursing bouts are typically much less frequent than those observed in primitive cultures. Cultural patterns, including time schedules, modern clothing, strollers and cribs, and inhibitions regarding nursing in public may reduce the mother-infant interactions.

Gussler and Briesemeister (1980) have summarized some of factors that can lead to insufficient milk. Mothers, who are typically unaware of the physiology of lactation, may attempt to schedule the baby's feeding times (often encouraged by hospital feeding patterns). Such attempts in conjunction with culturally suggested prohibitions on frequent daily or nocturnal feeding of the infant tend to inhibit milk production. The mother also may feel anxious about many things, including her own ability to supply the nutritional needs of the infant; stress or anxiety in turn, regardless of its source, can also contribute to a reduction in milk output. Concurrently, the infant may cry or fuss, creating further anxiety on the part of the mother, plus an increased need for food and possibly suckling difficulties on the part of the baby. If the mother responds to this situation by providing a supplemental bottle (or possibly even a pacifier) the suckling attempts of the infant at the breast may be reduced. It is probably not uncommon for a scenario such as this to develop into a true "insufficient milk syndrome." The mother's milk production is further reduced and if formula or other food is available the baby may wean itself.

NOCTURNAL NURSING AND SLEEPING
THROUGH THE NIGHT

There seems to be little doubt that nursing frequency plays a critical role in lactational success. Therefore, the informed mother will typically elect some form of on-demand feeding pattern, at least until lactation is well established.

At variance with truly on-demand feeding is another somewhat subtle but pervasive demand, at least in Western society. One of the most recurrent questions asked of new parents is "are you sleeping through the night?" This question may first be posed while the mother is still in the hospital (where routine procedures generally guarantee that no one sleeps through the night), and tends to be brought up by concerned friends and relatives over a period of several months or until the parents are able to answer affirmatively. In general it appears that babies that adopt the practice of sleeping for long periods of time are considered desirable and parents in possession of such children are to be congratulated. Practices such as supplementally feeding the infant just before bedtime, encouraging the father to give the baby a bottle at night or simply ignoring the infant if it cries at night are sometimes recommended.

Murray (1979) makes an excellent case for the hypothesis that infant crying is an "adaptive species-characteristic behavior that evolved as an emergency signal" which serves to "release parental behavior." Night-crying in particular seems to be resistant to modification (Blurton Jones, Rossetti Ferreira, Farquar Brown, & Macdonald, 1978). Nonetheless, Western cultural patterns of child care (including the reasonable desire to further involve the father in infant care, the placement of infants in separate beds and nurseries), in conjunction with the demands placed on working parents favor the development of "sleeping through the night" as a cultural norm.

In spite of its culturally determined advantages, sleeping through the night, at least in the absence of nocturnal nursing, may be at variance with our biological heritage. Nocturnal nursing may have particularly powerful physiological consequences for the mother. Prolactin, an essential hormone in lactation, has a circadian pattern of release and prolactin levels are highest at night (Sassin, Frantz, Weitzman, & Kapen, 1972). The contraceptive effects of nursing are most powerful if the nursing continues at night as well as in the day (Howie & McNeilly, 1982). Nocturnal nursing is a particularly important determinant of the length of suppression of menstrual cycles if it occurs in the later stages of lactation and after solid foods have been introduced. Women who nurse at night and delay supplemental feedings may postpone the resumption of menstrual cycles by 6 to 10 months in comparison to women who supplement early and/or reduce night nursing (Elias, Teas, Johnston, & Bora, 1986).

The mechanisms through which nocturnal nursing influences menstrual cycles are not known, however, Glasier, Howie, and McNeilly (1984) observed a larger suckling-induced surge of prolactin in feeds that occurred after, rather than before, mid-day. (This effect was observed in spite of the fact that the volume of milk taken by the baby was apparently constant throughout the day, indirectly indicating that the intensity of the infant's suckling did not differ in this study according to the time of feeding.) Pulses of luteinizing hormone (LH) from the pituitary, necessary for menstrual cyclicity and ovulation, are suppressed by nursing. When menstrual cycles resume following birth, surges of LH initially begin only at night (Yen, cited in Short, 1983).

In rats nocturnal nursing alone suppress the resumption of ovarian cycles (Gibber & Terkel, submitted). Also, in rats there is evidence to suggest that all successful nursing occurs when the mother is in deep (slow-wave) sleep. The mother rat sits down over her pups, they attach and she rapidly falls asleep. Only when she is in a deep sleep state does milk ejection actually occur (Voloschin & Tramezzani, 1979) and it is milk let-down which initiates sucking by the pups. Although, it is not necessary for human mothers to be asleep for milk ejection, as stated above, distractions can inhibit milk let-down. Human mothers and their infants can both be asleep while participating in the nursing process.

At present there do not appear to be any studies of the direct behavioral effects of nocturnal nursing on the mother or infant, but there is ample evidence that the hormones of the menstrual cycle can affect virtually every aspect of female physiology including the brain and its behavioral functions (Adler et al., 1986). There is one brief report that prolactin levels in cycling women are correlated with the percentage of paradoxical (rapid eye movement) sleep and with an increased "sleep efficiency index" (Petre-Quadens, 1979). The nature of this increase in sleep efficiency was not described, however, this report suggests the possibility that nursing women may be physiologically adapted to the demands of attending to an infant during the night.

It is likely that there are at least indirect behavioral consequences to the early postpartum resumption of menstrual cycles. Postpartum depression, or other less obvious hormonally related behavioral changes (such as fatigue in the presence of nocturnal attention to a child), might be influenced by lactation and associated endocrine events. Human responses may be analogous to those reported in rats (Smotherman et al., 1976; Thoman et al., 1970) and women who are lactating are apparently more insensitive to stress than nonlactating women (Wiesenfeld et al., 1985).

From the infant's perspective the presence of a parent at night could have immediate consequences for survival. Prior to modern housing and clothing a baby left alone at night for a prolonged period of time was likely to be a dead baby.

The nursing patterns of human infants can directly inhibit ovulation (Elias et al., 1986; Howie, McNeilly, Houston, Cook, & Boyle, 1982). Even without other methods of contraception, childbirth can be spaced at 3 or 4 year intervals in cultures with intensive nursing patterns (Konner & Worthman, 1980). Thus an infant that can effectively block her mother's ovulation, may assure herself of additional parental investments of time and resources. In other words, babies which, through any available means can reduce sibling competition may enhance their own survival. By demanding nocturnal nursing human infants can increase their access to their mother during a time of day when they may be particularly vulnerable; concurrently nocturnal nursing may enhance the mother's milk production and suppress her reproductive cycles.

BEHAVIORAL CONSEQUENCES OF BREASTFEEDING

Breastfeeding and associated phenomena may confer a number of benefits to both participants (Klaus & Kennell, 1982). The earliest sequelae of the decision to breastfeed might include an earlier onset of the mother-infant interaction.

It is becoming increasingly common for mothers to be encouraged to touch and nurse their infants immediately following delivery. A recent study of preterm neonates (Field, Schanberg, Scafidi, Bauer, Vega-Lahr, Garcia, Nystrom, & Kuhn, 1986) observed that tactile/ kinesthetic stimulation, for as little as three, 15-minute periods per day for 10 days, was associated with enhanced growth. When stimulated babies were compared to infants that were not stimulated, they had a 47% greater weight gain, other indications of more rapid maturation, and reduced durations of hospitalizations. Schanberg, Evoniuk, and Kuhn (1984) have demonstrated in rats that tactile stimulation is uniquely capable of enhancing metabolic growth processes. Infant rats deprived of touch showed, within a matter of hours, rapid reductions in growth hormone secretion and declines in other processes related to cellular growth.

Primate research, begun in the 1950s (Harlow, 1958), drew attention to the importance of physical contact and touch as an important modality (although not the only important sensory system) in the development of attachments. These studies also provided early documentation for the concept that the parent-infant attachment was based on more than a simple association between the mother and feeding. Nonetheless, feeding and physical contact are dominant behaviors in the mammalian mother-infant interaction, occupying a large proportion of the time in the newborn period. Therefore, the quality of the feeding experience may be of considerable practical significance.

Klaus and Kennell (1970, 1982) have argued that the initial mother-infant interactions can be uniquely important in developing an attachment or bonding between the mother and baby. In a recent survey of the effects of early mother-infant contact Klaus and Kennell (1982) noted that breastfeeding was continued for a longer period of time among mothers whose initial contact (occurring within the first hour after birth) including suckling. Carlsson and associates (1978) also found that extended contact immediately following birth was associated with a significant increase in contact behaviors, such as touching or holding the infant in the first few days of life, however, group differences between those with brief versus extended interactions were no longer apparent at 6 weeks of age. Recent reviews of the literature have suggested that strong conclusions are unwarranted regarding the uniqueness of maternal bonding (Lamb, 1982; McCall, 1982). Human parenting behavior is complexly determined. It should be noted that neither early contact nor nursing are essential to the development of an adequate mother-infant attachment. However, early contact and nursing may optimize lactation and provide foundations for subsequent attachment and bonding.

Mothers that breastfeed their infants tend to show more positive attitudes toward and quantitatively different patterns of interaction with their infants (Richards & Bernal. 1971). Wiesenfeld and associates (1985) also found evidence for more child-centered attitudes in breastfeeding mothers.

Dunn and Richards (1977) conducted an ethological analysis of mother-infant interactions during either bottle or breastfeeding. Even in the first few days of life breastfed babies were sucking longer, were allowed more control of their own feeding behavior, and were more likely to be touched while sucking. By 8- to 10-days-of-age these patterns of differential treatment were even more marked and additional differences became apparent. In general, breastfed infants were permitted more control over their own feeding patterns and were more likely to be touched by their mother. At 8-weeks-of-age differences between breast versus bottle-fed babies continued to be highly significant. The breastfeeding baby controlled the nipple and received more touching and more smiles from the mother. Alternatively, for the bottle-feeding infant the mother was more responsible for regulating the feeding patterns.

A massive psychology and child development literature supports the conclusion that the capacity to predict and/or control the environment can be a major determinant of behavior (see Mineka & Hendersen, 1985). Sucking is obviously among the earliest behaviors of newborn mammals. Piaget (1952) conceptualized the sucking response as a primary reflex which forms a foundation upon which more complex behaviors develop. According to Piaget (1952):

> Verbal or cogitative intelligence is based on practical or sensorimotor intelligence which in turn depends on acquired and recombined habits and associations. These presuppose, furthermore, the system of reflexes whose connection with the organism's anatomical and morphological structure is apparent. A certain continuity exists, therefore, between intelligence and the purely biological processes of morphogenesis and adaptation to the environment. (p. 1)

Piaget (1952) made detailed observations of infant sucking behaviors and suggested the following:

> The sequential manifestations of a reflex such as sucking are not comparable to the periodic starting up of a motor used intermittently, but constitute an historical development so that each episode depends on preceding episodes and conditions those that follow in a truly organic evolution. (p. 24–25)

A number of studies have investigated the possibility that infant feeding practices may be correlated with subsequent behavioral development. In the earlier part of this century such studies were often conducted with the intention of testing hypotheses generated by psychoanalysis. Based on theories formulated by Freud and his followers, it was postulated that sucking satisfied *oral* needs. The predictions generated by psychoanalytic theory are similar to those described in this paper in the context of on-demand feeding; i.e., infants that are permitted to engage in ad lib sucking should have opportunities to satisfy their oral needs and should experience later psychological or cognitive benefits.

Caldwell in a critical review of the relevant literature available in 1964 concluded that "at this point in the twentieth century, it is impossible to demonstrate any nutritional or health advantage for the infant or growing child associated with breast-feeding" (p. 25). In spite of her conclusions, Caldwell in fact surveyed a number of studies that suggested advantages for breastfed infants. As part of the Task force on Infant-feeding Practices commissioned by the Department of Health and Human Services, Kovar et al. (1984) surveyed the more recent literature dealing with potential psychological or cognitive differences associated with breastfeeding versus bottle-feeding. Most of the studies surveyed by the Task Force reported behavioral results favoring breast-fed children. Based on epidemiologic studies Kovar et al. conclude that there is "some evidence that children who are breast-fed have higher levels of intellectual functioning than children who are fed breast milk substitutes that are high in protein."

In one study Menkes (1977) reported that the incidence of referrals to a neurologist for learning disorders, versus referrals for other neurological problems such as seizures and headaches, was higher in bottle-fed children. All of the subjects were from white, upper middle-class families. Of the children with learning disorders 13.8% were breastfed; of the children referred for other disorders 47.2% were breastfed.

Rodgers (1978) analyzed data on intellectual development from the National Survey of Health and Development conducted in England. Based on data from 5362 births (1946 birth cohort), breastfed children as a group had higher scores on most of the variables derived from performance tests administered at 8 and 15 years-of-age. For example, sentence completion scores were highest in breastfed individuals and were progressively lower as a function of the amount of bottle-feeding (within the first 7 months of life). Rodgers used multiple regressions to statistically remove the effects of background differences between bottle and breastfed children. The magnitude of the effect of feeding variables was reduced, however, breastfeeding continued to be associated with a significantly higher performance on tests of picture intelligence, nonverbal ability, mathematics, and sentence completion.

An analysis of data for 13,135 children from the 1970 birth cohort of the National Survey of Health and Development (Taylor & Wadsworth, 1984) tended to support the general findings of Rodgers (1978). A positive correlation between the duration of breastfeeding and performance in tests of vocabulary and visuomotor coordination at 5-years-of-age remained significant even when allowances were made for potentially confounding variables, such as sex, social class, maternal age, maternal smoking during pregnancy, infant birth weight, and the presence of siblings.

Breastfed infants tend to have reliably superior performances on various tests given in later life. However, there are a number of indications that breastfed babies are more irritable and behaviorally aroused than bottle-fed infants (Bell, 1966; Korner & Thoman, 1972; Richards & Bernal, 1971).

DiPietro, Larson, and Porges (submitted) have replicated these findings and also have demonstrated physiological correlates of breastfeeding; specifically, they observed indications of higher levels of parasympathetic activity (i.e., vagal tone) in breastfed infants. These findings are especially interesting because they indicate that correlates of breastfeeding can be measured within a few days of birth and prior to the time that milk production begins. Such results could be used as further support for the hypothesis that preexisting differences (genetics, etc.) are of prime importance; other reported results may be due to the fact that breastfed infants have received less early food than bottle-fed babies. Alternative hypotheses may be considered. The physiological observations of Dipietro et al. (submitted) indicate that the breastfed infants may be in a more optimal physiological state than those that are bottle-fed; this tends to contradict the notion that breastfed infants are irritable because of hunger. Alternatively, DiPietro and associates, suggests that irritability or crying (Murray, 1979) could promote mother-infant interactions and thus enhance the infant's development. Nursing women are less easily upset by their infant's irritability than are nonlactating mother (Wiesenfeld et al., 1985). There may even be an activating agent in colostrum which could affect both the behavior and physiology of the newborn.

From a methodological perspective all of these studies are potentially confounded by preexisting differences between women who elect to breastfeed and those who do not. Conclusions concerning causal relationships are impossible. The magnitude of the statistical effect of infant feeding is typically reduced when intervening variables such as social class are statistically controlled. Nonetheless, there remains a positive association between breastfeeding and intellectual performance and other indices of good health in most of the available literature.

THE CONSEQUENCES OF BREAST
VERSUS BOTTLE-FEEDING

Feeding patterns affect everyone. Jelliffe (1976) summarizes this issue rather dramatically as follows:

> Only in the last 50 years or so has the widespread use of cow's milk for bottle-feeding come into being, and in some parts of the world has even come to be regarded as 'normal'. This perhaps represents the most widespread uncontrolled biological experiment that has ever taken place. Although not perceived as such, it is an even more profound change than that satirized by Aldous Huxley with his test-tube babies.

Breastfeeding remains largely a matter of parental decision. In the United States as recently as 1980 only slightly more than half of the women surveyed (Martinez et al., 1981) elected to breastfeed their infants in the hospital. Even among those mothers that try to breastfeed, many begin to supplement their milk almost immediately, often on the expressed assumption that the infant is not receiving adequate nutrition. For a variety of reasons, including insufficient milk or the need to return to work, many women discontinue nursing well before it is physiologically or psychologically desirable to wean the infant.

Various constraints can undermine successful breastfeeding: among these are maternal employment, cultural prohibitions against nursing in public or at night, and a general lack of knowledge among both parents and health-care professionals regarding the importance of nursing patterns to the establishment of lactation.

La Leche League International (Franklin Park, IL), and comparable grassroots organizations in other countries have arisen to provide education and encouragement to mothers who want to breastfeed. Practical information and encouragement for breastfeeding is available in publications such as "The Womanly Art of Breastfeeding" (La Leche League International, 1981), "You Can Breastfeed Your Baby" (Brewster, 1979), and "Nighttime Parenting" (Sears, 1985).

In spite of a growing literature many questions remain regarding the functional significance of patterns of nursing. La Leche League International and comparable groups tend to advocate patterns of infant care that are as close as possible to those believed to be *natural*. In general, research supports the biological wisdom of this approach. However, in many cases parents do not have the flexibility to follow these suggestions, particularly if the mother is employed.

Under contemporary constraints it is especially important to better understand the relative contributions of different behavioral patterns to the establishment and maintenance of adequate lactation. For example, it is possible that nocturnal nursing may play a unique role in lactational success. Perhaps nocturnal nursing can be exploited by working women to permit the maintenance of lactation during absences from the infant.

The role of lactation in the development of mother-infant interactions, postpartum depression and many other important processes remains largely unexplored. Patterns of nursing (frequency, time of day, age of introduction of solid foods, etc.) can be critical to lactational success; lactation in turn can interfere with the menstrual cycle and ovulation. These findings suggest that nursing patterns are powerful determinants of maternal physiology. Such effects may directly or indirectly impact on behavior.

An additional hypothesis considered here is the possibility that breastfeeding in general, and biologically appropriate nursing patterns in particular, may provide the infant with the opportunity to develop behavioral strategies of subsequent importance in stress management. This suggestion is based on admittedly rather loose inductive reasoning. However, testable and potentially important hypotheses can be generated by considering this possibility.

SPECULATIONS REGARDING THE ROLE OF ON-DEMAND NURSING IN STRESS MANAGEMENT

A major hypothesis arising from the existing literature is the suggestion that breastfeeding provides an early opportunity for the human infant to obtain both an optimal source of food and some degree of environmental control. Historically, the presence of either the biological mother or a lactating mother-substitute was necessary to infant survival. Viable alternatives, termed here in general as bottle-feeding, now exist.

Both life and relatively normal development can be sustained with bottle feeding and modern formulas (Kovar et al., 1984), at least under conditions of adequate sanitation and health care (Jason et al., 1984). Health differences between populations of breastfed and formula-fed babies may be relatively subtle and in many cases could reflect preexisting conditions related to the fact that women (or couples) who elect to breastfeed may otherwise treat their infants differently and possibly may even provide a different gene pool for their infants. At present it is impossible to dissect the relative contributions of the myriad of covariants that accompany the decision to breastfeed. In spite of the problems of interpretation, an overview of this literature indicates that in general breastfed infants are reliably advantaged in comparison to bottle-fed infants.

The earliest experiences of breastfed versus bottle-fed infants can be substantially different (Dunn & Richards, 1977). This observation leads to the hypothesis that these differential experiences could have developmental consequences that might impact on the amount of stress experienced by the individual and on the subsequent ability to manage stress.

At the simplest level, it is possible that suboptimal nutrition or food delivery could be stressful for the infant. In addition, there are clear indications that the immune systems of young babies that are exposed to foods other than human milk are not as efficient in preventing disease as those of breastfed babies. Breastfeeding may provide immunities, protecting the baby at least from the physiological stress of disease.

In young monkeys it has been reported that separation from the mother causes changes in the immune system (Reite, Harbeck, & Hoffman, 1981). Nutritional changes were confounded with maternal separation in these studies, as they are in many human child-rearing situations. Nonetheless, both nutrition and even very brief maternal separation could interact to at least slightly increase the susceptibility of the bottle-fed infant to disease.

Behaviorally, the breastfed baby may be more likely to have early positive experiences related to its ability to control the external environment. Both the animal and human literature in psychology strongly suggests that the absence of control can be detrimental, perhaps making the individual more susceptible to both physical and psychological illness.

CONCLUSIONS

Breastfeeding may provide benefits to both the mother and child. Human breast milk is an optimal and dynamically altered infant food. Breast milk contains anti-infective agents and substances that modulate growth. Cow's milk and other artificial formulas lack many of the advantages provided by breast milk and may actually introduce detrimental agents, such as foreign proteins, hormones, pesticides, etc. (Minchin, 1985).

The advantages of breastfeeding are now widely recognized. Nonetheless, many mothers do not breastfeed their children or may attempt breastfeeding for only a short time. A major factor in the decision to breastfeed is the attitude of the mother toward infant feeding. Attitudes and behavioral practices are also apparently major determinants of the ability to establish and maintain adequate lactation. Women who are encouraged to nurse their infants at frequent intervals are more successful at milk production and rarely suffer from milk insufficiency.

There are circadian rhythms in the production of the hormones associated with lactation and prolactin levels tend to be elevated at night. Based on the physiology of lactation, it appears that nocturnal nursing may play an important role in the establishment of lactation. Other possible functions of nocturnal nursing in the mother-infant interaction are discussed earlier.

In general there is little research on the functional significance of infant feeding patterns. Many otherwise carefully designed studies of newborns or the parent-infant interaction do not even mention the type of feeding procedures to which the child is exposed. In spite of inattention to the issue of infant-feeding practices, a growing literature suggests that the physiology and behavior of both the mother and infant are affected by the parental decision to nurse or not nurse.

The physiological systems that regulate lactation depend on behaviorally active substances such as dopamine and possibly the endogenous opiates (Short, 1984). These same chemicals have been implicated in organismic responses to environmental stressors and lactating females may have attenuated or more efficient stress responses (Adler et al., 1986; Smotherman et al., 1976; Wiesenfeld et al., 1985).

Feeding behaviors form a core of the experiences of newborn humans. Breastfeeding may provide infants with not only optimal nutrition, but in addition an optimal opportunity to develop coping skills. It is a major thesis of this paper that breastfeeding may provide experiences that are of value in later stress management. Many of the behavioral advantages associated with breastfeeding could be provided in other ways, through the wisdom or intuition of good parenting. However, in the absence of well-grounded principles for childrearing, more attention should be given to the importance of infant feeding practices. In fact it would seem wise to call a moratorium on "the most widespread uncontrolled biological experiment that has ever taken place" (Jelliffe, 1976).

ACKNOWLEDGMENTS

I am very grateful for the help of the following individuals in the development of this paper and the ideas expressed here: Eric Porges, Seth Porges, Stephen Porges, Janet DiPietro, Robert Hendersen, Ross Parke, Mary Frances Picciano and Tiffany Field. I want to particularly thank Roger V. Short for editorial comments and several recent references cited here.

REFERENCES

Adler, E. M., Cook, A., Davidson, D., West, C., & Bancroft, J. (1986). Hormones, mood and sexuality in lactating women. *British Journal of Psychiatry, 148,* 74–79.

Bell, R. Q. (1966). Level of arousal in breast-fed and bottle-fed newborns. *Psychosomatic Medicine, 28,* 177–180.

Blurton Jones, N. (1972). Comparative aspects of mother-child contact. In N. Blurton Jones (Ed.), *Ethological studies of child behavior* (pp. 305–328). Cambridge, England: Cambridge University Press.

Blurton Jones, N., Rossetti Ferreira, M. C., Farquar Brown, M., & Macdonald, L. (1978). The association between perinatal factors and later night waking. *Developmental Medicine and Child Neurology, 20,* 427–434.

Bowlby, J. (1969). *Attachment and loss. Volume I. Attachment.* New York: Basic Books.

Brewster, D. P. (1979). *You can breastfeed your baby.* Emmaus, PA: Rodale Press.

Caldwell, B. M. (1964). The effects of infant care. In M. L. Hoffman & L. W. Hoffman (Eds.), *Review of child development research* (Volume 1, pp. 9–87). New York: Russell Sage Foundation.

Carlsson, S. G., Fagerberg, H., Horneman, G., Hwang, C-P., Larsson, K., Rodholm, M., Schaller, J., Danielsson, B., & Gundewall, C. (1978). Effects of amount of contact between mother and child on the mother's nursing behavior. *Developmental Psychobiology, 11,* 143–150.

Carvalho, M. D., Robertson, S., Friedman, A., & Klaus, M. (1983). Effect of frequent breastfeeding on early milk production and infant weight gain. *Pediatrics, 72,* 307–311.

Chandra, R. K. (1979). Prospective studies of the effect of breast-feeding on incidence of infection and allergy. *Acta Paediatrica Scandinava, 68,* 691–694.

DiPietro, J. A., Larson, S., & Porges, S. W. (submitted). Behavioral and heart rate pattern differences between breast and bottle-fed neonates. *Developmental Psychology.*

Dunn, J. B., & Richards, M. P. (1977). Observations on the developing relationship between mother and baby in the neonatal period. In H. R. Schaeffer (Ed.), *Studies in mother-infant interaction* (pp. 427–455). New York: Academic Press.

Elias, M. F., Teas, J., Johnston, J., & Bora, C. (1986). Nursing practices and lactation amenorrhoea. *Journal of Biosocial Science, 18,* 1–10.

Ellis, D. J., & Hewat, R. J. (1984). Breast-feeding: Motivation and outcome. *Journal of Biosocial Sciences, 16,* 81–88.

Fergusson, D. M., Horwood, L. J., Shannon, R. T., et al. (1978). Infant health and breast-feeding during the first 16 weeks of life. *Australian Pediatric Journal, 14,* 254–258.

Field, T. M., Schanberg, S. M., Scafidi, F., Bauer, C. R., Vega-Lahr, N., Garcia, R., Nystrom, J., & Kuhn, C. M. (1986). Effects of tactile/kinesthetic stimulation on preterm neonates. *Pediatrics, 77,* 654–658.

Foucard, T. (1985). Development of food allergies with special reference to cow's milk allergy. *Pediatrics, 75* (Suppl.), 177–181.

Gaull, G. E., Wright, C. E., & Isaacs, C. E. (1985). Significance of growth modulators in human milk. *Pediatrics, 75* (Suppl.), 142–145.

Gibber, J. R., & Terkel, J. (submitted). Lactational acyclicity depends on time of day nursing occurs.

Glasier, A., Howie, P. W., & McNeilly, A. S. (1984). The prolactin response to suckling. *Clinical Endocrinology, 21,* 109–116.

Gussler, J., & Briesemeister, L. (1980). The insufficient milk syndrome: A biocultural explanation. *Medical Anthropology, 4,* 145–162.

Hamosh, M., Bitman, J., Wood, L., Hamosh, P., & Mehta, N. T. (1985). Lipids in milk and the first steps in their digestion. *Pediatrics, 75* (Suppl.), 146–150.

Hanson, L. A., Ahistedt, S., Andersson, B., Carlsson, B., Fallstrom, S. P., Mellander, L., Porras, O. Soderstrom, T., & Eden, C. S. (1985). Protective factors in milk and the development of the immune system. *Pediatrics, 75* (Suppl.), 172–175.

Harlow, H. F. (1958). The nature of love. *American Psychologist, 13,* 673–685.

Howie, P. W., & McNeilly, A. S. (1982). Effect of breast feeding patterns on human birth intervals. *Journal of Reproduction and Fertility, 65,* 545–557.

Howie, P. W., McNeilly, A. S., Houston, M. J., Cook, A., & Boyle, H. (1982). Fertility after childbirth: Post-partum ovulation and menstruation in bottle and breast feeding mothers. *Clinical Endocrinology, 17,* 323–332.

Jason, J. M., Nieburg, J., & Marks, J. S. (1984). Mortality and infectious disease associated with infant-feeding practices in developing countries. *Pediatrics, 74* (suppl), 702–727.

Jelliffe, D. B. (1976). Community and socio-political considerations of breast feeding. In *Breastfeeding and the mother.* Ciba Foundation Symposium 45. Amsterdam: Elsevier.

Jelliffe, D. B., & Jelliffe, E. F. P. (1978). Human milk in the modern world. Oxford, England: Oxford University Press.

Klaus, M. H., & Kennell, J. H. (1970). Mothers separated from their newborn infants. *Pediatric Clinics of North America, 17,* 1015–1037.

Klaus, M. H., & Kennell, J. H. (1982). *Parent-infant bonding.* St. Louis, MO: C. V. Mosby.

Konner, M. J. (1972). Aspects of the developmental ethology of a foraging people. In N. Blurton Jones (Ed.), *Ethological studies of child behaviour* (pp. 285–304). Cambridge, England: Cambridge University Press.

Konner, M. J., & Worthman, C. (1980). Nursing frequency, gonadal function, and birth spacing among !Kung hunter-gathers. *Science, 207,* 788–791.

Korner, A. F., & Thoman, E. B. (1972). The relative efficacy of contact and vestibular-proprioceptive stimulation in soothing neonates. *Child Development, 43,* 443–453.

Kovar, M. G., Seidula, M. K., Marks, J. S., & Fraser, D. W. (1984). Review of the epidemiologic evidence for an association between infant feeding and infant health. *Pediatrics, 74* (Suppl.), 615–638.

Lamb, M. E. (1982). Early contact and maternal-infant bonding: One decade later. *Pediatrics, 70,* 763–678.

Lawrence, R. A. (1980). Breast-feeding, a guide for the medical profession. St. Louis, MO: C. V. Mosby.

Martinez, G. A., Dodd, D. A., & Samartgedes, J. A. (1981). Milk feeding patterns in the United States during the first 12 months of life. *Pediatrics, 68,* 863–868.

McCall, R. B. (1982). A hard look at stimulating and predicting development: The cases of bonding and screening. *Pediatrics in Review, 3,* 205–212.

Menkes, J. H. (1977). Early feeding history of children with learning disorders. *Developmental Medicine & Child Neurology, 19,* 169–171.

Minchin, M. (1985). *Breastfeeding matters.* Sidney, Australia: Alma Press and George Allen & Unwin.

Mineka, S., & Hendersen, R. W. (1985). Controllability and predictability in acquired motivation. *Annual Review of Psychology, 36,* 494–529.

Murray, A. D. (1979). Infant crying as in elicitor of parental behavior: An examination of two models. *Psychological bulletin, 86*, 191–215.

Neville, M. C., & Neifert, M. R. (1983). *Lactation, physiology, nutrition, and breastfeeding.* New York: Plenum Press.

Newton, N., & Newton, M. (1967). Psychologic aspects of lactation. *New England Journal of Medicine, 277,* 1179–1188.

Newton, M., & Newton, N. R. (1968). The let-down reflex in human lactation. *Journal of Pediatrics, 33,* 698–704.

Oski, F. A. (1985). Is bovine milk a health hazard? *Pediatrics, 75* (Suppl.), 182–185.

Petre-Quadens, O. (1979). Hormones and sleep. *Journal of Physiology, 293,* 70–71P.

Piaget, J. (1952). *The origins of intelligence in children.* Translated by M. Cook. New York: W. W. Norton.

Reite, M., Harbeck, R., & Hoffman, A. (1981). Altered cellular immune response following peer separation. *Life Sciences, 29,* 1133–1136.

Richards, J. E. (1985). Respiratory sinus arrhythmia predicts heart rate and visual responses during visual attention in 14 and 20 week old infants. *Psychophysiology, 22,* 101–108.

Richards, M. P. M., & Bernal, J. F. (1971). An observational study of mother-infant interaction. In N. Blurton-Jones (Ed.), *Ethological studies of child behaviour* (pp. 175–198). Cambridge, England: Cambridge University Press.

Rodgers, B. (1978). Feeding in infancy and later ability and attainment: A longitudinal study. *Developmental Medicine and Child Neurology, 20,* 421–426.

Salariya, E. M., Easton, P., & Cater, J. (1980). Breastfeeding and milk supply failure. *Journal of Maternal and Child Health, 5,* 38.

Sassin, J. F., Frantz, A. G., Weitzman, E. D., & Kapen, S. (1972). Human prolactin: 24-hour pattern with increased release during sleep. *Science, 177,* 1205–1207.

Sears, W. (1985). *Nighttime parenting.* Franklin Park, IL: LaLeche League International.

Schanberg, S. M., Evoniuk, G., & Kuhn, C. M. (1984). Tactile and nutritional aspects of maternal care: Specific regulators of neuroendocrine function and cellular development. *Proceedings of the Society for Experimental Biology and Medicine, 175,* 135–146.

Short, R. V. (1983). Biological basis for the contraceptive effects of breast-feeding. In L. Reid (Ed.), Neuroendocrine aspects of reproduction (pp. 325–343). New York: Academic Press.

Short, R. V. (1984). Breast feeding. *Scientific American, 250,* pp. 35–41.

Smotherman, W. P., Wiener, S. G., Mendoza, S. P., & Levine, S. (1976). Pituitary-adrenal responsiveness of rat mothers to noxious stimuli and stimuli produced by pups. In *Breast-feeding and the Mother.* Ciba Foundation Symposium 45 (pp. 5–25). Amsterdam: Elsevier.

Stern, J. M., Goldman, L., & Levine, S. (1973). Pituitary-adrenal responsiveness during lactation in rats. *Neuroendocrinology, 12,* 179–191.

Taylor, B., & Wadsworth, J. (1984). Breast feeding and child development at five years. *Developmental Medicine and Child Neurology, 26,* 73–80.

Thoman, E. B., Conner, R. L., & Levine, S. (1970). Lactation suppresses adrenal corticosteroid activity and aggressiveness in rats. *Journal of Comparative & Physiological Psychology, 70,* 364–369.

Thoman, E. B., Leiderman, P. D., & Olson, J. P. (1972). Neonate-mother interaction during breast-feeding. *Developmental Psychology, 6,* 110–118.

Voloschin, L. M., & Tramezzani, J. H. (1979). Milk ejection reflex linked to slow wave sleep in nursing rats. *Endocrinology, 105,* 1202–1207.

Walker, W. A. (1985). Absorption of protein and protein fragments in the developing intestine: Role in immunological-allergic reactions. *Pediatrics, 75* (Suppl.), 167–171.

Wiesenfeld, A. R., Malatesta, C. Z., Whitman, P. B., Grannose, C., & Vile, R. (1985). Psychophysiological response of breast-and bottle-feeding mothers to their infants' signals. *Psychophysiology, 22,* 79–86.

3
The Mutual Regulation Model: The Infant's Self and Interactive Regulation and Coping and Defensive Capacities

A. Gianino
McLean Hospital, Belmont, MA

E. Z. Tronick
University of Massachusetts, Amherst

COPING WITH INTERACTIVE STRESS IN INFANCY

Psychopathology in infancy is often attributed to abnormal interactive experiences. For example, social withdrawal (Bakeman & Brown, 1977; Brazelton, Kowslowski, & Main, 1974; Field, 1977; Massie, 1978; Stern, 1971, 1977), failure to thrive (Greenspan, 1982), and depression (Cohn & Tronick, 1983; Zahn-Waxler, McKnew, Cummings, Davenport, & Radke-Yarrow, 1984) have been linked to aberrant interpersonal relations. The underlying view is that the infant who experiences abnormally stressful interactions learns to cope with them in a particular fashion, but that his learned pattern of social interaction and coping is also abnormal. Consequently, when the infant utilizes his pattern in other, potentially normal, interactions, it distorts them, making them abnormal, too. This engenders an insidious, self-reinforcing, interactive cycle in which the infant's repeated distortion of otherwise normal interactions stresses him, compelling him again and again to adopt his coping response, which further reinforces the learned, or *internalized*, aberrant pattern.

Unfortunately, the interactive details of such abnormal social exchanges typically remain unexamined, as do the specific ways in which infants cope with interactive stress (but see Brazelton et al., 1974; Massie, 1978; Stern, 1971). In addition, none of the available data indicate when an infant's pattern of coping with an interactive stress becomes a stable individual characteristic. Thus the connection between the infant's manner of coping with interaction stress and other developmental changes remains unclear (Campos, Barrett, Lamb, Goldsmith, & Sternberg, 1983; Gianino, 1982, 1985; Hodapp & Mueller, 1982; Parke & Asher, 1983).

47

In this paper we present a system for describing the infant's capacities for coping with stressful interactions, and we summarize data on the developmental changes and stability of these capacities. Our work has been guided by what has become known as the Mutual Regulation Model of social engagement. In particular, we have elaborated on the model's hypothesis that the infant's coping capacities develop from his behavioral repertoire for regulating social and object engagement.

THE MUTUAL REGULATION MODEL

The Mutual Regulation Model (MRM) of mother-infant interaction (Brazelton, 1982; Brazelton et al., 1974; Tronick, 1980, 1982) proposes that mother and infant have an interactive goal and a set of capacities to help attain the goal. It suggests that their goal is to achieve a state of mutual regulation, or reciprocity, and that to attain it they *jointly* regulate the interaction with interactive behaviors. The MRM further proposes that the interactive behaviors are primarily affective displays.

Research supporting the MRM's assumption of the infant's active role in the regulation of his interactions includes studies such as those on the infant's differential reactions to mothers, fathers, and strangers (Dixon, Yogman, Tronick, Adamson, Als, & Brazelton, 1981; Parke, 1979; Parke, O'Leary, & West, 1972); significant differences between the observed distribution of mother-infant joint behaviors and their expected distribution predicted from the distributions of their independent behaviors (Bullowa, 1975; Tronick, Krafchuk, Ricks, Cohn, & Winn, 1985); specificity and modification in the infant's response to distortions in his partner's behaviors (Beebe, Jaffe, Feldstein, Mays, & Alson, 1985; Cohn & Tronick, 1983; Fogel, Diamond, Langhorst, & Demos, 1983; Trevarthan, 1977; Tronick, Ricks, & Cohn, 1982); contingencies between infant smiles and vocalizations and specific maternal turn-yielding signals (Anderson, Vietze, & Dokechi, 1977; Mayer & Tronick, 1985); and contingencies between infant averting and maternal behaviors (Bloom, 1977; Brazelton et al., 1974; Field, 1977; Massie, 1978; Stern, 1977).

Studies by Stern (1974), Brazelton et al. (1974), Tronick, Als, and Adamson (1978), and Beebe and Stern (1977) support the MRM's assumption that the interactants have a goal of achieving a state of reciprocity. Note that "reciprocity" is used to cover a range of somewhat unspecified terms, such as *matching, attunement, synchrony, mutual delight, mutual regulation,* etc. These terms are not equivalent, but in the current context the differences are not central, with one exception. These terms differ in the relative weight they give to the interactive *process* as opposed to the interactive *outcome,* or goal. The process is a feedback-regulated control system, which primarily operates as an affective process.

The goal is some interpersonal state, e.g., intimacy, connectedness, sociality, oneness, love, attachment. *Reciprocity,* for example, focuses on the process, while *mutual delight* focuses on the hedonic outcome.

In support of its claim that the infant's affective system plays a crucial role in regulating social interaction, the MRM contends that the infant's affective system is differentiated at birth. Following models suggested by Izard (1978) and Campos et al. (1983), the MRM proposes that by the middle of the infant's first year he has the capacity to experience and express at least seven primary emotions, *viz.,* joy, interest, sadness, anger, fear, surprise, and distress. According to this view, each of the infant's affective responses entails a qualitatively different *evaluation* of the events impinging on him. The infant's affective responses are said to be evaluative in the sense that they invest these events with personal significance and meaning; there is no implication that the process involves higher order cognitions or conscious reflection. To accomplish this evaluation—referred to as an "appraisal" by Bowlby (1969) and as an "appreciation" by Campos et al. (1983)—the infant's affective system appraises the impinging events in terms of their bearing on his current goals. The appraisal process is differentiated in that each of the infant's emotions expresses a different categorization of how the impinging events affect the infant's goal attainment. For instance, the difference between an infant's joyful, angry, and sad response, according to Campos et al., is due to the following difference in the infant's appraisal: A joyful response occurs when the infant's appraisal is that he is obtaining his goal; an angry response occurs when the infant's appraisal is that his goal is being obstructed but that it is *obtainable* under the circumstances, i.e., given the stimulus conditions; and a sad response occurs when the infant's appraisal is that his goal is being obstructed but that it is *un*obtainable under the circumstances.

These recent advances in our understanding of the development and complexity of the infant's affective system have supported the MRM's claim that the infant's affective responses have an important interpersonal function. The function, to communicate the infant's ongoing appraisal of the interaction, is accomplished because the infant's appraisal is automatically expressed through his affective displays. This affords the infant significant communicative power, particularly with a sensitive and responsive partner, enabling him to initiate, modify, and maintain the exchange.

Although the MRM contends that the interactants have a goal of achieving a state of reciprocity, it emphasizes that such a state is not always achieved. Imperfections occur for a number of reasons: mistimed behavior; a misreading by one partner of the other partner's signals, producing behavior that does not match the expectation of the other; differences in each partner's immediate goal; or the older partner's attempt to encourage the infant to expand his capabilities (Tronick et al., 1978). Moreover, instances of imperfection are remarkably common. In a recent study of 3-, 6-, and 9-month-old infants (Cohn, Krafchuk, Ricks, Winn, & Tronick, 1985), it was found that mother and infant were in mismatched states 70% of the time. This is hardly the romantic synchrony of mutual delight.

The Mutual Regulation Model takes account of the imperfections inherent in the interactive process by proposing that a "normal disruption"—referred to here as a *mismatch* (Stern, 1977; Tronick, Als, & Brazelton, 1980; Tronick, Krafchuk, Ricks, Cohn, & Winn, 1985; and Fafouti-Milenkovic & Uzgiris, 1979)—motivates the infant to adjust to it or modify it by employing his interactive skills. To do this, the infant employs the same affective displays and interactive behaviors that allow him to initiate, modify, and maintain the well-regulated interaction, since these also enable him to repair, avoid, or terminate a mismatched exchange.

During a normal interaction, positive affect is generated by well-regulated exchanges, and negative affect is generated by mismatched exchanges. Both positive and negative affect manifest themselves in affective expressions and, motivationally, in interactive behavior. Specifically, the infant's expressions of joy and interest indicate his positive emotional evaluation of the ongoing interaction and communicate to the partner that she should interact or continue to engage in what she is doing (Tronick, Als, & Adamson, 1978). The infant's negative appraisal of a mismatched interaction (Campos et al., 1983)—manifested in distress, anger, and sadness—signals to the partner to change her behavior. Together, positive and negative affect enable the infant to regulate the interaction to achieve mutual regulation. As noted earlier, however, this is true with one qualification. The infant's affective displays regulate the interaction when he is with a sensitive partner who is willing to modify her own behavior to match her reading of his communications.

An important implication of the MRM's position that the infant uses his affective system to regulate his interactions is that the infant has a capacity for regulating his affective responses (Brazelton, 1974; Field, 1977; McCall & McGhee, 1977; Spitz, 1965; Stern, 1974, 1977). This follows because the infant must regulate two aspects of affect while interacting. The first aspect is the qualitative dimension, that is, the particular affective state the infant is feeling and expressing. The second aspect is the quantitative dimension, that is, the temporal and intensive parameters of affect, typically measured in terms of the threshold, latency, rise time, intensity, and recovery time of an affective occurrence. When a mismatch occurs, both types of affective self-regulation are usually facilitated through the communicative effects of the infant's affective expressions. With a sensitive partner, the infant's affective displays alter a mismatch, a situation which would continue to generate increasingly strong negative affect if allowed to continue. The interactive reparation accomplished by the infant's affective displays (with the partner's cooperation) fosters at least a reduction in negative affect, if not a change toward positive affect. In this sense, the infant's interactive repertoire facilitates his self-regulation of emotional states while he is interactively engaged.

This perspective casts a different light on what are commonly thought to be the important aspects of social interaction for the infant's development. Although it is generally agreed that mismatches are normal and occur with some frequency, many researchers, including ourselves, have typically proposed that the degree of reciprocity or mutual delight evidenced in an interaction is most important to the development of the infant. From the point of view of the MRM, reciprocity is still important, but the successful resolution of mismatches is more central, serving a multiplicity of developmental functions.

Psychodynamic theorists from Freud to Mahler, as well as developmentalists (Stechler & Halton, 1982; Trevarthan, 1977), have propounded that otherwise apparently frustrating experiences allow for self-other differentiation. Stern (1977) and Tronick, Als, and Adamson (1978) have argued that mismatches provide the infant with opportunities to further broaden and develop his interactive skills. Tronick (1980) has expanded on that claim by suggesting that insofar as the infant is able to repair mismatches, the infant is more likely to develop a sense of effectance in the interactive sphere. We propose two further functions of mismatches. First, mismatches compel the infant to develop his self-regulatory skills. Second, the infant's experience in managing mismatches develops his self-regulatory skills into skills which are useful for coping with prolonged, exaggerated, or aberrant forms of interactive stress. As we will argue in the Discussion, however, we also propose that the second function can be derailed if the interaction is chronically aberrant.

The facilitative effects of ordinary mismatches on normal development need to be contrasted to the potentially deleterious consequences of prolonged, exaggerated, and/or aberrant forms of interactive stress, what we call PRESAS (pronounced "presses") for short. PRESAS stress not only the infant's resources for regulating social exchanges, but also his capacity for regulating the accompanying negative affect. The MRM hypothesizes that when the infant experiences a significant and prolonged distortion of reciprocity, one he is unable to repair by altering the interaction to achieve his goal, the amount of stress and negative affect increase significantly (Gianino, 1982; Tronick et al., 1982).

Such effects have been consistently demonstrated in studies of relatively prolonged perturbations of the normal interaction. The studies include both experimental designs and clinical investigations. For example, there are studies of infants interacting with strangers (Dixon et al., 1981) or interacting with their mother while she remains still-faced or simulates depression (Cohn & Tronick, 1983; Fogel et al., 1983; Gianino, 1982; Tronick, Als, Adamson, Wise, & Brazelton, 1978); and there are studies in which the infant's mother is clinically depressed (Tronick, Cohn, & Shea, 1985; Zahn-Waxler et al., 1984) or for other reasons behaves inappropriately (Massie, 1978, 1982; Stern, 1977). In all the studies two things occur. On the one hand, the infant's attempts to repair the distortion through affective displays fail as long as the distortion persists, and, on the other hand, negative affect is generated as long as the infant remains motivated to interact while continuing to fail in his reparative attempts. Consequently, the studies repeatedly show that the PRESAS tax the infant's capacity for sustaining interactive engagement while maintaining self-regulation (Brazelton et al., 1974; Gianino, 1982; Massie, 1978; Stern, 1974; Tronick et al., 1982). Following Brazelton (1974), Gianino (1982) has observed that in order to manage the negative affect generated by PRESAS, even those experimentally induced, the infant is sometimes compelled to utilize other coping behaviors in addition to, or instead of, his interactive skills.

But one note of clarification is needed. There is no exact boundary between self-regulation and coping, just as there is no clear boundary between normal and abnormal input. In general, we try to use the term self-regulation when the infant is confronted by the mismatches and other imperfections characteristic of normal interactions and the term coping when the infant is attempting to regulate distortions that fall outside the normal range, i.e., PRESAS. Thus in this paper we typically refer to "coping" behaviors because we are focusing on interactions we have experimentally manipulated to simulate PRESAS, even though they are short-lived simulations. But, more generally, we believe that from a developmental point of view there is a great deal of overlap between the sets of behaviors which serve self-regulatory and coping functions, with self-comforting being a notable exception. The primary difference is in the way the two sets of behaviors are deployed, e.g., with regard to flexibility and persistence. Furthermore, as will be discussed at the end of this paper, there are the additional, complicated relations among self-regulatory, coping, and defensive behaviors.

According to Brazelton et al. (1974), even 1-month-old infants have several behavioral strategies for coping with stress, whether the stress is induced by the infant's interaction with people or objects. In addition to being able to signal both positively and negatively with affective displays, infants are able to reject or push away the stressful object; they are able to withdraw from the stressor by sharply turning or arching away and even by loosing postural control; and they are able to decrease their perceptual receptivity to the stressful stimuli by, what is in effect, looking without seeing.

All four coping strategies produce a reduction in the amount of negative affect experienced by the infant. A significant difference between signaling and the other strategies is that by signaling the infant preserves his goal of maintaining engagement with the partner; Beebe (1975) has made a similar point. When the infant adopts any of the other coping strategies, he forgoes social engagement in order to maintain internal regulation.

Gianino (1982) has noted that when an infant turns away from his partner in an effort to terminate or avoid a stressful exchange, he can exert control over his attentional process in one of two ways (Derryberry & Rothbart, 1984). In the first way, the infant can scan the environment without fixing his focus, causing his attention to remain "free floating." In the second way, the infant can redirect his attention to a surrounding object, including his own body. Both allow the infant to reorient away from the stressful stimuli, enabling him to control the timing and duration of his focus on the stressor and, according to Brazelton et al. (1974), providing him with a recovery period. However, the two ways of controlling his attentional processes are not equivalent. Although scanning the surround without pausing to attend to the mother or a particular object allows the infant to reduce the stressful input, it precludes his engagement with the object world as well as his reengagement with the mother; this strategy is "autistic" in the nonpathological sense. By redirecting his attention to a particular object, however, the infant is able to avoid the stressful stimuli while at the same time retaining his capacity for engaging in an affectively positive activity. Functionally, the attention directed to an object entails a switch in the infant's operative goals, since in withdrawing interest from his partner and attending to an object the infant becomes motivated more by object exploration than by social interaction. A potential advantage of coping with PRESAS by switching goal orientations from social engagement to object exploration is that the infant can make more adaptive use of his time and energy while maintaining his self-regulation.

INFANT COPING IN RESPONSE TO THE STILL-FACE, SIMULATED DEPRESSION, CLINICAL DEPRESSION, AND THE STRANGE SITUATION

To examine the infant's coping capacities, we have engaged in a number of studies in which we look at the infant's reaction to a particular interactive stress, *viz.*, the mother behaving still-faced. In this manipulation, the mother is in the normal face-to-face position, but she does not react at all to her infant; she remains expressionless and unresponsive. Tronick, Als, Adamson, Wise, and Brazelton (1978) have argued that the still-face is stressful because gaze contact functions as a crucial context marker which affects the regulative meaning of the accompanying emotional displays (Bloom, 1977; Fogel et al., 1983). In the still-face, the mother's *en face* position and eye contact with her infant present him with a signal that invites social interaction, while her expressionless and unresponsive face denies it. It is as if the mother is saying hello and good-bye at the same time, leaving the infant trapped between the two messages. Insofar as the infant is primed for interaction by the mother's *en face* position and eye contact, as well as by his own interactive goals, the mother's still-face often results in infant bids to initiate social interaction. Because the mother remains unresponsive, however, there is no possibility for the infant to repair the interaction; the infant's attempts are repeatedly frustrated. For this reason the still-face is a stress

TABLE 3.1
Infant Coping Behavior System

---

1. SOCIAL ATTEND: Looks at mother without signaling.

2. SIGNAL: Acts in a way which functions to modify
   mother's behavior.
   Positive--Signals with a positive affective tone,
       e.g., smile or coo face.
   Neutral--Signals with neutral affective tone, e.g.,
       pick-me-up gesture.
   Negative--Signals with negative affective tone,
       e.g., fuss or cry.

3. OBJECT ATTEND: Focuses attention on something other
       than mother.
   Other--Focuses on object with or without manipulation
       of it, e.g., strap of chair.
   Self--Focuses on part of own body with or without
       manipulation of it, e.g., toes.

   SELF-COMFORT: Uses own body or object to provide
       self-comforting stimulation.
   Oral-Self--Sucks on part of body, e.g., fingers.
   Oral-Other--Sucks on object, e.g., strap of chair.
   Self-Clasp--Clasps hands together.
   Rock--Rocks from side to side or to and fro.

5. ESCAPE: Attempts to increase the physical distance
       from mother by turning, twisting, or arching away.

6. AVERT/SCAN: Looks away from the mother, but does not
       successfully maintain attention to something else.

7. WITHDRAWAL: Utilizes motor, attentional, and percep-
       tual processes to minimize social engagement.
   Motor--Gives up postural control.
   Perceptual--Looks "dull" or "glassy-eyed."

---

outside the normal range. Unless the infant is able to adopt some other measure to cope with his predicament, he will likely become increasingly distressed as the experiment continues.

To assess the infant's coping response to the interactive stress, Gianino (1982) developed the Infant Coping Behavior System (ICBS). The system combines (a) observations by Brazelton et al. (1974) on how the infants respond to stress, (b) Gianino's hypothesis about the infant's use of object exploration as a coping strategy, and (c) elements of Tronick, Als, and Brazelton (1980) Modified Monadic Phase Scoring System. The major categories of the system are presented in Table 3.1. Social Attend, Self-Comfort, and Escape were added after the first study, as well be discussed below. Coding with Gianino's system was done from videotapes on a slow motion videodeck.

In our first still-face study, we compared the behavior of 54 mother-infant dyads, 18 each at 3, 6, and 9 months (Gianino, 1982). Each dyad played normally for 2 minutes, experienced the still-face for 2 minutes, and played again for 2 minutes. We found that the infant's tendency to use Object Attend increased with development. We also found that compared to 9-month-old infants, 3- and 6-month-olds were more likely to use Object Attend for either very brief or very long bouts. That is, 3- and 6-month-olds were less able than 9-month-olds to sustain their attention to an object or to withdraw it from an object once it was fixed. We believe this indicates the greater ability of 9-month-olds to modulate their attentional involvement with objects while interactively stressed and thus to use object exploration as an effective coping strategy without forsaking their goal of reengaging the mother. Piaget's (1968) observation that from 4 to 10 months the infant's horizon extends outward from his body to objects in the surround, manifesting itself in a change from primary to secondary circular reactions, was supported by our finding that the use of Self-Object Attend peaked at 3 months while that of Other-Object Attend peaked at 6 months. We were suprised to find that the frequency of Positive Signal did not increase with development, while the frequency of Negative Signal did. However, the mean bout length of Negative Signal dropped eight-fold from 3 to 9 months, which suggests that 3-month-olds were least capable of soothing themselves once they became distressed enough to cry, and 9-month-olds were most capable. Furthermore, there is a qualitative change between 3 and 9 months in the use of Negative Signal that is not captured by the coding system in that the 3-month-olds appeared more distressed and the 9-month-olds more angry.

We also found that Motor and Perceptual Withdrawal were seldom used by these normal infants, particularly after they reached 3-months-of-age. This is not surprising since Motor and Perceptual Withdrawal are relatively primitive forms of coping, involving the type of pervasive disengagement from the surround more typical of very young infants. We also observed that the amount of body tension, evidenced in hand clenching and heavy breathing, decreased with development. For 3- and 6-month-olds, body tension is a somewhat primitive phenomena. The younger infant is a more biosocial creature than the older infant and as such is more prone to relatively nonspecific physiological reactions to many forms of stress, including interactive stress (Sander, 1977).[1] The last finding we would like to mention was a significant decrease in the variability of the frequency of all coping behaviors, suggesting that as infants become older they become more alike in their coping tendencies.

In order to assess the organization and structure of the infant's response, a within group analysis of the transition matrices at each age was performed with the infant's behavior scored using Tronick, Als, and Brazelton's (1980) Modified Monadic Phase Scoring System. The Monadic System was used because the ICBS was not exhaustive when first designed, which precluded a sequential analysis of the infant's behavior. In terms of the data presented here, the relevant differences between the ICBS and the Monadic Scoring System are twofold:

---

[1]While we are focusing on affective regulation for purposes of discussing coping, we agree with Sander (1962) that there are different tasks at different developmental periods which require other forms of regulation. As Sander notes, the task preceding the period we are discussing has to do with physiological regulation.

First, Self-Comfort, Escape, and Withdrawal are scored in the ICBS, but not in the Monadic System; second, "Wary," a subcategory of "Social Attend," in which the infant looks at the mother warily, is scored in the Monadic System, but not in the ICBS.

An integral feature of the organization of infant behavior at all three ages was the infant's tendency to cycle from Social Attend to Avert and from Avert to Object Attend (see Fig. 3.1). Regardless of age, infants first attempted to terminate and avoid the stressful interaction by Averting their gaze from the mother. After Averting, they were more likely to switch their attention from the interaction to the surround, as evidenced in the low probability that they would go from Avert to Social Attend and the increased probability that they would go from Avert to Object Attend. Among the significant main effects for age was a difference in how infants tended to respond after Object Attend. Whereas 9-month-olds were more likely than expected to Avert again after Object Attend, 6-month-olds were more likely than expected to Social Attend and 3-month-olds to Protest. This finding indicates the 3-month-old's greater difficulty with switching goals as a way of self-regulating. Furthermore, after Protesting, 9-month-olds were the only group who were more likely than expected to Object Attend, suggesting better coping capacity than 3- or 6-month-olds.

More generally, the developmental differences in the infant's coping response were marked by a significant increase in behavioral complexity and organization. There were increases in the number of coping behaviors from 3 to 9 months (225, 320, 348, respectively) and in the frequency of transitions from one behavior to another. Furthermore, there was an increase in predictibility, in that the number of transitions which had a conditional probability significantly different from expected went from 6 at 3 months, to 8 at 6 months, to 13 at 9 months. In general, it was found that the older the infant, the more behavioral options he had available and the greater his capacity to employ these options to sustain self-regulation while interpersonally stressed.

In another study in our laboratory (Cohn & Tronick, 1983), we asked each mother to simulate depression with her 3½-month-old-infant. Specifically, we asked the mother to flatten her affect, restrain the expressiveness of her voice, and to limit the use of her hands. Because simulated depression is a dynamic display, the mother mistimed and mismatched many of her infant's signals, making it a more stressful PRESAS than the still-face. What we found was that there was less social engagement by the infant than in the still-face situation. In terms of the sequential organization of behavior, there was a very tight cycle of Avert, Wary, and Negative Signal, which the infant found difficult to escape from.

In order to better understand infant coping, Cohn and Tronick are now carrying out a naturalistic study of 7-month-old infants whose mothers evidence depressive symptoms and other signs of disturbance (Cohn, Matias, Tronick, Connell, & Lyons-Ruth, 1987). The mothers are rated in the clinical range on the

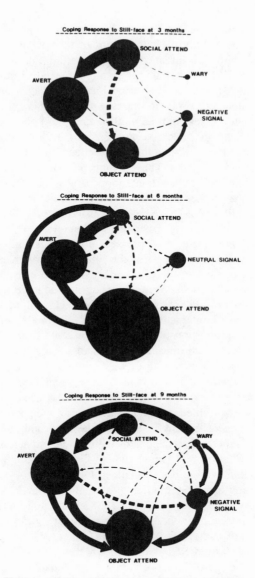

FIG. 3.1. The size of the circle represents the proportion of time infants were in each phase. The solid arrows are excitatory transitions,
those conditional probabilities that significantly ($p < .05$) exceeded the
independent probability of one transition, and broken arrows are in-
hibitory transitions, those conditional probabilities that significantly
($p < .05$) reduced the independent probability of the transition. The
wider the arrow the greater the likelihood of occurrence.

CES-D depression scale. The families are also participating in one of two clinical interventions. To better study the interactions of these dyads, the mothers are being asked to play with their infants at their homes. In preliminary analyses, the findings appear very much like what we found in our experimental studies except that these infants look much more distressed and disengaged than do infants in the simulated situation. For example, the depressed mothers engage in play less than 10% of the time, whereas normal mothers engage in play more than 42% of the time (Tronick, Krafchuk, Ricks, Cohn, & Winn, 1985). A second finding is that there is a profound distortion in the infant's behavior when they are interacting with their depressed mothers. These infants play only about 5% of the time, whereas infants of normal mothers play about 13% of the time. Moreover, the extant of play by the mother is strongly related to the amount of play by the infant, with a correlation of .51. We believe this indicates the extent to which the mother's behavior is influencing the infant's behavior.

Looking at the same group of depressed mothers and infants, we are also finding a disruption in other aspects of the infant's behavior in addition to the amount of play. In particular, there is a marked decrease in the percentage of time the infants are able to focus on an object during the interaction. In a normal interaction, the 6-month-old infant spends about 41% of the time in Object Attend. When a normal interaction is disturbed, as in the still-face, there is nonetheless a similar proportion of object engagement. In these situations, the infant directs his attention to objects as a way of coping, i.e., he switches his goal to object exploration as a way of maintaining self-regulation. However, when we look at the interactions of infants and their depressed mothers, there is a marked decrease in the proportion of time the infants engage objects. So not only has prolonged exposure limited the infant's available coping strategies by inhibiting his capacity to use Positive Signal to repair the distortion, it has also begun to disrupt the infant's emerging engagement with the inanimate environment.

The question we are now asking is when infants develop stable individual differences in dealing with stress. Some results have suggested that styles of coping are stabilizing around 6-months-of-age (Brazelton, 1974; Cohn & Tronick, 1983; Frosch, 1983; Massie, 1977, 1978, 1982; and Stern, 1971, 1977). However, the stability found in these studies was either short-term within-session effects, based on a few subjects, or drawn from clinical evidence. To address this situation, we recently completed a study in which we looked at the stability of infant reactions to the still-face at 6-months-of-age (Gianino, 1985). We had 52 infants interact with their mothers on two occasions, separated by 7 days. We then compared infant coping behaviors on visit 1 with their coping behaviors on visit 2. Gianino's Infant Coping Behavior System was used, modified to include three new codes based on the work reported earlier:

1. Self-Comfort—to capture the infant's attempts to use his own body or nearby objects to provide self-comforting stimulation; it includes the categories Oral-Self, Oral-Other, Rock, and Self-Clasp;

2. Escape—to capture the infant's attempts to increase his physical distance from the mother by turning, twisting, or arching away and to distinguish this behavior from the more serious forms of Motor Withdrawal in which the infant gives up postural control and collapses in his seat; and

3. Social Attend—to capture the times the infant monitors the mother without attempting to Signal her and to make the scoring system exhaustive.

The addition of Self-Comfort was particularly important, since our studies of simulated PRESAS indicated that infants often resorted to this coping behavior, sometimes to the exclusion of their other self-regulatory behaviors and sometimes in conjunction with them. Overall, we found that of the 33 correlations of behavior from visit 1 to visit 2 which we analyzed 18 were significant, ranging between .29 and .50. Only Scan and Social Attend failed to exhibit stability for all three dependent measures (frequency, total duration, and bout length) from visit 1 to visit 2. Since the literature on the stability of *discrete* behaviors in infancy has seldom demonstrated significant relationships (Sroufe & Waters, 1977), correlations of this size suggest an emergent pattern of stability in coping strategies. We offer two examples (see Table 3.2). First, we found that the total duration of all 3 categores of Signal (Positive, Neutral, and Negative) were positively correlated, indicating that infants displayed some stable tendencies in their use of Signal when presented with a particular interactive stress. When these 3 categories were collapsed, the evidence for stability in the use of Signal was even stronger. Significant correlations were found in how often the infants Signaled, how long they sustained each attempt, and the total time they employed it. If signaling the partner when distressed is an especially adaptive coping strategy, as we claim, then it is significant that 6-month-old infants are

TABLE 3.2
Correlations of Self-Regulatory Behaviors Visit One With Visit Two

Behavior	Total [a] Frequency	Total [a] Duration	Bout Length
Signal	.43[b]	.41[b]	.32[b]
Positive Signal	.36[b]	.50[b]	.20
Neutral Signal	-.03	.29[b]	.31[b]
Negative Signal	.22[b]	.35[b]	.20
Self-Comfort	.46[b]	.35[b]	.33[b]
Oral-Self	.47[b]	.31[b]	.45
Oral-Other	.30[b]	.34[b]	.32
Rock	.71[b]	.99[b]	.71

[a] Total duration and bout length measured in seconds.
[b] $p < .05$

already exhibiting some stable individual differences in this regard. Second, we found that 3 out of the 4 categories of Self-Comfort (the exception being Self-Clasp) were significantly correlated for the same three measures, i.e., frequency, total duration. and bout length. If tendencies to Self-Comfort in response to stress are predictive of certain patterns of personality development and defensive patterns, as hypothesized by generations of psychodynamic theorists, then evidence indicating the presence of stable individual differences in these tendencies at 6 months, at least in response to an interactive stress, suggests that certain aspects of character may be present as early as 6 months.

In a longitudinal study (Tronick et al., 1982), we related whether 6-month-old infants Signaled or failed to Signal (e.g., Scanned) in response to the still-face with their classification of attachment at 1 year, using Ainsworth's strange situation. From our perspective, the strange situation assesses the quality of the infant's ability to cope with an age appropriate stress, i.e., the mother leaving the infant in a strange situation. We found that those infants who Signaled at 6 months were classified as securely attached at 1 year, while those infants who failed to Signal were classified as insecurely attached. Thus there is evidence of stability between coping with an interpersonal stress at 6 months and interpersonal competence at 12 months.

The results of our two studies on the stability of individual differences in coping with interpersonal stress provide support for the view that two of the infant's more important coping strategies (Signal and Self-Comfort) are beginning to stabilize by 6 months. Remarkably, this is at least a month or two before most infants evidence a strong, discriminating attachment to their mother (Bowbly, 1969).

THE INTERCONNECTIONS AMONG SELF
AND MUTUAL REGULATION, OBJECT
EXPLORATION, COPING, AND DEFENSE

Our study of the ontogeny of infant coping behaviors from 3 to 9 months has shown that coping patterns are modified by the developmental level of the infant. Maturation and experience combine to expand the infant's initial self-regulatory repertoire. With development, the infant acquires greater skill and capacity in a number of areas. As Stern (1977) has pointed out, the infant's communicative repertoire, e.g., the range and use of facial expressions and vocalizations, broadens with development. At the same time, the infant's capacity to interpret the mother's expressions also increases as the infant begins to master subtleties of affective displays and social cues as well as nuances in the communicative meanings of changes in tempo and rhythm. The stabilization of the mother-infant relationship between 3 and 9 months facilitates this learning, enhancing the infant's ability to predict the mother's interactive patterns (Tronick et al., 1982).

The enhancements in the infant's ability to signal and decode interactive behaviors enables the infant to more effectively communicate his appraisal of a distorted interaction.

A most dramatic change comes between 4 and 7 months with the incorporation of objects into the interaction, affording the infant greater flexibility in switching his immediate goal away from social interaction when such interaction proves overly stressful. Considering these factors together, an infant of 9-months-of-age will have notably more skills available than a 3-month-old for coping with such sources of interactive stress as occasional maternal unresponsivity to the infant's signals (Stern, 1977; Tronick et al., 1982). Additionally, the older the infant the greater the complexity and flexibility of responses to interactive stress. Thus coping strategies are part of and arise out of the infant's behavioral repertoire for regulating social and object engagement. They are supplemented by the infant's ability to control his attentional, perceptive, and motor capacities, all of which afford him a further measure of behavioral and psychological control over the source of his distress.

It appears for at least some infants that coping patterns are beginning to stabilize by the time the infants reach 6-months-of-age and that the social competency exhibited in these emergent patterns might be related to the social competency evidenced in the infant's quality of attachment at 12 months (Tronick et al., 1982). Thus there is now evidence that infants have specific coping patterns and that they exhibit individual differences in the deployment of these coping patterns when confronted with an interactive stress. Furthermore, there is now reason to believe that a prolonged distortion of the interactive process, such as having a depressed mother, distorts and modifies both the infant's social and object skills.

We think these studies indicate that infant coping skills partly arise out of the infant's normal interactive behaviors. The skills required to regulate a normal interaction are employed whenever the flow of the interaction is disrupted by a mismatch. The negative affect which is briefly produced by a mismatch is typically modulated when the infant successfully regulates the interaction with his social skills. According to the MRM's account of the process, the infant signals the partner to change her mismatched behavior by expressing his appraisal that the interaction is distressing. The resulting change in the (sensitive and responsive) partner's behavior typically helps alleviate the infant's distress, since it alters the state of the interaction, which enables the infant to self-regulate his affective state. In short, interactive regulation and self-regulation complement each other: The infant's affective displays alter the partner's behavior and the interaction, which facilitates the infant's attempts to regulate his affective state. During those periods when the interactive stress is markedly prolonged, exaggerated, or distorted, however, the infant is unable to readjust the interaction. This engenders greater negative affect which often compels the use of other regulatory—or what we call coping—strategies, e.g., self-comforting.

The intimate connection between self-regulation and interactive regulation within the MRM has led us to conclude that it is important to consider them together when discussing the infant's social behavior. Since even normal interactions typically involve a number of mismatches, we believe this point applies to *normal* as well as *distorted* interactions. In a sense we are saying that the infant must be viewed from two perspectives, but that like the Necker Cube the perspectives are on one object, the infant.

The first perspective views the infant as regulating his social interactions to achieve a goal-determined interactive state. Although this regulatory task has been given more attention than the task of self-regulation by researchers studying social interaction, there is still no consensus on how to classify the interactive goal. As mentioned earlier, in addition to Brazelton's (1974) suggested term "reciprocity," which we use in this paper to designate both a goal and a dynamic process, there are the concepts "mutual delight" (Stern, 1977), "affective attunment" (Beebe & Stern, 1977), "intersubjectivity" (Trevarthan, 1977), "coherence" (Lester, Hoffman, & Brazelton, 1985; Gottman, 1979), "matching" (Tronick, Als, & Adamson, 1978) and "shared directional tendencies" (Tronick et al., 1982). In spite of these differences, there *is* agreement that the infant's behavior is *directed* towards social interaction once the corresponding behavioral system has been activated by social stimuli or internal processes. There is also agreement that the infant's behavior is modified by the feedback he receives from his interactive partner; Bowlby (1969) employs the term "goal-corrected" to describe this type of complexly motivated behavior.

In the second perspective, once the infant has set a goal for social interaction, he must regulate a variety of emotions appropriate to the goal and the conditions confronted. Each of these emotions is qualitatively different from the others (or they include blends, cf. Ekman, 1980), and each has an intensity dimension. The infant must regulate both the quality, i.e., which affective state predominates, and quantity, i.e., the intensity or fullness within an affective state. Others (Brazelton, 1974; Field, 1977; Sroufe, 1979; Stern, 1977) have argued that the infant is regulating a level or dimension of arousal. We believe this to be incorrect. Consider whether the infant is more *aroused* when smiling or when showing intense interest. Indeed, it is not at all clear how the arousal model accounts for the affective and behavioral specificity evidenced by the infant. Very similar critiques have been made of the "discrepancy hypothesis" which—although primarily a cognitive hypothesis—invokes a quantitative model of degree of discrepancy to account for the infant's differential reactions. On our view, the *arousal* which the infant must regulate is the intensity dimension of his affective states. But these differences notwithstanding, whatever we choose to call the "what" that is being regulated, these models agree it is something internal.

What may unite these two perspectives on the infant's regulatory tasks—one unobservable, endogenous, and subjective/experiential, the other observable, exogenous, and interactive—is that both see the process of regulation as involving the affective system with its simultaneous dualities of internal states and internal experiences manifested in external emotional expressions and interactive communication. It is because the infant's internal affective regulators use the exogenous input he is receiving to help modify both his internal affective state and his interactive communication to his partner that self-regulation and interactive regulation can occur at the same time. Again, since the exogenous input emanating from a social partner can be modified through the infant's communicative behaviors when the partner is willing to be sensitively responsive to the infant's signals, the infant can regulate the interaction at the same time that he regulates his affective state. For example, when the infant smiles in response to maternal play, it is an act of self-regulation which has resulted in pleasure, indicating that the infant has achieved some goal, and it is a socially regulatory act, communicating that the partner should continue to engage in her activity. Thus regulation takes place inside and outside the organism.

This view does not require that the infant make a distinction between self and other. In fact, it may be advantageous to an infant with a sensitive partner not to make the distinction and instead believe that all changes emanate from himself, since the resulting well-regulated interaction will further his sense of effectance (Tronick et al., 1982). On the other hand, the inability to distinguish between self and other can be disadvantageous—indeed, deleterious—when the interactive partner is insensitive. With such a partner, the infant's inability to discriminate the actual source of his distress will teach him that he is incapable of exerting any control over his social realm, which will inhibit his development of a sense of effectance.

In this paper, we have noted that the disruption of object engagement observed in infants interacting with their depressed mothers entails a disruption of their capacity to use such engagement as a self-regulatory, or coping, strategy. We recognize that the disruption in object engagement is directly due to a disruption in the behavioral system which controls object engagement rather than to a disruption in the system which controls social engagement (Brazelton et al., 1974; Trevarthan & Hubley, 1978; Tronick, Krafchuk, Ricks, Cohn, & Winn, 1985). However, we also believe that the two systems are organized hierarchically, with the social engagement system primary and the object engagement system partly dependent on it (Tronick, 1980). The disruption seen in object engagement occurs because the depressed mother's interaction profoundly disrupts the infant's ability to control his social engagement, and without that control the infant cannot go on to engage objects. This interpretation is similar to Ainsworth's interpretation of a balance between attachment and exploration. In her view, when the attachment is disrupted, causing the infant to feel insecure, the infant is unable to move on to explore the environment. We are making the further claim that when the infant has a history of abnormally stressful interactions, he becomes unable to recruit his object engagement system for self-regulatory purposes. The infant's ability to deploy his object engagement system to regulate his affective state as well as his involvement with objects parallels his ability to use his social skills for both self- and interactive regulation. From this point of view, he is able to use both sxstems for internal and external regulatory functions (the Necker Cube, again).

As a last point we might begin to think about the development of defensive behaviors. We introduce defensive behaviors into this discussion because we believe they have a functional relationship to coping behaviors in that both serve self-regulatory objectives. Since we are looking at the normal development of coping skills and arguing that they evolve out of the normal interaction, particularly aspects of the interaction that involve mismatching, we think it is important to consider the connection these functions have to the emergence of infant defensive skills. Drawing upon case studies by Brazelton, Young, and Bullowa (1971), Stern (1971, 1977), Massie (1977, 1978, 1982), and Adamson, Als, Tronick, and Brazelton (1977), Gianino (1982) has hypothesized that defensive behaviors can evolve out of the infant's attempts to cope with a history of chronic PRESAS to his primary social relationships. Experience, constrained by temperament (Derryberry & Rothbart, 1984), teaches the infant which coping behaviors are most effective in regulating the distress (Sullivan, 1953). The transition from coping behaviors to defensive behaviors occurs once the infant begins to employ them automatically, inflexibly, and indiscriminantly, and thus even with a partner who does nothing to warrant them. They are ''defensive'' because they are adopted to *preclude* the experience of interactive stress, that is, to preclude the experience of anxiety generated by the infant's interactive experience. Once the infant begins to automatically deploy defensive behaviors, he will adopt them even if they are so extreme as to constrict his overall ability to maintain engagement with the surround and, more generally, even if they restrict his immediate and longer term options; in short, even if they curtail his autonomy. Such is the primacy of the infant's need to self-regulate his affective state.

To illustrate the difference we see between coping and defense, consider the following example. We have found that among normal infants a prolonged avert is a common response to an interactive stress. In a normal population an avert is adaptive since it allows the infant to self-regulate and does not preclude him from returning to the mother when she makes herself more available. As long as the mother is not habitually unavailable, the infant experiences many occasions in which he successfully engages her and many occasions in which he first averts from her to cope with a mismatch but then returns to find her ready to reengage him. With this interactive history, the infant develops a sense of confidence in his mother's availability (Ainsworth, Bell, & Stayton, 1974) and a sense of competence in his own ability to regulate mismatches (Tronick et al., 1982; White, 1959). But consider an infant who repeatedly resorts to an avert in order to cope with a mother who routinely rebuffs his social elicitations. We speculate that after many such experiences the infant will tend to automatically disengage from the mother in order to immediately minimize his distress. His tendency will be to disengage, perhaps involving himself in the surround, even before he has begun to interact with her. And with the cumulative impact of these experiences, he will develop a sense of ineffectance or helplessness and be biased towards withdrawal (Seligman, 1975). Furthermore, we expect that his sense of ineffectance and tendency towards withdrawal will be carried into his other relationships, even with partners who are more sensitive (see Massie, 1978; Stern, 1977). We believe that in situations such as described in the hypothetical example above, the infant's deployment of his normal social skills fails to regulate the distorted interaction. As this begins to compel the infant to make self-regulation a preeminent goal, he begins to turn inward. Once the infant's experience with this kind of failure of interactive regulation is reiterated enough, he begins to withdraw and to come into new situations already withdrawn, already biased not to react to the situation appropriately. We think that the reiteration of experiences which prevent normal interactive regulation is the basis of the defensive patterns of behavior and, indeed, the pathology we see in failure to thrive, depressed, and withdrawn infants.

We believe that coping with an interpersonal stress is an important adaptive task for normal infants during the first year and that such coping may have a predictive relationship to later measures of social competency. Certainly more research is needed on the origin of individual differences in the patterning of coping strategies, or what we call coping styles. Research of this type is needed on both normal and at risk populations and should consider variables such as infant temperament and maternal sensitivity. We believe the resulting data will broaden our understanding of both normal and abnormal developmental processes.

REFERENCES

Adamson, L., Als, H., Tronick, E., & Brazelton, T. B. (1977). The development of social reciprocity between a sighted infant and her blind parents. *Journal of the American Academy of Child Psychology, 16,* 194–207.

Ainsworth, M., Bell, S., & Stayton, D. (1974). Infant-mother attachment and social development: "Socialization" as a product of reciprocal responsiveness to signals. In M. P. M. Richards (Ed.), *The integration of a child into a social world.* London: Cambridge University Press.

Anderson, B. J., Vietze, P., & Dokechi, P. R. (1977). Reciprocity in vocal interaction of mothers and infants. *Child Development, 48,* 1676–1681.

Bakeman, R., & Brown, J. V. (1977). Behavioral dialogues: An approach to the assessment of mother-infant interaction. *Child Development, 48,* 195–203.

Beebe, B. (1975). *The regulation of interpersonal space through the creation of visual spatial boundaries, and implications for defensive processes: One case study at 4 months.* Unpublished Manuscript, Albert Einstein University Psychiatric Institute.

Beebe, B., Jaffe, J., Feldstein, S., Mays, K., & Alson, D. (1985). Matching of timing: The application of an adult dialogue model to mother infant vocal and kinesic interactions. To appear in T. Field (Ed.), *Infant Social Perception.* Norwood, NJ: Ablex.

Beebe, B., & Stern, D. (1977). Engagement-disengagement and early object experience. In M.

Freedman & S. Grenel (Eds.), *Communicative structures and psychic structures*. New York: Plenum.

Bloom, K. (1977). Operant baseline procedures suppress infant social behavior. *Journal of Experimental Child Psychology, 23*, 128–132.

Bowlby, J. (1969). *Attachment and Loss, Vol 1, Attachment*, New York: Basic Books.

Brazelton, T. B. (1974). Does the neonate shape his environment? In *Birth Defects, Original Articles Series, The National Foundation, The infant at risk, 10*(32), 131–140.

Brazelton, T. B. (1982). Joint regulation of neonate-parent behavior. In E. Tronick (Ed.), *Social interchange in infancy: Affect, cognition, and communication*. Baltimore, MD: University Park Press.

Brazelton, T. B., Koslowski, B., & Main, M. (1974). The origin of reciprocity: The early mother-infant interaction. In M. Lewis & L. Rosenblum (Eds.), *The effect of the infant on its caregiver*. New York: Wiley.

Brazelton, T. B., Young, G. G., & Bullowa, M. (1971). Inception and resolution of early developmental pathology: A case history. *Journal of the American Academy of Child Psychiatry, 10*, 124–35.

Bullowa, M. (1975). When infant and adult communicate, how do they synchronize their behaviors? In A. Kendon, R. M. Harris & M. R. Key (Eds.), *The organization of behavior in face-to-face interaction*. The Hague: Mouton.

Campos, J., Barrett, K., Lamb, M., Goldsmith, H., & Sternberg, R. (1983). Socioemotional development. In P. Mussen (Eds), *Handbook of child development*. New York: Wiley.

Cohn, J., Krafchuk, E., Ricks, M., Winn, S., & Tronick, E. (1985). Continuity and change from three to nine months-of-age in the sequencing of mother-infant dyadic states during face-to-face interaction. Accepted for publication, *Developmental Psychology*.

Cohn, J., Matias, R., Tronick, E. Z., Connell, D., & Lyons-Ruth, K. (1987). Face-to-face interactions of depressed mothers & their infants. In E. Tronick & T. Field, (Eds.), *Maternal depression & infant disturbance*. San Francisco: Jossey-Bass.

Cohn, J., & Tronick, E. Z. (1983). Three-month-old infant's reaction to simulated maternal depression. *Child Development, 54*, 185–193.

Derryberry, D., & Rothbart, M. (1984). Emotion, attention, and temperament. In C. Izard, J. Kagan, & R. Zajoc (Eds.), *Emotion, cognition and behavior*. New York: Cambridge University Press.

Dixon, S. D., Yogman, M., Tronick, E., Adamson, L., Als, H., & Brazelton, T. B. (1981). Early infant social interaction with parents and strangers. *Journal of American Adademy of Child Psychiatry, 20*, 32–52.

Ekman, P. (1980). Biological and culture contributions to body and facial movement in the expression of emotions. In A. Rorty (Ed.), *Explaining emotions*. Berkeley: University of California Press.

Fafouti-Milenkovic, M., & Uzgiris, I. C. (1979). The mother-infant communication system. *New Directions for Child Development, 4*, 41–56.

Field, T. M. (1977). Effects of early separation, interactive deficits, and experimental manipulations on infant-mother face-to-face interaction. *Child Development, 48*, 763–771.

Fogel, A., Diamond, G. R., Langhorst, B. H., & Demos, V. (1983). Affective and cognitive aspects of the 2-month-old's participation in face-to-face interaction with the mother. In E. Z. Tronick (Ed.), *Social interchange in infancy: Affect, cognition, and communication*. Baltimore, MD: University Park Press.

Frosch, E. (1983). *Re-establishing equilibrium: A study of the ontogeny of transition strategies*. Unpublished manuscript, Amherst College.

Gianino, A. (1982). *The ontogeny of coping responses in infancy*. Unpublished manuscript, University of Massachusetts.

Gianino, A. (1985). *The stability of infant coping with interpersonal stress*. Unpublished doctoral dissertation, University of Massachusetts.

Greenspan, S. (1982). *Psychopathology and adaptation in infancy and early childhood: Principles of clinical diagnosis and preventive intervention*. New York: International University Press.

Gottman, J. M. (1979). Detecting cyclicity in social interaction. *Psychological Bulletin, 86*, 338–348.

Hodapp, R., & Mueller, E. (1982). Early social development. In B. Wolman (Ed.), *Handbook of developmental psychology*. Englewood Cliffs, NJ: Prentice-Hall.

Izard, C. E. (1978). On the ontogenesis of emotions and emotion-cognition relationships in infancy. In M. Lewis & L. Rosenblum (Eds.), *The development of affect*. New York: Plenum.

Lester, B. M., Hoffman, J., & Brazelton, T. B. (1985). The rhythmic structure of mother-infant interaction in term and preterm infants. *Child Development, 56*, 449–452.

Massie, H. N. (1977). Patterns of mother-infant behavior and subsequent childhood psychosis. *Child Psychiatry and Human Development, 7*, 211–230.

Massie, H. N. (1978). The early natural history of childhood psychosis. *Journal of American Academy of Child Psychiatry, 17*, 29–45.

Massie, H. N. (1982). Affective development and the organization of mother-infant behavior from the perspective of psychopathology. In E. Tronick (Ed.), *Social interchange in infancy: Affect, cognition and communication*. Baltimore, MD: University Park Press.

Mayer, N., & Tronick, E. (1985). Mother turn-giving signals and infant turn-taking in mother-infant interaction. In T. Field & N. Fox (Eds.), *Social perception in infants*. Norwood, NJ: Ablex.

McCall, R. B., & McGhee, P. E. (1977). The discrepancy hypothesis of attention and affect in infant. In E. C. Uzgiris & F. Weismann (Eds.), *The structuring of experience*. New York: Plenum.

Parke, R. (1979). Perspectives on father-infant interaction. In J. Osofsky (Ed.), *Handbook on infant development*. New York: Wiley.

Parke, R., & Asher, S. (1983). Social and personality development. In M. Rosenzweig & L. Porter (Eds.), *Annual Review of Psychology, 34*.

Parke, R. D., O'Leary, S. E., & West, S. (1972, September). Mother-father-newborn interaction: Effects of maternal medication, labor, and sex of infant. *Proceedings of the 18th Annual Convention*, American Psychological Association, Washington, D.C.

Piaget, J. (1968). *Six psychological studies*. New York: Vintage Books.

Sander, L. (1962). Issues in early mother-infant interaction. *Journal of the American Acadamy of Child Psychiatry, 1*, 141–166.

Sander, L. W. (1977). The regulation of exchange in the infant-caregiver systems and some aspects of the context-contest relationship. In M. Lewis & L. Rosenblum (Eds.), *Interaction, conversation and the development of language*. New York: Wiley.

Seligman, M. E. P. (1975). *Helplessness: On depression, development and death*. San Francisco: W. H. Freeman.

Spitz, R. (1965). *The first year of life*. New York: International University Press.

Sroufe, L. (1979). Socioemotional development. In J. Osofsky (Ed.), *Handbook of infant development*. New York: Wiley.

Sroufe, L., & Waters, E. (1977). Attachment as an organizational construct. *Child Development, 48*, 1184–1199.

Stechler, G., & Halton, A. (1982). Prenatal influences on human development. In B. Wolman (Ed.), *Handbook of developmental psychology*. Englewood Cliffs, NJ: Prentice-Hall.

Stern, D. A. (1971). A micro-analysis of mother-infant interaction: Behavior regulating social contact between a mother and her 3½ month old twins. *Journal of the American Academy of Child Psychiatry, 10*, 501–517.

Stern, D. (1974). The goal and structure of mother-infant play. *Journal of the American Academy of Child Psychiatry, 13,* 402–421.

Stern, D. (1977). *The first relationship.* Cambridge, MA: Harvard University Press.

Sullivan, H. S. (1953). *The Interpersonal Theory of Psychology.* New York: Norton.

Trevarthan, C. (1977). Descriptive analyses of infant communicative behavior. In H. R. Schaffer (Ed.), *Studies in mother-infant interaction* . London: Academic Press.

Trevarthan, C., & Hubley, P. (1978). Secondary inter-subjectivity: Confidence, confiding and acts of meaning in the first year. In A. Lock (Ed.), *Action, gesture and symbol: The emergence of language* . New York: Academic Press.

Tronick, E. (1980). On the primacy of social skills. In D. B. Sawin, L. O. Walker, & J. H. Penticuff (Eds.), *The exceptional infant, Vol. 4: Psychosocial risks in infant-environmental transactions* . New York: Bruner/Mazel.

Tronick, E. (Ed.). (1982). *Social interchange in infancy: Affect, cognition, and communication.* Baltimore, MD: University Park Press.

Tronick, E., Als, H., & Adamson, L. (1978). Structure of early face-to-face communicative interactions. In M. Bullowa (Ed.), *Before speech: The beginning of interpersonal communication.* Cambridge, England: Cambridge University Press.

Tronick, E., Als, J., Adamson, L., Wise, S., & Brazelton, T. B. (1978). The infant's response to entrapment between contradictory messages in face-to-face interaction. *Journal of American Academy of Child Psychiatry, 17,* 1–13.

Tronick, E., Als, H., & Brazelton, T. B. (1980). Monadic phases: A structural descriptive analysis of infant-mother face-to-face interaction. *Merrill-Palmer Quarterly of Behavior and Development, 26,* 1–24.

Tronick, E. Z., Cohn, J., Shea, E. (1985). The transfer of affect between mothers and infants. In T. B. Brazelton & M. Yogman (Eds.), *Affective development in infancy.* Norwood, NJ: Ablex.

Tronick, E., Krafchuk, E., Ricks, M., Cohn, J., & Winn, S. (1980). *Social interaction "normal and abnormal" maternal characteristics, and the organization of infant social behavior.* Paper presented at the Seminar on the Development of Infants and Parents, Boston.

Tronick, E., Krafchuk, E., Ricks, M., Cohn, J., & Winn, S. (1985). *Mother-infant face-to-face interaction at 3, 6, and 9 months: Content and matching.* Manuscript submitted for publication.

Tronick, E. Z., Ricks, M., & Cohn, J. F. (1982). Maternal and infant affective exchange: Patterns of adaptation. In T. Field and A. Fogel (Eds.), *Emotion and interaction: Normal and high risk infants.* Hillsdale, NJ: Lawrence Erlbaum Associates.

White, R. (1959). Motivation reconsidered: The concept of competence. *Psychological Review, 66,* 297–33.

Zahn-Waxler, C., McKnew, D. H., Cummings, M., Davenport, Y. B., Radke-Yarrow, M. (1984). Problem behaviors and peer interactions of young children with a manic-depressive parent. *American Journal of Psychiatry, 141*(2), 236–240.

II CHILDHOOD

4 Antecedents of the Coronary-Prone Behavior Pattern

Barbara S. McCann
Karen A. Matthews
University of Pittsburgh

The Type A behavior pattern is defined as ". . . a characteristic action-emotion complex which is exhibited by those individuals who are engaged in a relatively chronic struggle to obtain an unlimited number of poorly defined things from their environment in the shortest period of time, and if necessary, against the opposing efforts of other things or persons in this same environment" (Friedman, 1969). The major overt manifestations of this behavior pattern are extremes of aggressiveness, an easily aroused hostility, excessive competitive achievement striving, and heightened impatience. Individuals who display a preponderance of these behaviors are called Type As, whereas those who do not are called Type Bs. Type As are at approximately twice the risk for coronary heart disease as Type Bs (Haynes, Feinleib, & Kannel, 1980; Rosenman, Brand, Jenkins, Friedman, Straus, & Wurm, 1975). This elevated risk remains when the major risk factors for coronary heart disease are simultaneously controlled.

Given the health consequences of Type A behavior, it is important to understand its origins. The present chapter provides an overview of what is known, as of late 1984, about the development of Pattern A. It begins by laying out the assumptions underlying our research in this area. We then describe how Type A can be assessed in the developing individual. Here we discuss the reliability and behavioral validity of available methods. The next section considers the relationship of children's Type A behaviors and related psychophysiological processes to those exhibited by adults. The fourth section evaluates familial factors affecting the development of Pattern A and the final section describes our current research efforts.

MAJOR RESEARCH ASSUMPTIONS

Our research program is based on six major assumptions. First, it is assumed that the study of the pediatric origins of the risk factors for coronary heart disease is important for prevention of disease in healthy individuals and for intervention with high risk persons. Although manifest coronary heart disease is rare among the young, it does not strike out of the blue. It is typically the consequence of a life-long development of atherosclerosis in the coronary arteries. This condition, called coronary artery disease in its advanced form, arises from the interplay of certain genetic, biological, and life style factors that can begin to exert their pathogenic influence prior to or during the second decade of life. Indeed, the early beginning of coronary artery disease may be quite prevalent. Over half of the adolescent war victims in two autopsy studies showed some signs of coronary atherosclerosis (Enos, Holmes, & Beyer, 1953; McNamara, Molot, Stremple, & Cutting, 1971). As a consequence of these and other data, scientists are investigating the prevalence and development in the young of the specific features or risk factors known to characterize adults prone to coronary artery and heart disease. It is in this context that we are studying the development of the Type A behavior pattern.

A second assumption is that Pattern A is a multidimensional construct. Pattern A is not a single behavior, but a set of behaviors. Thus, the developmental pathways for the individual components may be quite different. This possibility has led us to study both the development of overall Pattern A and its individual components.

The third assumption of our research derives from the second. Behavior pattern classification is based on a simple preponderance of discrete Type A behaviors. Thus, not all Type As display all Type A behaviors, nor do all Type Bs display none. Consequently it is possible that some Type A characteristics are more important than others in accounting for Type A's association with coronary artery and heart disease. A reanalysis of a subset of data from the Western Collaborative Group Study was undertaken to test this proposition (Matthews, Glass, Rosenman, & Bortner, 1977). The Structured Interview responses of the first 62 men under the intake age of 50 years diagnosed with coronary heart disease during the first 4½ years of the study were compared to those of 124 healthy controls matched for age and place of employment. Of the more than 40 ratings of the Structured Interview, the following eight discriminated cases and controls: overall ratings of potential for hostility and vigorous answers; and self-reports that anger is frequent and outward, that the person gets irritated when waiting, that he/she is competitive with peers, and that he/she senses time passing too rapidly. Thus, only some aspects of Type A were related to risk for coronary heart disease in this sample and we are assuming in our research that only some aspects of Type A may be important for understanding the origins of coronary risk.

A fourth assumption concerns the fact that while we are psychologists by training, we do not believe that the origins of Type A are merely psychological in nature. Rather, we assume that a complex interplay of biological, genetic, psychological, and cultural factors plays a role in the development of the coronary-prone aspects of Type A. This assumption is based in part on data showing cross-cultural differences in the prevalence of Type A behavior (e.g., Cohen, Syme, Jenkins, Kagan, & Zyzanski, 1979) and in part on data demonstrating biological correlates of Type A men's responses to psychological stress (see Houston, 1983 for a review).

The fifth assumption concerns our model of development of Type A. In general, models of development can be categorized into two major types: stage and linear. A stage model presumes that the development of a behavioral characteristic, e.g., competitiveness, entails a series of transformations of behavior where new, previously unused rules, styles, and motives appear and are different in substance from previous rules, styles, and motives used to guide behavior. In contrast, a linear model of development of competitiveness assumes a remarkable consistency in competitive behavior over the life span. This is not to say that a behavior like competitiveness never changes in a linear model approach, but that its form in adulthood, e.g., playing a cutthroat game of bridge, is recognizable from its childhood manifestation, e.g., aspiring to be the best student in class. In our research, we have assumed a linear model of development, not because it may be entirely true, but because it is a simpler model. We will move to the more complex, stage model as the data push us in that direction. At the present time, however, data from longitudinal studies of the development of personality characteristics resembling Type A do indicate some stability in those characteristics. For example, the level of achievement striving by elementary school-aged children relative to others their age is similar to their relative level in adulthood (Block, 1971; Moss & Kagan, 1961). Impulsivity, which is related to Pattern A probably via its association with impatience, demonstrates an unusually high persistence over time (Block, 1971).

Data from these longitudinal studies also support our final assumption: the development of Pattern A may be different for males and females. Longitudinal data demonstrate continuity from childhood to adulthood for males, not females, in competitiveness, anger arousal, and aggressiveness (Block, 1971; Moss & Kagan, 1961; Olweus, 1979). Modes of experiencing and expressing anger may differ for the sexes. Achievement behaviors of women are thought to be affected to a greater degree by a fear of success than those of men (Horner, 1972). Not only do we believe that the development of Pattern A is different for men and women, but we think the available longitudinal data indicate that it may become stable later for women.

ASSESSMENT OF TYPE A BEHAVIOR IN CHILDREN
AND ADOLESCENTS

In investigating the antecedents of Pattern A, it is necessary to develop an adequate method for identifying children who exhibit Type A or Type B behavior. In this section, we review the available instruments for assessing Pattern A in children and adolescents, namely, the Adolescent Structured Interview (ASI), the Hunter-Wolf A-B Rating Scale, and the Matthews Youth Test for Health (MYTH).

ASI.   Siegel and Leitch (1981) explored the feasibility of adapting the Structured Interview (SI; Rosenman, 1978) for use with adolescents. They developed the Adolescent Structured Interview (ASI), which contains 22 questions about the interviewee's characteristics in a variety of settings. Its administration is different from the administration of the SI. Unlike the SI, the degree of challenge in the ASI is minimal because adolescents in pilot testing withdrew from such challenges. Siegel and Leitch (1981) administered the interview to 204 male and female adolescents, ranging in age from 13 to 18 years. Results revealed good interrater agreement (75%). There were no sex or age effects on behavior classifications.

In a later study, Siegel, Matthews, and Leitch (1981) rated these same interviews for interruption of the interviewer, loud or explosive speech, response latency, passive hostility, and competition for control of the interview, i.e., for content and speech stylistics. These ratings were subjected to factor analysis and yielded three factors: Interview Behaviors, Impatience and Harddriving. Two of the three factors from the ASI were only weakly associated with the global classification: Impatience and Harddriving. Only the Interview Behaviors factor was correlated with the global rating ($r = .81$). Adolescents who scored above the median on this last factor rated themselves as more active, angry, and controlling than those who scored below the median. High-scoring subjects on the Impatience factor indicated they felt a sense of time urgency, and strove for both recognition and achievement. Finally, high-scoring subjects on the Harddriving factor reported being competitive, hard working, desiring recognition, and active.

In a subsequent study, Siegel (1982) assessed the relationship between the ASI and cardiovascular arousal and sleep disturbances in 213 adolescents. The Impatience factor of the ASI was strongly related to reports of cardiovascular arousal. A weak relationship was found between the Harddriving factor and cardiovascular arousal. No such relationship was found for the Interview Behaviors factor. There were no significant relationships between sleep disturbances and any of the factors.

Although preliminary data show the ASI to be a valid instrument for determining Type A classification and related components in the adolescent population, further research is needed to assess the validity of this instrument for predicting behavior in the school or home. The ASI is related to self-reported behaviors, but it may or may not be related to actual Type A behaviors of adolescents. In addition, the feasibility of employing this measure in the assessment of a younger sample (below age 13) should be investigated. However, initial comparisons between the ASI and the MYTH (Matthews & Jennings, 1984) do indicate that these two measures correlate quite well among 4th and 5th grade male children ($r = .42$).

Hunter-Wolf A-B Rating Scale. The second method of assessing Type A in children is the A-B Rating Scale developed by Hunter, Wolf, and their associates (Wolf, Hunter, & Webber, 1979). The current version of this self-report questionnaire contains 24 items rated on a 7-point scale. The items were derived from the Bortner A-B rating scale, which assesses Pattern A in adulthood (Bortner, 1969), and from the MYTH. Sample items (reflecting time urgency) are: "I feel the time passes quickly, I think about many things at the same time." In one sample of 85 8th-grade children, test-retest reliability of the Hunter-Wolf A-B rating scale across 6 weeks was .53. While there were no gender differences in this sample, there was a racial difference such that Caucasians scored higher on the A-B scale than did blacks. Also, children who scored high on the scale had a lower self-concept than did children who scored low on the scale, in contrast to Type A college students who have higher self-esteem (Glass, 1977).

In another study, the construct validity of the Hunter-Wolf scale was examined using a subsample of participants in the Bogalusa Heart Study (Wolf, Sklov, Wenzl, Hunter, & Berenson, 1982). A total of 160 black and Caucasian male and female children from 5th and 6th grade classrooms completed the Hunter-Wolf scale and participated in six tasks designed to elicit Type A behavior. For half the children, emphasis was placed on speed and competition for the tasks. The remaining children completed the tasks without these instructions; these children comprised the control condition. As predicted, Type A children generally responded to the majority of tasks in an accelerated and/or competitive manner. It was not found, however, that Type A children performed at an accelerated rate regardless of task instructions, while Type Bs performed quickly only when speed and competition were emphasized.

In sum, the Hunter-Wolf Rating Scale is useful because it can be self-administered and because available validity data are good. Reliability data for periods longer than 6 weeks should be collected. It is not clear, however, if the instrument would be useful with children younger than 12-years-old.

MYTH. The final scale is the Matthews Youth Test for Health, or MYTH (Matthews & Angulo, 1980). This scale contains 17 statements that describe competitive achievement-striving, aggressiveness-hostility, and a sense of time urgency in children. A sample item is, "When working or playing, she/he tries to do better than other children.'' Another illustration is, "This child is patient when working with children slower than she/he is.'' Each statement is rated by an external observer, the child's classroom teacher, on a scale of 1 (extremely uncharacteristic) to 5 (extremely characteristic). After three items are reverse coded (because they describe Pattern B), the scores are summed to yield an overall score that can range from 17 to 85. Two subscale scores are also available in the MYTH. One is the sum of all the items describing children's competitiveness and achievement behavior. The second is the sum of all items describing children's aggressiveness, hostility, and a sense of time urgency. These two subscales were developed because repeated factor analyses of the MYTH items in various samples consistently yielded the above two dimensions.

Normative, reliability, and validity data on the MYTH were gathered in a sample of approximately 500 elementary-school-age children residing in a small midwestern town (Matthews & Angulo, 1980). The children were enrolled in grades kindergarten, 2, 4, and 6, and were predominantly Caucasian and from middle socioeconomic families. Children in the study represented 95% of the potential participants. All participants were evaluated on the MYTH scale three times by their classroom teachers.

The results revealed that while the total MYTH scores did not vary by grade, boys did have higher MYTH scores at all grades than did girls in this sample. This gender difference in rated Type A is consistent with gender differences in adult Pattern A (Waldron, 1979) and in children's aggressive and competitive behavior (Maccoby & Jacklin, 1974), two components of Pattern A. Thus, it appears likely that the gender differences in Pattern A in adulthood have their beginning in childhood.

The stability and reliability of the MYTH assessment of Type A behavior have been assessed within the context of a longitudinal study (Matthews & Avis, 1983). School children from two different communities were rated on the MYTH by their classroom teachers for 2 consecutive years. A total of 248 children from a small Kansas community were assessed on two occasions, and 385 children were assessed who lived in an affluent Pittsburgh suburb.

To assess the intrarater reliability of the MYTH, children in the Kansas sample had repeated MYTH ratings within 3 weeks by the same teachers. This analysis yielded high correlations on all MYTH scores, ranging from $rs = .84$ to .87. Calculation of Pearson correlation coefficients yielded correlations between repeated MYTH scores over the 2 years which ranged from $rs = .47$ to .59. Correlations were greatest with the older children in the study, suggesting that behavior patterns become more stable over time. Similar trends were noted for the competitive achievement and impatience-aggression subscales of the MYTH. Analysis of sex and community differences revealed that boys from the Pittsburgh sample were rated less consistently over time than the remaining subjects. This finding raises the possibility that environmental factors might differentially affect ratings of boys' and girls' Pattern A behaviors.

The reliability of MYTH Type A behaviors has also been studied in preschool-age children. Murray, Bruhn, and Bunce (1983) found that teachers' ratings of 219 4-year-olds yielded factors similar to those described previously (Matthews & Angulo, 1980). These investigators also assessed changes in MYTH scores over time. Fifty-four of the students rated initially at age 4 were rated again when they were age 5. No MYTH differences between ages 4 and 5 were found. An additional 56 students rated at age 4 were rated again at age 6. Within this subsample, boys at age 6 scored lower on the total Type A scale and on the impatience/aggression subscale than they had at age 4. No age differences were found for girls. In another study (Murray & Bruhn, 1983), the MYTH was completed by teachers of 114 4-year-old preschool children. The MYTH was administered again 3 months after the initial administration. Test-retest correlations for the subscales of the MYTH ranged from .68 to .73.

The validity of the MYTH has been tested by a series of laboratory studies. For example, in a study in which 2nd- and 6th-grade children were asked to perform a frustrating task, observers' ratings of children's impatient behaviors revealed that MYTH Type A children were significantly more impatient than Type B children (Matthews & Angulo, 1980). MYTH Type As sighed, were restless, and interrupted the experimenter. Similar behaviors are diagnostic criteria of Pattern A in the adult interview (Scherwitz, Berton, & Leventhal, 1977; Schucker & Jacobs, 1977).

Type A adults have been shown to have high aspirations for their performance (Mettlin, 1976; Snow, 1978). Matthews and Siegel (1983) have demonstrated that Type A children have higher standards for evaluation of their performance than do Type B children, regardless of the presence or absence of an explicit standard. Type B children, in contrast, choose a higher standard only in the absence of a specific standard. Also, Type A children in this study choose to compare their performance with a hypothetical child who performs exceptionally well, despite being told that their own performance is "pretty good."

Corrigan and Moskowitz (1983) studied the construct validity of the MYTH in a sample of 48 preschool-age children. The children were classified as A or B using the MYTH. Children were assigned to a choice reaction time visual task with or without incentives. As expected, Type B children with no incentives had significantly slower reaction times than the Type As in the two groups or the Type Bs with an incentive. Correlational analyses revealed an inverse relationship between the MYTH scores and reaction time. In addition, the MYTH scores were significantly positively correlated with classroom impatience ratings. The results of the study are consistent with similar studies of the effects of deadlines and incentives on task performances in Type A and Type B adults (Burnam, Pennebaker, & Glass, 1975; Manuck & Garland, 1979).

A similar finding has emerged in two studies of grade-school children conducted by Matthews and Volkin (1981). In one of the studies reported, MYTH Type As outperformed Type Bs on a series of arithmetic problems administered with or without a time deadline. This effect was due to As outperforming Bs when no deadline was given. In the second study, Type A boys were found to hold a weight 50% longer than Type B boys and to underreport their subjective fatigue. In general, results of laboratory studies have been supportive of the reliability and construct validity of the MYTH.

Summary.   Each of the aforementioned assessment techniques may be useful in certain settings. For example, the Hunter-Wolf A-B rating scale may measure adolescents' Type A behaviors and perhaps children's when teachers are unavailable to rate them. The MYTH requires the cooperation of teachers, but it does permit the rating of young children in a setting which is likely to elicit characteristic Type A behaviors. Finally, the ASI is valuable in its similarity to the adult SI and it makes scoring of speech stylistics possible. Thus, several techniques show promise as satisfactory measures of children's and adolescents' Type A behaviors. With continued psychometric research, it is likely that Pattern A can be adequately assessed via the above measures. In addition, in the process of validating any of the instruments, a more precise, rigorous conceptualization of Pattern A than is currently available may be developed.

PSYCHOPHYSIOLOGICAL CHARACTERISTICS
OF TYPE A CHILDREN

Numerous investigations have documented that when Type A adults are presented with situations which tap the major components of the Type A construct, they respond with heightened physiological arousal (see Houston, 1983, for a review). For example, Type A adults show greater increases relative to resting conditions in blood pressure, heart rate, and catecholamines when exposed to a harassing confederate than do Type B adults (Glass, Krakoff, Contrada, et al., 1980). Only a handful of psychophysiological investigations have been conducted among children identified as Type A. We now turn to a review of these studies.

Lawler, Allen, Critcher, and Standard (1981) studied blood pressure, heart rate, and skin conductance responses of children 11- and 12-years-old for whom MYTH and Bortner test battery performance scores (Bortner, Rosenman, & Friedman, 1970) were available. The latter test battery score consists of a composite of five behavioral measures thought to reflect Type A characteristics. Physiological responses were monitored during a reaction time task and an anagram solution task, both of which were accompanied by a small monetary incentive. When subjects were classified according to the Bortner battery, Type As showed a tendency toward higher systolic blood pressure levels and greater systolic blood pressure reactivity to both tasks. Type As also showed greater heart rate reactivity and variability during the task and at rest, respectively. In addition, Bortner-classified Type As had greater skin conductance responses to the reaction time signals. With the MYTH classification, only Type A females showed greater systolic blood pressure and heart rate reactivity. Type A females also showed lower mean heart rate and quicker reaction times. Type A males had greater mean heart rate levels overall.

Matthews and Jennings (1984) classified 4th and 5th grade boys as Type A or Type B on the basis of both the ASI and the MYTH. In the first of two experiments, 34 5th grade boys played two versions of a computer game called handball that tests speed and accuracy and should elicit competitiveness in Type As. During the first game, subjects were asked to keep the ball in play for 3 minutes with as few misses as possible. During the second game, they played against the computer. Blood pressures were measured at rest, and during and after the game. Heart rate and pulse transit time were measured throughout. In the second experiment, children played three games. One game required them to trace the outline of a star by viewing only the mirror image of their hand. Blood pressure was measured during this task. Another game entailed serial subtraction by 3's, 4's, and 2's in three trials of 60 seconds duration. Blood pressure was measured during each trial. In the final game, children were instructed to press a response key as quickly as possible after they saw the word "draw" on a computer monitor. If they pressed the key more than 400 msec after "draw" or if they pressed the key before "draw," they were "shot." Blood pressure was monitored three times during the course of this game. Heart rate and pulse transit time were measured throughout all three tasks.

Results revealed that all tasks for both experiments produced reliable increases in heart rate and blood pressure. During the first experiment, ASI-defined Type As showed greater heart rate reactivity than similarly defined Type Bs. During the second game, more extreme Type A behavior was associated with greater elevations in both systolic and diastolic blood pressure. The only significant finding in the first experiment using the MYTH for behavior classification showed that Type As and Type Xs (subjects with an equal representation of A and B characteristics) decreased in diastolic blood pressure from the first to the second task. Type Bs remained the same across the two tasks.

In the second experiment, behavior pattern classifications based on the ASI failed to yield A-B effects on the cardiovascular measures. However, the MYTH classification revealed that Type As had enhanced systolic blood pressure responses to the tasks in the second experiment. These subjects also experienced increasing heart rate relative to their MYTH-defined Type B counterparts. Therefore, support for the ability of both the ASI and the MYTH to predict cardiovascular reactivity was demonstrated, although a priori predictions about which tasks produced the effects were not made.

In a nonexperimental investigation, Siegel, Matthews, and Leitch (1983) assessed the relationship between Type A behavior and blood pressure variability in 211 male and female adolescents, 13- to 18-years-of-age. The empirical basis of this study was the findings reported by Manuck, Corse, and Winkelman (1979) showing that among lawyers, Type As had greater blood pressure variability and peak systolic blood pressure values during the workday than did Type Bs. In the Siegel et al. study, Type A was assessed using the ASI. Blood pressure was measured initially in a seated position following 5 minutes of rest. Approximately 8 months later, blood pressure was measured three times during the course of a physical examination. All assessments were conducted in subjects' schools. An analysis of covariance with weight and initial blood pressure as covariates revealed that extreme Type A (A1) adolescents showed the greater systolic blood pressure variability. However, subjects classified as incomplete Type As (A2s) did not differ from subjects with an equal representation of A and B characteristics (Type X). Diastolic blood pressure was not affected by behavior type. Behavior pattern was also associated with peak systolic blood pressure, with Type As showing greater peak systolic pressure than Type Bs. Similar effects for peak diastolic pressure were not noted.

Lundberg has examined the physiological responsivity of much younger children (Lundberg, 1983a, 1983b). In one study, he measured catecholamine and cortisol excretions in 15 boys and 11 girls 3- to 6-years-of-age. Type A scores were obtained using the MYTH. Catecholamine and cortisol excretion was measured at a daycare center and at home. Boys obtained higher MYTH Type A scores than girls and excreted more adrenaline and noradrenaline. No differences were found on the basis of behavior type alone, however.

In another study by Lundberg (1983b), fifteen 3- to 6-year-old boys were classified as either Type A or Type B based on MYTH scores. Blood pressure and heart rate were monitored at rest, and while the boys were engaged in a physical and an emotional challenge. The physical challenge consisted of asking subjects to run as fast as possible up and down a 20 meter corridor. In the emotional challenge, subjects were asked to play a game in which they pretended that they were a sleeping bear who awoke and grabbed another child. Heart rate and blood pressure measurements were obtained immediately after each situation. Type A boys responded with greater systolic blood pressure increases than Type B boys during the physical challenge. They did not differ during rest or during the emotional challenge.

The early development of psychophysiologic responsivity among Type A males at least suggests the origins of Type A might be traced back to very early childhood. It also suggests the possibility that early familial and genetic factors might play a crucial role in the early development of Type A. In the next section, we review evidence regarding the familial factors in Type A.

FAMILIAL FACTORS IN TYPE A BEHAVIOR

The genetic influence on the development of Type A behavior has been investigated in studies of twins. The twin method is based on genetic differences between monozygotic and dizygotic twins. Monozygotic or identical twins share 100% of their genes in common, while dizygotic or fraternal twins share 50% of their genes, on the average. If the degree of similarity on an attribute between monozygotic twins is greater than the degree of similarity between dizygotic twins, then it is assumed that there is a genetic component to the attribute in question. This method of analysis also assumes that the environmental factors which determine the attribute are no more similar for monozygotic twins than for dizygotic twins.

Such concordance analyses provide a means for determining the heritability of Type A behavior. In particular, if Type A behavior has a heritable base, monozygotic twins should have a higher concordance rate than dizygotic twins. Rosenman and colleagues tested the hypothesis that Type A is heritable by administering the Structured Interview to a sample of 89 monozygotic and 93 dizygotic adult twin pairs (Rahe, Hervig, & Rosenman, 1978). The interview classification was based on five categories: A1 (fully developed Type A), A2 (incomplete Type A), X (an equal representation of Type A and Type B characteristics), B3 (incomplete Type B), and B4 (fully developed Type B or complete absence of Type A). Using a definition of concordance in which the two twins were in the exact same category or in adjacent categories, concordance rates were 79% for monozygotic twins and 69% for fraternal twins. Although both of these rates are greater than chance, they are not significantly different from each other. However, some of the self-report inventories which are significantly correlated with global Type A showed significant heritability, such as the Thurstone Temperament Survey. The authors concluded that the significant concordance rate for both monozygotic and dizygotic twins reflected similarities in early learning experiences and that the pattern of concordance rates on some of the self-report scales, particularly items reflecting heightened motor activity, may have a heritable base.

While the Structured Interview was originally developed to provide a global estimate of the presence or absence of Type A characteristics, the interview, like the ASI, can be rated on the basis of speech stylistics and interview-behavior as well as rated on the content of subjects' responses. Factor analyses of ratings of self-reported and observable Type A behaviors and speech stylistics indicative of the Type A behavior pattern during the SI in adult males have yielded four dimensions in several samples: clinical ratings, primarily of speech stylistics; and self-reports of anger, pressured drive, and competitiveness (Matthews, Krantz, Dembroski, & MacDougall, 1982). These findings raise the possibility that some dimensions of Type A as measured by the SI may have a heritable base, whereas others may not.

To assess this possibility, taperecorded interviews of 80 MZ and 80 DZ twin pairs from the Rosenman study were coded for self-reported and observable Type A behaviors (such as signs of hostility and extremes of competition for control), and speech stylistics indicative of Pattern A (Matthews, Rosenman, Dembroski, et al., 1984). Analyses revealed that for the clinical ratings factor, the MZ intraclass correlations were about twice the size of the comparable DZ correlations factor and that the estimates of genetic variance approached significance, which is the pattern of results expected for an additive model of genetic variance. In addition, three of the six ratings on this factor, loud voice, competition for control, and potential for hostility, did show significant heritability. The findings for the remaining factors were not consistent with a genetic hypothesis.

These results are intriguing because individual differences in the clinical ratings factor may show a common element. All may reflect a general hyperresponsivity to environmental challenge, and in this case, to the challenge presented in the SI. Consistent with this notion are data showing that specific overt Type A behaviors exhibited during an interview, e.g., frequent interruptions of the interviewer and a loud voice, can be the result of mutual imitation between the interviewer and interviewee (Matthews, 1982); that they can be used to dominate and control social interactions (Dembroski, MacDougall, & Musante, 1984); and that they are reduced in intensity following beta-adrenergic blockage (Schmeider, Friedrich, Neus, et al., 1983). In addition, cardiovascular hyperreactivity to environmental challenge, which characterizes the Type A adult male, may have a heritable base (Matthews & Rakaczky, 1986; Rose, Miller, & Grim, 1982a, 1982b). Should there be a modest heritable base in individual differences in the clinical ratings factor, the available findings may indicate that underlying Pattern A is a general hyperresponsivity that has a heritable base. Stated differently, what may be underlying Pattern A is a general temperament to be responsive to environmental demands and stressors.

A temperament is considered to be a broad predisposition to behave in a certain style that emerges early in life, is relatively consistent over time, and has a heritable component. Building upon this predisposition are the early familial and cultural factors that shape the specific ways the individuals perceive, understand, and respond to their environment. Similarly, in the case of Type A, the early familial and cultural factors may build upon the proposed temperament substrate, and given the twin data, these factors certainly play the greatest role in shaping the ways the individual with the Type A pattern perceives, understands, and behaves in western society—with heightened competitive achievement-striving, aggressiveness, time urgency and hostility toward others. Nonetheless, according to the temperament perspective, underlying the development of Type A is a general, perhaps heritable hyperresponsivity to environmental challenge.

Despite evidence that Pattern A may have a heritable component, the twin data also suggest that family environment experiences might play a crucial role in the development of Pattern A. Children tend to imitate the behavior of same-sex models who are reinforced for their behavior (Bandura, 1969; Cohen, 1976). Given the general belief that our culture reinforces Type A behavior (Margolis, McLeroy, Runyan, & Kaplan, 1983), it seems likely that children might model their same-sex parent's Type A behavior. Support for this hypothesis was found in a study of twins enrolled at the University of Texas at Austin (Matthews &

Krantz, 1976). The twins in this sample had an average age of 21.2 years and an average educational level of 15.5 years. Their parents had an average age of 52.4 years and an average educational level of 14.7 years. Both the parents and twins completed the JAS. The association of the average twin JAS scores and the parents' scores was computed. Results revealed that the JAS scores of female twins were significantly related to their mother's, not to their father's scores. Among male twins only the correlation with the father's scores approached significance. Nonetheless, these findings provide some support for the notion that children, particularly females, tend to model their same-sex parents' Type A behavior.

In a similar study, male adolescents ages 11 and older and their fathers were assessed on the Bortner test battery (Bortner, Rosenman, & Friedman, 1970). The correlation between the fathers' and sons' test scores was .16. Another way to examine the relationship of fathers and their sons is to examine the similarity of their A-B classifications. A significant contingency coefficient of .31 was yielded from this approach, thus demonstrating weak but positive evidence for father-son similarity in Pattern A.

While these studies are instructive, they probably underestimate the magnitude of the parental modeling effect on children. It is unlikely that children imitate all of their parents' Type A behaviors. Instead, they probably imitate a subset of them. Thus, the weak association between the children's and parents' global Type A scores may not be an accurate reflection of the association between parents and children in individual Type A behaviors. Such was certainly the case in the aforementioned heritability studies, where a subset of Type A behaviors appeared to be heritable, but the global Type A classification was not. Hence, a fruitful approach in future research would be to examine parent-child similarity of individual Type A behaviors, including nonverbal behaviors associated with Pattern A (e.g., Hughes, Jacobs, Schucker, Chapman, Murray, & Johnson, 1983).

Whether or not parental modeling of specific Type A behavior contributes strongly to the development of Pattern A, parents may substantially affect their children in other ways. One way is through the nature of their parents' childrearing practices. Evidence regarding the childrearing practices associated with the development of Pattern A comes from two observational studies of the childrearing practices used with Type A and Type B sons. In the first of these studies (Glass, 1977), mothers interacted with their elementary school-aged sons, who had been rated by their teachers as exhibiting Type A or Type B behavior on an early version of the MYTH. The boys were required to complete three tasks: stack a set of odd-shaped blocks with one hand while blindfolded; copy a pictorial representation of a geometric figure with a set of cubes; and throw bean bags into a basket. The mothers were allowed to assist their sons in any way they wished, with the exception of completing the tasks for the children. An observer present in the testing room coded the behavior of the mothers and children. After completion of the testing period, the mothers administered the Type A Structured Interview. In this way, the childrearing practices used by Type A and Type B mothers with their Type A and Type B boys would be examined.

The results revealed that Type A boys were treated differently from Type B boys. Specifically, Type A and Type B mothers gave fewer positive evaluations of task performance to Type A boys than to Type B boys, and Type A boys were pushed to try harder than were Type B boys, particularly by Type B mothers. An example of the latter is, "You're doing fine, but next time, let's try for 5." Because of the nature of the study, it could not be concluded that the differences in childrearing practices associated with the Type A and Type B boys caused the children's behavior pattern. In fact, children have such an impressive range of effects on caregivers that the differences in maternal behavior may have been elicited by the children's characteristic behavior (Harper, 1975).

To test this possibility, the study was essentially repeated with two modifications (Matthews, 1977). First, the boys in this study were actual As or Bs who exhibited Type A or Type B behavior respectively according to a prearranged script. They did this during the performance of the bean bag toss task while a female stranger, a mother of another same-age boy, observed. In this way, the women had an opportunity to form an initial impression of the children's behavior. The second modification was that following the bean bag performance, the children interacted with the women on the other two tasks. The boys did not follow a script during this portion of the experiment. It was expected that if the female strangers responded to Type A and Type B boys in a manner similar to the mothers in the previous study, then it is likely that the maternal childrearing practices in the previous study were not caused by the children and may have contributed, in fact, to the children's Type A behavior.

Analyses of the coded interactions of the children and women revealed that in contrast to the previous findings, Type A boys received more positive evaluations of their task performance than did Type B boys from female strangers. Similar to the previous findings, Type A boys were pushed to accelerate their efforts more often than were Type B boys. However, only the Type B women consistently showed the above pattern of results.

Taking the results of the two studies together, it seems probable that the Type A boys do not cause their own mothers to give them few positive evaluations because they do not elicit such from female strangers. Rather, a low intrafamilial frequency of positive evaluation of task performance and high extrafamilial frequency may play a causal role in the development of Pattern A. On the other hand, it does appear that Type A behavior by boys elicits comments designed to improve the children's performance from Type B mothers and strangers. In this way, a curious phenomenon results: Type A boys elicit precisely that behavior from Type B women that may encourage them to continue striving to achieve everescalating goals. Thus, this adult-Type A child interaction is likely to be a self-perpetuating dynamic, which also should maintain the Type A child's continual struggle to achieve into adulthood.

CURRENT RESEARCH

Given the importance of familial factors to the development of Type A, we are now investigating in a population of families the extent to which families predispose, model, and pattern children's Type A behaviors and their associated cardiovascular responses to stress. We are particularly interested in the impact of gender and familial history of cardiovascular disease as they interact with childrearing practices, coping methods, and stress to impact on the development of Type A.

To address these issues, we have asked children enrolled in a longitudinal cohort study begun in 1979, their siblings, and their parents to participate in an individually administered experimental session. During this session, all participants perform a difficult cognitive task, a frustrating psychomotor task, and isometric exercise. Heart rate and blood pressure are monitored intermittently throughout these tasks. Subjects are administered the Type A interview and several questionnaires on coping with anger and anxiety. Parents complete indices of family interactions and childrearing practices. We expect that this study will allow us to address many of the issues and questions raised in this chapter, including whether:

1. the global Type A behavior pattern and its components cluster within families;
2. family childrearing practices foster the development of Pattern A in children;
3. behaviorally induced cardiovascular reactivity is a response style that clusters in families; and
4. the predictors of cardiovascular reactivity are the same in children as in adults.

We expect to complete data analyses in our current study by the spring of 1987. Overall, the data should assist us in a better understanding of how it is that Type A behavior emerges early in life, what combination of factors lead to the development of Pattern A, and, ultimately, how one might pursue the mechanisms linking the Type A behavior pattern to the development of coronary artery disease.

REFERENCES

Bandura, A. (1969). *Principles of behavior modification*. New York: Holt, Rinehart & Winston.
Block, J. (1971). *Lives through time*. Berkeley, CA: Bancroft.
Bortner, R. W. (1969). A short rating scale as a potential measure of Pattern A behavior. *Journal of Chronic Diseases, 22*, 87–91.
Bortner, R. W., Rosenman, R. H., & Friedman, M. (1970). Familial similarity in Pattern A behavior. *Journal of Chronic Diseases, 23*, 39–43.

Burnam, M. A., Pennebaker, J. W., & Glass, D. C. (1975). Time consciousness, achievement striving and the Type A coronary-prone behavior pattern. *Journal of Abnormal Psychology, 84,* 76–79.

Cohen, J. B., Syme, S. L., Jenkins, C. D., Kagan, A., & Zyzanski, S. J. (1979). Cultural context of Type A behavior and risk for CHD: A study of Japanese American males. *Journal of Behavioral Medicine, 2,* 375–384.

Cohen, S. (1976). *Social and personality development in childhood.* New York: Macmillan.

Corrigan, S. A., & Moskowitz, D. S. (1983). Type A behavior in preschool children: Construct validation evidence for the MYTH. *Child Development, 54,* 1513–1524.

Dembroski, T. M., MacDougall, J. M., & Musante, L. (1984). Desirability of control versus locus of control: Relationship of paralinguistics in the Type A interview. *Health Psychology, 3,* 15–26.

Enos, W. F., Holmes, R. H., & Beyer, J. (1953). Coronary disease among U.S. soldiers killed in action in Korea. *Journal of the American Medical Association, 152,* 1090–1093.

Friedman, M. (1969). *Pathogenesis of coronary artery disease.* New York: McGraw-Hill.

Glass, D. C. (1977). *Behavior patterns, stress, and coronary disease.* Hillsdale, NJ: Lawrence Erlbaum Associates.

Glass, D. C., Krakoff, L. R., Contrada, R., Hilton, W. F., Kehoe, K., Mannucci, E. G., Collins, C., Snow, B., & Elting, E. (1980). Effect of harassment and competition upon cardiovascular and plasma catecholamine responses in Type A and Type B individuals. *Psychophysiology, 17,* 453–463.

Harper, L. (1975). The scope of offspring effects: From caregiver to culture. *Psychological Bulletin, 82,* 784–801.

Haynes, S. G., Feinleib, M., & Kannel, W. B. (1980). The relationship of psychosocial factors to coronary heart disease in the Framingham study. III. Eight-year incidence of coronary heart disease. *American Journal of Epidemiology, 111,* 37–58.

Horner, M. S. (1972). Toward an understanding of achievement-related conflicts in women. *Journal of Social Issues, 28,* 157–175.

Houston, B. K. (1983). Psychophysiological responsivity and the Type A behavior pattern. *Journal of Research in Personality, 17,* 22–39.

Hughes, J. R., Jacobs, D. R., Schucker, B., Chapman, D. P., Murray. D. M., & Johnson, C. A. (1983). Nonverbal behavior of the Type A individual. *Journal of Behavioral Medicine, 6,* 279–289.

Lawler, K. A., Allen, M. T., Critcher, E. C., & Standard, B. A. (1981). The relationship of physiological responses to the coronary-prone behavior pattern in children. *Journal of Behavioral Medicine, 4,* 203–216.

Lundberg, U. (1983a). Sex differences in behaviour pattern and catecholamine and cortisol excretion in 3–6 year old day-care children. *Biological Psychology, 16,* 109–117.

Lundberg, U. (1983b). Note on Type A behavior and cardiovascular responses to challenge in 3–6-year-old children. *Journal of Psychosomatic Research, 27,* 39–42.

Maccoby, E. E., & Jacklin, C. N. (1974). *The psychology of sex differences.* Stanford, CA: Stanford University Press.

Manuck, S. B., Corse, C. D., & Winkelman, P. A. (1979). Behavioral correlates of individual differences in blood pressure reactivity. *Journal of Psychosomatic Research, 23,* 281–288.

Manuck, S. B., & Garland, F. N. (1979). Coronary-prone behavior pattern, task incentive, and cardiovascular response. *Psychophysiology, 16,* 136–142.

Margolis, L. H., McLeroy, K. R., Runyan, C. W., & Kaplan, B. H. (1983). Type A behavior: An ecological approach. *Journal of Behavioral Medicine, 6,* 245–258.

Matthews, K. A. (1977). Caregiver-child interactions and the Type A coronary-prone behavior pattern. *Child Development, 48,* 1752–1756.

Matthews, K. A. (1982). Psychological perspectives on the Type A behavior pattern. *Psychological Bulletin, 91,* 293–323.

Matthews, K. A., & Angulo, J. (1980). Measurement of the Type A behavior pattern in children: Assessment of children's competitiveness, impatience-anger, and aggression. *Child Development, 51,* 466–475.

Matthews, K. A., & Avis, N. E. (1983). Stability of overt Type A behaviors in children: Results from a one-year longitudinal study. *Child Development, 54,* 1507–1512.

Matthews, K. A., Glass, D. C., Rosenman, R. H., & Bortner, R. W. (1977). Competitive drive, Pattern A, and coronary heart disease: A further analysis of some data from the Western Collaborative Group Study. *Journal of Chronic Diseases, 30,* 489–498.

Matthews, K. A., & Jennings, J. R. (1984). Cardiovascular responses of boys exhibiting the Type A behavior pattern. *Psychosomatic Medicine, 46,* 484–497.

Matthews, K. A., & Krantz, D. S. (1976). Resemblance of twins and their parents in Pattern A behavior. *Psychosomatic Medicine, 28,* 140–144.

Matthews, K. A., Krantz, D. S., Dembroski, T. M., & MacDougall, J. M. (1982). The unique and common variance in the Structured Interview and Jenkins Activity Survey measures of the Type A behavior pattern. *Journal of Personality and Social Psychology, 42,* 303–313.

Matthews, K. A., & Rakaczky, C. J. (1986). Familial aspects of the Type A behavior pattern and physiologic reactivity to stress. In T. H. Schmidt, T. M. Dembroski, & G. Blumchen (Eds.), *Biological and psychological factors in cardiovascular disease.* Berlin: Springer-Verlag.

Matthews, K. A., Rosenman, R. H., Dembroski, T. M., Harris, E. L., & MacDougall, J. M. (1984). Familial resemblance in components of the Type A behavior pattern: A reanalysis of the California Type A twin study. *Psychosomatic Medicine, 46,* 512–522.

Matthews, K. A., & Siegel, J. M. (1983). Type A behaviors by children, social comparison, and standards for self-evaluation. *Developmental Psychology, 19,* 135–140.

Matthews, K. A., & Volkin, J. I. (1981). Efforts to excel and the Type A behavior pattern in children. *Child Development, 52,* 1283–1289.

McNamara, S. S., Molot, M. A., Stremple, J. F., & Cutting, R. T. (1971). Coronary artery disease in combat casualties in Vietnam. *Journal of the American Medical Association, 216,* 1185–1187.

Mettlin, C. (1976). Occupational careers and the prevention of coronary-prone behavior. *Social Science and Medicine, 10,* 367–372.

Moss, H. A., & Kagan, J. (1961). Stability of achievement and recognition seeking behavior from early childhood through childhood. *Journal of Abnormal and Social Psychology, 62,* 504–513.

Murray, J. L., & Bruhm, J. G. (1983). Reliability of the MYTH scale in assessing Type A behavior in preschool children. *Journal of Human Stress,* 23–28.

Olweus, D. (1979). Stability of aggressive reaction patterns in males: A review. *Psychological Bulletin, 86,* 852–875.

Rahe, R. H., Hervig, L., & Rosenman, R. H. (1978). Heritability of Type A behavior. *Psychosomatic Medicine, 40,* 478–486.

Rose, R. J., Miller, J. Z., & Grim, C. E. (1982a, October). *Familial factors in blood pressure response to laboratory stress: A twin study.* Paper presented at the annual meeting of the Society for Psychophysiological Research, Minneapolis.

Rose, R. J., Miller, J. Z., & Grim, C. E. (1982b, March). *Blood pressure response to laboratory stressors in young normotensive twins and singletons.* Paper presented at the annual meeting of the American Heart Association Council of Epidemiology, San Antonio.

Rosenman, R. H. (1978). The interview method of assessment of the coronary-prone behavior pattern. In T. M. Dembroski, S. M. Weiss, J. L. Shields, S. G. Haynes, & M. Feinleib (Eds.), *Coronary-prone behavior.* New York: Springer-Verlag.

Rosenman, R. H., Brand, R. J., Jenkins, C. D., Friedman, M., Straus, R., & Wurm, M. (1975). Coronary heart disease in the Western Collaborative Group Study: Final follow-up experience of 8½ years. *Journal of the American Medical Association, 233,* 872–877.

Scherwitz, L., Berton, K., & Leventhal, H. (1977). Type A assessment and interaction in the behavior pattern interview. *Psychosomatic Medicine, 39,* 229–240.

Schucker, B., & Jacobs, D. R. (1977). Assessment of behavioral risk of coronary disease by voice characteristics. *Psychosomatic Medicine, 39,* 219–228.

Schmeider, R., Friedrich, G., Neus, H., et al. (1983). The influence of beta blockers on cardiovascular reactivity and Type A behavior pattern in hypertensives. *Psychosomatic Medicine, 45,* 417–424.

Siegel, J. M. (1982). Type A behavior and self reports of cardiovascular arousal in adolescents. *Journal of Human Stress,* 24–30.

Siegel, J. M., & Leitch, C. J. (1981). Assessment of the Type A behavior pattern in adolescents. *Psychosomatic Medicine, 43,* 45–56.

Siegel, J. M., Matthews, K. A., & Leitch, C. J. (1981). Validation of the Type A interview assessment of adolescents: A multidimensional approach. *Psychosomatic Medicine, 43,* 311–321.

Siegel, J. M., Matthews, K. A., & Leitch, C. J. (1983). Blood pressure variability and the Type A behavior pattern in adolescence. *Journal of Psychosomatic Research, 27,* 265–272.

Snow, B. (1978). Level of aspiration in coronary prone and non-coronary prone adults. *Personality and Social Psychology Bulletin, 4,* 416–419.

Waldron, I. (1979). Sex differences in the coronary-prone behavior pattern. In T. M. Dembroski, S. M. Weiss, J. L. Shields, S. G. Haynes, & M. Feinleib (Eds.), *Coronary-prone behavior.* New York: Springer-Verlag.

Wolf, T. M., Hunter, S. M., & Webber, L. (1979). Psychosocial measures and cardiovascular risk factors in children and adolescents. *Journal of Psychology, 101,* 139–146.

Wolf, T. M., Sklov, M. C., Wenzl, P. A., Hunter, S. M., & Berenson, G. S. (1982). Validation of a measure of Type A behavior pattern in children: Bogalusa Heart Study. *Child Development, 53,* 126–135.

5 Type A Behavior in Preschool Children

Nitza Vega-Lahr
Tiffany Field
Sheri Goldstein
Deborah Carran
University of Miami Medical School

In the 1950s, Friedman and Rosenman (1959) observed that, compared to the noncardiac patients they were treating, those suffering from cardiac disorders seemed to present a particular constellation of behavioral characteristics. Unsatisfied with the predictive validity of traditional risk factors for coronary heart disease (e.g., hypertension, serum cholesterol level, and smoking), Friedman and Rosenman (1974) focused on the systematic observation of that collection of behaviors now identified as the Type A Pattern. They described Pattern A as an "action-emotion complex that can be observed in a person who is aggressively involved in a chronic, incessant struggle to achieve more and more in less and less time, and if required to do so, against the opposing efforts of other things and of other persons" (p. 67).

Overt manifestations of Pattern A include extremes of aggressiveness, easily aroused hostility, a sense of time urgency, a tendency to challenge and compete with others, an explosive and accelerated speech pattern, and a high level of restlessness. Type B individuals, on the other hand, are relatively free of these characteristics. Friedman and Rosenman (1971) further stated that Pattern A emerges only when certain conditions of the milieu arise that elicit these particular responses in certain individuals. This description of Pattern A behavior is consistent with contemporary interactionist models of personality, emphasizing the interaction of individual predispositions and contextual variables. Thus, the Type A pattern is a set of overt behaviors that is elicited in susceptible individuals by a particular constellation of environmental events. The type A Pattern is conceptualized as a behavioral continuum, ranging from extreme Type A to extreme non-Type A, or Type B; Type A individuals are expected to differ from Type Bs only when confronted with a specific set of situations or events.

Since the time when the Type A pattern was first described, many studies have investigated its role as an independent risk factor for coronary heart disease and for atherosclerosis, the underlying chronic disease process (Matthews, 1982). More recently, investigators have examined Pattern A from a psychological perspective. In this paper, research relating to the etiology of Type A behavior is reviewed in light of a theoretical perspective introduced by Glass (1977). Furthermore, research efforts focusing on the emergence of Type A behavior in early childhood are described, and future directions for investigation are suggested.

Before reviewing this research one important matter to consider is the assessment of Type A behavior. To distinguish individuals along the Type A continuum, research with adults has primarily relied on either a standardized Structured Interview developed by Rosenman et al. (1975) or a 54-item self-administered instrument called the Jenkins Activity Survey, or JAS (Jenkins, Zyzanski, & Rosenman, 1971). In either case, the adults are asked about their characteristic response mode in the face of situations that should elicit Type A behavior. In a series of retrospective and prospective studies, Type A behavior, as measured by either of these techniques, has been associated with an increased risk for coronary heart disease, as compared to Type B (Rosenman et al., 1975). Although both methods have been found to be reliable, the Structured Interview appears to be a better predictor of heart disease and physiological response to challenge than the JAS (Dembroski, MacDougall, Shields, Petitto, & Lushene, 1978). Evidently, observations of the Type A behavior pattern exhibited during interview procedures provide a more sensitive measure of coronary-prone behavior of adults than the self-perception of the type A behavior alone.

Although Type A has been extensively described and researched in adulthood, its origins have not received as much attention. It is conceivable that the antecedents of type A can be traced to experiences arising in early childhood (Matthews & Angulo, 1980). In order to investigate the developmental antecedents of Type A in children, a new instrument was developed by Matthews (1977). The Matthews Youth Test for Health (MYTH) is a 17-item scale of statements that characterize overt behaviors typically attributed to Type A adults; ratings from 1 to 5 for each item are summed to yield an overall Type A score, as well as two subscale scores representing two orthogonal factors (competitiveness and impatience-aggression). The MYTH has been established as a valid and reliable instrument, as evidenced by investigations with preschool and elementary school-aged children (Corrigan & Moskowitz, 1983; Matthews & Angulo, 1980; Whiting, 1981). Furthermore, the factors yielded by the MYTH bear some resemblance to the factors that emerge from the JAS, allowing comparison of adult and child behaviors.

Research in the area of Type A behavior has recently included the identification of environmental or situational variables. Investigations conducted by Glass and his colleagues (Glass, 1977) have highlighted the influence of environmental variables on task performance by Type A and Type B adults. Their studies have shown that Type As work hard to succeed, suppress subjective states (such as fatigue) that might interfere with task performance, and conduct their activities at a very rapid pace. Similar characteristics were noted in a study by Carver, Coleman, and Glass (1976) who required Type A and Type B males to complete a treadmill test (walking on a motorized surface at increasingly sharp angles of incline). Results from their study showed that compared to the B males, Type As worked at a level closer to the limits of their endurance and, at the same time, expressed less overall fatigue than did Bs. This tendency may be understood in terms of the achievement-oriented characteristics of the Type A individual. Their results were replicated in a study with 6th grade boys, using a different task. Matthews and Volkin (1981) found that Type A boys held a weight longer than did Type B boys and underreported their subjective fatigue.

Another difference between As and Bs is their sense of time urgency. Type A individuals become more impatient with delays and report, for example, that a time interval of 1 minute elapses reliably sooner than it does for Type Bs (Burnam, Pennebaker, & Glass, 1973). Furthermore, Burnam et al. (1973) found that Type A and B individuals worked at comparable rates when given explicit deadlines for solving mathematical problems, but without the external imposition of a deadline, Type B subjects worked at a slower pace.

The arousal of impatience has behavioral consequences as well. Glass, Snyder, and Hollis (1974) reported that Type As did more poorly than Type Bs on a timing task that required a delayed response, i.e., a task involving differential reinforcement of low rates of responding (DRL). On a DRL task, the subject must wait during the fixed time interval before responding; this type of task is difficult and requires considerable patience. Type A individuals performed poorly because they were unable to wait long enough following reinforcement before emitting subsequent responses.

The role of incentives provided for successful performance has also been investigated for Type A–Type B differences. Manuck and Garland (1979) established that both Type A and B subjects performed at comparable rates when an extrinsic reinforcer was made contingent upon successful task performance, but when no incentives were offered, Type Bs solved fewer test problems correctly than did Type A subjects.

Very few studies have been published on Type A behavior in young children. In an effort to validate the MYTH scale as an assessment device for Type A behavior in school-age children, Matthews and Angulo (1980) investigated differences between Type A and Type B children in their responses to three experimental tasks. Type A children won a race against a female experimenter by a larger margin than did Type Bs; the A subjects aggressed against a Bobo doll on an earlier trial than did Bs; and the frequency of impatient behaviors during a frustrating drawing task was greater for the Type A than for the Type B children.

Investigations of Type A behavior in preschool children are limited to two studies (Corrigan & Moskowitz, 1983; Whiting, 1981). The Corrigan and Moskowitz study showed that Type As and Type Bs, participating individually in a visual discrimination task, behaved differently depending upon the presence or absence of a time constraint and incentive. As predicted, the reaction times of Type B children who worked without time limits and an incentive were significantly longer than those of both A and B children who worked with a time limit and incentive (Corrigan & Moskowitz, 1983). The authors also recorded impatient behaviors exhibited during task performance, but no significant differences were found between As and Bs on their impatient behaviors. Although impatient behavior was exhibited uniformly by all children, the investigators believe that the lack of significant differences and low variability in this behavior may have been due to the difficult nature of the task and the short attention span of the preschool children.

From an operant framework, Whiting (1981) explored the effects of three environments on rates of time-urgent behavior in preschool children. Analogues of two type A and one type B environment were designed, and preschoolers individually participated in a simple problem-solving task in the presence of alternating environmental contingencies. One type A setting provided positive consequences for task completion within a fixed time interval, while another type A setting offered the same consequences together with negative outcomes if the task was not completed within the time period. The type B setting also offered positive consequences, but the reward was not as great, and there was no time limit. In a repeated-measures design, each child was assigned to one of four environmental sequences. Results indicated that differentially structured Type A environments produced varied rates of Type A behavior. However, type A and B children's behaviors significantly differed only when the B environment was presented first in the sequence.

These results, taken together, indicate the important role of environmental dimensions in the differential response patterns of Type A and Type B individuals. All of the studies in some way provide evidence for the Type A individual's attempts to achieve, excel, or operate instrumentally on his environment. These results have been found in children and adults alike. What explanations are offered?

Though many efforts have been made to conceptualize the Type A pattern, one of the most comprehensive and systematic approaches comes from the work of Glass (1977). Glass has suggested that Type A characteristics are exhibited in the interest and with the purpose of maintaining and asserting control over environmental demands and requirements, or even to counteract stressful aspects of the environment (i.e., uncontrollable events). Glass and Singer (1972) suggest that Type As are engaged in a struggle for control, whereas Type Bs are relatively free of such concerns and hence, do not exhibit the characteristic Pattern A behavior.

This concept of uncontrollability is defined by Glass and Singer (1972) in terms of the outcomes of a behavior: When an individual perceives that his responses will not determine what he gets, the outcome is uncontrollable. By contrast, controllability involves the subject's perception of a contingency between responding and outcome. An uncontrollable event elicits an initial reaction in Type As called by Glass hyper-responsiveness as it is assumed to reflect considerable effort to assert control over the situation. In comparison to B individuals, Type A persons experience increased motivation to master and control uncontrollable events. According to Glass, the B individuals exhibit hypo-responsiveness in the face of the same uncontrollable situations. These theoretical assumptions have been tested in a series of experiments in which control of the task was manipulated. In general, results have shown that the expected initial high-amplitude reaction of Type A individuals to uncontrollable events occurs only when the events are very salient or compelling of attention in adults (Glass, 1977) or children (Matthews, 1979).

Responses of Type A and Type B individuals to uncontrollable events have been tested via the learned helplessness paradigm developed by Seligman (1975). In a study by Krantz, Glass, and Snyder (1974), salience of the uncontrollable event was varied by the intensity of an uncontrollable noise during a pretreatment phase. Following this phase under high salience conditions, Type As were extremely slow to terminate the noise during test phase when control of the noise was feasible. However, when the noise was of relatively low intensity, they did not show learned helplessness deficits. These findings suggest that Type As give up after continued failure to control a salient uncontrollable event, but do not give up after failure to control an event of low salience.

Glass and others have suggested a cognitive interpretation for these findings. Individuals learn the noncontingency between responses and outcomes, but in the case of the Type As, this loss of control is not encoded effectively unless there are explicitly salient cues in the environment signalling the noncontingency. This interpretation underlines the role of the environment in the control and maintenance of Type A behavior. However, as we have seen, little effort has been made to systematically investigate the specific setting maintenance mechanisms that shape and perpetuate Type A behavior.

To complete the biobehavioral model of uncontrollability, evidence from several studies shows that uncontrollability also elicits hyper-responsiveness in physiological behavior including increases in heart rate and blood pressure and enhanced secretion of norepinephrine, epinephrine, and cortisol (Glass, Krakoff, Contrada et al., 1980; Williams, Kuhn, Melosh, White, & Schanberg, 1982). This heightened sympathetic nervous system activation, specifically associated with Type A behavior, is hypothesized to mediate the tendency of Type As to develop atherosclerosis and coronary heart disease.

Although no evidence exists linking Type A behavior in young children with subsequent development of heart disease, the study of both behavioral and physiological responses in children is critical to the understanding of the development of type A behavior. If no associations between the behavior and the physiological responses are found in children, then it could be said that the pathology may develop only later, after several years of Type A behavior.

Finally, an interesting but rarely investigated variable is the social dimensions of the environment that may be related to the production of Pattern A behavior. Several theorists have suggested that parents might model Type A behavior for their children. Thus, parents and children would exhibit similarities along the Type A continuum (Matthews, 1978). For children younger than 11 years, however, no relationship between parent-child scores has been found (Matthews, 1978). Nonetheless, childrearing practices of the parents are likely to play a critical role in the development of Pattern A. In a study on mother-child interactions, Matthews (1977) observed Type A and B male children (ages 4–10) while working with their mothers on three tasks. Mothers of extreme Type A children more frequently disapproved and encouraged them to try harder following good performance than the mothers of extreme Type Bs. Because a mother's childrearing practices and interaction style are characteristically affected by the behavior pattern of her child, it is equally possible that the child's behavior pattern also contributes to the development of a particular style of childrearing via shaping and reinforcement mechanisms.

In the same vein, peers, who are also considered agents of the social environment, might also influence or elicit Type A behavior in an individual. Thus, the interaction patterns between Type A and Type B individuals might vary as a function of the dyad members involved. Only one study has examined this issue (Van Egeren, 1979). Dyads of different configurations (Type A–Type A, Type A–Type B, and Type B–Type B) played a modified Prisoner's Dilemma game. Results showed that Type As elicited more competitiveness and angry feelings from both A and B partners than did Type Bs. In fact, Type Bs were just as angry as As when interacting with As. Verbal threats and behavioral challenges characterized the dyads in the following ascending order: B–B, A–B, and A–A. These findings indicate that As do engage in more aggressive and competitive behavior, particularly with other As. Moreover, Bs became annoyed, competitive, and aggressive when interacting with As. It does appear, then, that the Type A behavior pattern itself plays a role in eliciting Pattern A characteristics in others, which in turn, might lead the individual to display higher frequencies of this behavior.

In summary, there is converging evidence that physiological and behavioral differences exist between Type A and Type B adults, and, at this time, at least similar behavioral differences have also been observed in children. Efforts have been made to identify and assess Type A behaviors, and the importance of specific eliciting situational variables has been illustrated by the empirical evidence. Research on Type A behavior in children is still in a formative stage of development, yet there are many promising avenues of investigation. Although the Type A pattern has not been identified as coronary-prone at early ages, it does seem important to assess this behavior in childhood in order to learn more about the etiology, development, and stability of its components.

The present investigation represents an initial step in a program of research on Type A behavior in early childhood. The major objectives included the assessment of behavioral differences in preschool children varying along the Type A continuum, both in an ecological setting (the classroom) and in a more controlled environment (the laboratory). Using the MYTH as the technique for assessment of Pattern A, it was predicted that Type A children would exhibit more impatience, aggression, and competitiveness than Type B children. The procedures included assessment of type A in the children and their parents using the standardized MYTH and JAS questionnaires, naturalistic observations of the children's play behaviors (in the classroom and in a laboratory playroom), a series of competitive tasks (car race and tower building), and an interview designed to elicit Type A behavior in the children. In these situations type A/type B children were observed together in dyads inasmuch as peer interaction behaviors of type A children have not yet been investigated, and a dyadic interactive context has been considered moderately competitive as compared to individually performed tasks. Finally, the study investigated the differences in speech behavior of Type As and Type Bs during an interview relating to the laboratory tasks.

METHOD

Sample

The subjects were 48 preschool-age children (24 boys and 24 girls) who attended an all-day nursery school. Their parents were Caucasian, middle-income, medical school staff or faculty. The children ranged in age from 29 to 50 months at the time of testing (mean boys' age = 38 months; mean girls' age = 41 months). The IQ scores of the children based on the McCarthy scales averaged 122.

Procedure

The children were first rated on the MYTH questionnaire. Their behaviors were then observed during classroom freeplay observations. Following these observations, type A–Type B same sex dyads were formed based on the MYTH ratings, and these dyads were taken to a laboratory playroom for dyadic freeplay observations, competitive tasks and an interview.

MYTH ratings.   Each child was rated on the Matthews Youth Test of Health (MYTH) by the head teacher, an assistant teacher, an examiner acquainted with the children, and each of the child's parents. In addition, the parents completed the Jenkins Activity Survey (JAS), a self-report measure for adults tapping Type A behavior.

For purposes of classifying the children into Type A and Type B groups, a composite score based on the average on the MYTH ratings given by the examiner and the head teacher was computed for each child. The subjects were then divided by a median split (within same sex group) on the basis of this score, and thus were categorized as either Type A or Type B. Scores for the type A boys ranged from 51 to 61 (M = 56.8), and scores for Type A girls ranged from 55 to 67 (M = 60.0). Scores for type B boys ranged from 36 to 48, (M = 41.8) and for type B girls, the range was 37 to 50 (M = 45.3). The mean age for the type A group was 40.8 months and for the type B group, 40.3 months. Type A–B dyads of the same sex were then formed, matching the children on age (maximum age difference within a dyad was three months). These dyads were subsequently observed during laboratory freeplay, competitive tasks, and interviews.

Classroom observations. The preschool classroom environment where the observations took place emphasized free play, creative arts, and school readiness curricula. This classroom (9m x 8m) featured a number of learning centers and special play areas partitioned by barriers scaled to child-height (e.g., art-science learning center, a block area, kitchen-dollhouse area, and a manipulative play area contained in a large multilevel structure). The teacher-child ratio in the room was 1:12. The observations were conducted during the children's free play period in the morning, a time when the children are encouraged to engage in activities on their own and teacher intervention and direction are minimal.

The classroom observations were conducted by two research assistants naive to the hypotheses of the study and to the classification (by type) of the children. Three 10-minute time sample unit observations at 10-second intervals were made of each child, spanning a period of 8 weeks. Behaviors coded during these observations included: vocalizations, expiratory sighs, tongue clicking, verbal frustration, excessive physical gesturing, gross motor activity, activity change, facial annoyance, interruptions, aggression, and solitary play. These behavior categories were included because some had been noted in Type A adults (Friedman & Rosenman, 1974), and most had been observed in young Type A children (Corrigan & Moskowitz, 1983; Matthews & Angulo, 1980; Whiting, 1981). These behaviors were assumed to represent the three components of Type A behavior: impatience, aggression and competitiveness–achievement striving. Observers of the classroom freeplay sessions were initially trained by observing freeplay sessions until the level of interobserver agreement reached at least .80. Interobserver agreement during subsequent reliability checks on ⅓ of the observation periods ranged from .75 to .95 (M = .88).

Laboratory observations. The type A/type B same-sex dyads were accompanied to the laboratory playroom by two research assistants for these observations. The dyads first engaged in a 10-minute freeplay session followed by two competitive tasks (car race and tower building) and an interview. The laboratory playroom is a miniature of the classroom. It contained a variety of popular preschool toys such as Lego blocks, storybooks, dress-up props, puzzles, a kitchen center, dolls, etc. In addition, a "Bobo doll" inflatable punching bag was placed on the edge of the play area.

1. *Freeplay observation.* During the 10-minute free play session the children were instructed to play with any of the toys for a short time while the experimenters attended to a task in the adjoining (videomonitor) room. The dyads' behaviors were videotaped by a ceiling height videocamera with a wide angle lens covering the playroom area but remaining unobtrusive to the children.

The tapes were later coded by two trained observers for the following behavioral categories: punches Bobo doll (initiator or imitator), structures/organizes play episode, commands, challenges/competes, imitates, vocalizes, gross motor activity, and activity change. These behaviors were thought to reflect the components of Type A behavior mentioned earlier and to measure efforts to control and structure the play episode. The tapes were coded at 10 sec. time sample unit intervals. Upon termination of the play period, the subjects engaged in a car race and a tower-building race.

2. *Car race.* For the car race each child chose a toy automobile to race against each other. On the floor in a room adjoining the laboratory playroom was a "racetrack," a 10 ft. long strip of masking tape marked off in half-foot segments. One of the experimenters demonstrated the appropriate behavior for the race, telling the children to keep their hands on the cars at all times, and instructing them to crawl across the floor towards the goal as well as urging the children to hurry. The two children then raced their cars on either side of the track on a series of two trials. The experimenter recorded the winner of the race and the margin of victory in half-foot segments. Physical characteristics of the children were thought to be insignificant since both members of the dyad were of comparable size and physical constitution.

3. *Tower-building race.* After completion of the car race, the experimenter removed the cars and presented a basket of 21 large wooden blocks for the tower-building race, placing it between the two children seated side-by-side on the floor. The children were asked to build their own "very high tower" against the wall. While the experimenter urged the children to hurry, the subjects built their towers, which were considered completed upon depletion of the block supply. The experimenter then noted which child had built the highest tower and the total number of blocks he or she had used.

4. *Interview.* Subsequent to the block task, the children were asked to sit side-by-side, facing the experimenter for an interview. They were asked to respond to some questions relating to the "games" they had just played. A tape recorder was placed in a midway position in front of the children for recording their verbal responses. The questions were directed to neither child in particular, and the interviewer was instructed not to elaborate on a given child's answer. Questions were as follows: How did you like the playroom? Which toy did you like the best? Who beat up the bouncing clown? Who had the fastest car? Who likes to win at games? Who built the highest tower with the blocks? Who can run faster? Who can climb higher? Who has a pet at home? This interview was used

primarily to observe the children's speech behavior. The interview was also considered an opportunity to elicit competitive and impatient behaviors. At the end of the interview the experimenter completed ratings of each child based on their behavior during the laboratory races and interviews along the following dimensions: affect, cooperation, impatience, aggression, restlessness, attention, and activity level. These were rated on a 5-point Likert type scale, from low to high. The children were then given a "magic" sticker, thanked for their participation, and returned to the classroom. The interview tapes were then immediately transcribed to preserve the identity of the children's voices. They were then coded for the percentage time talking (using a stop watch), number of interruptions, number of questions answered, and number of questions answered first by each child.

RESULTS

Relationships Between Type A in Children and Parents

Correlation analyses were first performed on the MYTH ratings of type A in the children and the relationships between the type A ratings of the children and type A ratings of their parents. As can be seen in Table 5.1 there were a number of significant, although moderate, coefficients of interrater agreement between parents, teachers and the researcher on the summary score of the MYTH assessment of children's type A. Based on Matthews' factor loadings (Matthews & Angulo, 1980) competitiveness and impatience–aggression factor scores were derived. Several of the coefficients were significant for the competitiveness factor of the MYTH. However, interrater agreement for the impatience–aggression factor was only reliable for the teachers and researcher. Correlations between these factor scores and the overall MYTH scores for each of the raters also appear in Table 5.1. These correlations were moderately high.

Table 5.2 illustrates the correlation coefficients for the type A (Jenkins, Zyzanski, & Rosenman, 1971) self-ratings and factors (impatience, job striving, and competitiveness) of the mothers and fathers. Except for the job factor, the type A and factor scores of the mothers and fathers (most particularly the impatience factor) appeared to be highly correlated. That the job factor was not correlated is somewhat surprising given that both parents of these children were medical professionals. However, the correlations between the job factor and the overall Type A scores for both the mothers and fathers were somewhat low.

Also, in Table 5.2 the correlation coefficients for type A scores (and factors) for mothers and fathers and MYTH scores (and factors) for children (as rated by parents) are given. Surprisingly, none of the mothers' self-ratings on the type A questionnaire were related to their own ratings of their child on the MYTH. However, moderately high correlations were found for fathers' self-ratings and

TABLE 5.1
Interrater Agreement for MYTH Scores and Factors, and Relationships
Between MYTH Factors and Overall Score

| | Interrater Agreement on MYTH Scores | | | | |
	Father	Mother	Head Tchr.	Asst. Tchr.	Researcher
Father	--				
Mother	.41*				
Head Tchr.	.23	.61*			
Asst. Tchr.	.24	.35	.52*		
Researcher	.39*	.38*	.53*	.48*	--

| | MYTH Competitiveness Factor | | | | |
	Father	Mother	Head Tchr.	Asst. Tchr.	Researcher
Father	--				
Mother	.61*				
Head Tchr.	.26	.66*			
Asst. Tchr.	.21	.52*	.68*		
Researcher	.22	.34	.45*	.55*	--

| | MYTH Impatience-Aggression Factors | | | | |
	Father	Mother	Head Tchr.	Asst. Tchr.	Researcher
Father	--				
Mother	.34				
Head Tchr.	.16	.11			
Asst. Tchr.	.03	.02	.41*		
Researcher	.30	.16	.52*	.50*	--

| | Relationship MYTH Factors to Overall Score | |
	Type A & Comp.	Type A & Imp./Aggr.
Father	.82*	.72*
Mother	.80*	.68*
Head Tchr.	.82*	.86*
Asst. Tchr.	.84*	.76*
Researcher	.80*	.82*

*Significant coefficients at $p < .05$ or better

ratings of their children (except for the job factor of the father). In addition, curiously, the mothers' ratings of type A behavior in herself were moderately highly correlated with the fathers' ratings of type A in their children.

Classroom Freeplay

For the remaining data, multivariate analyses of variance followed by univariate analyses of variance and post hoc comparisons by Bonferroni t tests (Myers, 1977) were performed. Prior to the data analyses, the following classroom play categories were excluded due to their extremely low frequencies: expiratory sighs, tongue clicks, and verbal frustration.

TABLE 5.2
Relationships Between Type A (and factors) Ratings of Mother and Father

	Mother				Father			
	TYPEAM	IMPM	JOBM	COMPM	TYPEAF	IMPF	JOBF	COMPF
TYPEAM	--							
IMPM	.64*							
JOBM	.44*	.34						
COMPM	.67*	.49*	.63*	--				
TYPEAF	.64*	.52*	.29	.41*				
IMPF	.59*	.77*	.17	.45*	.55*			
JOBF	.34	.24	.30	.03	.38*	.21		
COMPF	.46*	.23	.22	.49*	.80*	.33	.30	--

Relationships Between Type A (and factors) for Mothers/
Fathers and MYTH Scores (and factors) for Children

Mother Rating Child	Mother Self-Rating			
	TYPEAM	IMPM	JOBM	COMPM
TYPEACH	.08	.19	-.15	-.01
IMPCH	-.12	.32	-.02	-.06
COMPCH	.32	.15	-.11	.10

Father Rating Child				
	TYPEAF	IMPF	JOBF	COMPF
TYPEACH	.62*	.62*	.37	.53*
IMPCH	.60*	.50*	.36	.33
COMPCH	.35	.33	.21	.44*

Father Rating Child				
	TYPEAM	IMPM	JOBM	COMPM
TYPEACH	.71*	.65*	.34	.45*
IMPCH	.51*	.65*	.39*	.36
COMPCH	.51*	.29	.13	.29

*Significant coefficients at $p < .05$ or better.

For the behaviors observed in the classroom (means are presented in Table 5.3) children classified as Type A engaged in more frequent interruptions, displayed more facial annoyance, and exhibited more gross motor activity than children classified as Type B. These findings are consistent with the expected direction of results.

Laboratory Freeplay

Consistent with the classroom freeplay situation, gross motor activity was also more frequent among the Type A children as compared to Type B's (see Table 5.4). Also, as expected, Type A children initiated punching of the Bobo doll more frequently and punched the Bobo doll more frequently than the Type B

TABLE 5.3
Mean Percentage Time Behaviors Occurred During Classroom Freeplay

Classroom Freeplay Measures	Type A		Type B		Effects
	Male	Female	Male	Female	
Vocalizations	34.8	44.8	35.8	37.2	N.S.
Gestures	.8	.9	.3	.7	N.S.
Gross motor activity	51.9	51.6	41.6	46.6	A^1
Activity change	8.8	6.1	5.3	7.4	N.S.
Facial annoyance	1.4	2.4	.6	1.2	A^2
Interruptions	.4	.6	.3	.1	A^1
Aggression	2.1	2.0	2.8	2.0	N.S.
Solitary play	19.0	14.6	27.1	18.0	N.S.

A = Type A > B; 1 = $p < .05$, 2 = $p < .01$

TABLE 5.4
Means for Laboratory Freeplay, Races and Interview Measures

	Type A		Type B		Effects
	Male	Female	Male	Female	
Laboratory Freeplay Measures (% Time)					
Punches Bobo first	60.0	80.0	30.0	30.0	A^2
Punches Bobo	8.8	5.3	1.5	2.0	A^3
Structures play	14.8	11.6	8.1	13.4	N.S.
Commands	15.0	21.6	17.6	25.2	N.S.
Challenges/Competes	1.7	2.3	2.3	2.8	N.S.
Imitates	4.1	5.2	4.7	3.8	N.S.
Vocalization	68.8	78.7	56.0	80.0	F^2
Gross motor activity	84.8	74.8	71.0	65.8	A^1
Activity change	36.7	29.3	35.8	30.5	N.S.
Correct guess	80.0	60.0	90.0	60.0	M^1
Race Measures					
Victory car race (%)	60.0	70.0	40.0	30.0	A^1
# Segments victory	3.6	2.7	1.3	1.3	A^1
Victory tower race (%)	60.0	80.0	40.0	20.0	A^1
# Blocks tower	10.8	11.3	10.3	9.8	A^1
Ratings					
Attention	4.8	4.5	4.9	4.5	M^1
Cooperation	4.6	4.8	4.6	4.8	N.S.
Persistence	2.2	1.4	1.3	1.5	N.S.
Affect	4.0	4.3	4.1	4.3	N.S.
Activity	4.4	3.3	3.8	3.2	M^1
Restlessness	2.3	1.3	1.7	1.3	M^1
Aggression	3.2	1.8	2.3	1.4	M^3
Interview Measures					
% Time talking	13.0	13.6	11.7	15.7	N.S.
Interruptions	1.3	1.3	1.0	1.3	N.S.
Questions answered	8.1	8.0	7.2	7.2	A^1
Questions answered first	6.3	6.5	4.0	3.9	A^4

A = Type A > B; F = Female > Male, M = Male > Female
1 = $p < .05$; 2 = $p < .01$; 3 = $p < .005$; 4 = $p < .001$

children. Analyses contrasting males and females revealed significant differences for 2 categories: Girls vocalized more frequently, and boys were more often correctly assessed (by type) than girls by a naive observer.

Races

Results in this series of tasks also conformed to expectations (Table 5.4). In the car race event, type A children were more frequently the winners as compared to type B children; furthermore, the margin of victory, measured by the number of race track segments, was significantly greater for the type As. Similar findings were revealed by the analysis of the block tower-building data. Type A children more frequently built taller towers, and, consequently, used more blocks than type B children.

For the ratings assigned by the observer at the end of the session, no differences were noted between type A and B children. However, sex differences occurred for the ratings of aggression, restlessness, attentiveness, and activity, with males receiving higher ratings than females on all of these dimensions.

Interview

Surprisingly, no differences were found in terms of percentage time talking or total number of interruptions for type A and B children during the interviews. However, Type A children answered more questions than children categorized as type B, and As more frequently answered the questions first than did Bs.

DISCUSSION

In this study type A behaviors were explored in preschool children using questionnaires, observations, and competitive tasks. With respect to the questionnaire data, the interrater agreement on the summary MYTH (Matthews, 1977) scores, though only moderately significant, suggests that this instrument is a reliable assessment of type A behavior in preschool children. These findings corroborate those of others who have used this scale with preschool (Corrigan & Moskowitz, 1983) and school-age children (Matthews & Angulo, 1980). An analysis of the two independent factors comprising the MYTH yielded significant interrater reliability across all raters for the competitiveness factor. For the impatience–aggression factor interrater agreement was reliable only for the teachers and researcher. One plausible explanation is that the impatience–aggression items largely refer to socially undesirable behaviors, such as getting into fights and becoming easily irritated, while competitive-achievement striving items connote a socially desirable quality. These associated valences may have led parents to distort ratings on the impatience–aggression items, while teachers and researchers may have offered a more objective evaluation of the children's impatience–aggression behavior.

The correlations between Type A ratings of mothers and fathers (on the JAS) including the global type A rating and the impatience and competitiveness factors were moderately high. This is perhaps not surprising inasmuch as both the mothers and fathers are medical professionals with presumably similar achievement-striving and time-urgency characteristics. For the same reason, however, it is surprising that the job factor correlation for mothers and fathers was not significant. However, as already mentioned, the correlations between the job factor and the overall type A scores for both the mothers and fathers were somewhat low, suggesting that this factor might be unreliable, or at least less related to global type A ratings. Unfortunately no other studies on the relationship between type A in spouses could be found in the literature for data comparison purposes.

For the analyses on the relationships between parents' ratings of themselves (on the JAS) and their MYTH ratings of their children, high correlations were obtained only between (1) father's type A scores and child's type A score, as assessed by the father; and (2) mother's type A scores and child's type A scores also assessed by the father. The mother's ratings of herself and of her child yielded no significant correlations. The absence of a relationship between mothers' self ratings and the ratings of their child is consistent with the literature. Evidence from other studies suggests that when instruments used to assess type A behavior in mothers and their children are different (as in this case), and the children are younger than eleven, no relationship has been found (Matthews, 1978). However, the fact that both the fathers' and the mothers' self-ratings are highly correlated with the fathers' ratings of the child raises the possibility that there are relationships between parent and child type A behaviors, and the fathers are simply more objective in rating their children. Other studies (Matthews, 1978) may have failed to find correlations between type A in parents and children simply because they were tapping mothers' assessments of type A in themselves and their children.

Although several theorists have suggested that parents may be a model of type A behavior for their children, and thus, parents and children would exhibit similarities along the type A dimension, it is still unclear how these relationships develop. Childrearing practices of the parents in general and patterns of parent-child interaction in particular would seem to be critical in the development and maintenance of Type A behavior. Although Matthews and her colleagues have addressed this issue (Matthews, 1978) further research is needed to clarify the independent effects of parental characteristics on the formation of Type A behavior in young children. Unfortunately, in this study parent-child interaction behaviors were not observed.

Analyses of the classroom freeplay behaviors revealed that Type A children showed more frequent interruptions, displayed more facial annoyance and exhibited more gross motor activity than the Type B children. However, no differences between Type A and B children were observed for the majority of those behaviors selected to tap impatience-aggression and competitiveness. This relative absence of behavioral differences between the types suggests that the freeplay, unstructured classroom environment may not possess the necessary characteristics to elicit the salient components of Type A behavior. During freeplay children are free to choose from an array of activities, and the supply of play equipment and materials is more than sufficient for all children; thus the environment may not be conducive to competitiveness or impatience–aggression. Furthermore, no time constraints are imposed on their activities, and socially undesirable behaviors, such as aggression towards peers, excessive competition, and neglect of turn-taking and sharing are routinely discouraged by the classroom teachers. All of these programmatic environmental conditions may affect the display of Type A behavior. Even though most of these behaviors on the impatience–aggression and competitive dimensions have been observed in preschool children, they were primarily demonstrated in studies using structured tasks specifically designed to elicit them (Corrigan & Moskowitz, 1983; Matthews & Angulo, 1980; Whiting, 1981). The findings of this study support the notion that type A behavior occurs as a function of setting characteristics that selectively elicit this pattern in some individuals, but not others.

The freeplay sessions in the laboratory yielded results that approximated those of the classroom freeplay session. Although the lab environment was a miniature replica of the classroom, it offered one additional feature. A Bobo doll (inflatable punching toy) was included in an effort to elicit aggressive play. As mentioned in the results, children classified as type A initiated more approaches to the Bobo doll and more frequently punched the doll than did children categorized as type B. These results are consistent with those of Matthews & Angulo (1980) on older school-age children.

A constellation of behaviors related to control of the environment (e.g., commands, structures play) was included to tap type A/type B differences. No differences were found, perhaps suggesting that efforts to control are mainly displayed by type A preschool children under conditions of high salience and loss of control (Glass, 1977; Matthews, 1979). Since the freeplay sessions in the lab were also unstructured, they apparently did not feature sufficiently stressful conditions for the children to experience "loss of control."

One finding common to both the classroom and the laboratory freeplay observations was that type A children engaged in more frequent gross motor acitivity (running, jumping, climbing, moving about) than did type Bs. Although not directly related to any of the typically described components of type A behavior, differences between As and Bs along this dimension raise interesting possibilities to be explored in future investigations.

Results from the car races and tower building tasks are consistent with findings from a study on older children (Matthews & Angulo, 1980). Type As won the car race more often and by a significantly greater margin than Bs did. Likewise, compared to Bs, children classified as As built taller towers, consequently drawing more blocks from a common supply. Both of these experimental tasks were aimed at assessing competitive behavior in the children. Due to the young age of our subjects, interpeer racing was considered a potentially more competitive task than the typically studied procedure of racing against an adult experimenter (Matthews & Angulo, 1980). These findings suggest that type As worked harder and faster than Bs to achieve the goals, and thus displayed more competitive behavior in these challenging situations. Similar behaviors were observed by Matthews & Angulo (1980) in their school-age children, but when children raced against a female experimenter.

Because speech pattern differences have been noted in type A adults, a short interview on questions relating to the experimental tasks was included at the end of the children's laboratory session. No differences between Type A and B children were noted for the total time talking or for the number of interruptions. These findings suggest that differences in speech characteristics may well occur only along the qualitative dimension. In general, type A adults exhibit an explosive speech pattern, speaking more quickly, louder and using longer sentences. As a way of showing their impatience, they also interrupt the examiner more often, particularly when the latter purposefully hesitates or speaks slowly. In the present study, these speech qualities were too difficult to code from the children's voices on the audiotapes, and hence, little can be said in reference to this dimension. The children's verbal skills were not very mature, sophisticated or elaborate, and their speech was often unclear, limiting the coding of speech stylistics. In addition, these young children may have felt shy in this unfamiliar, structured situation, perhaps accounting for the low frequencies of interruptions observed. On the other hand, the fact that the type A children were more frequently the first to respond to questions, and responded to a greater number of questions than the Bs, reflects their competitive behavior in this situation. Taken together, these results point to the potential utility of the interview, perhaps not as an assessment instrument, but as a verification of other observable Type A behaviors.

FUTURE DIRECTIONS

Although it has long been argued that the etiology of Pattern A may well be linked to the individual's environmental history, few studies have attempted to systematically identify those particular aspects of the environment that contribute to the development and maintenance of this behavior pattern, or to the plasticity of Type A behavior in diverse settings, particularly in early childhood.

Most studies have concentrated on the assessment of Type A behavior in individually based situations, with the exception of the studies of mother-child interaction by Matthews (1978) and the Van Egeren study (1979) with adults, and have typically involved some level of time constraint, reinforcement, or uncontrollability. No efforts have been directed to the study of interactions between Type A and Type B children under specific environmental conditions, although the importance of both types of social agents (parents and peers) has been noted. Type A behavior itself may serve as an environmental *elicitor* of Type A behavior in others. Thus, the patterns of interaction occurring between dyads differing in their Type A–B configuration can be expected to vary accordingly. The social interaction patterns of all types of dyads (Type A–A, Type A–B, and Type B–B) could be studied under multiple conditions of uncontrollability (salience of loss of control) to investigate this possibility. In accordance with Glass's model that uncontrollability is the noncontingency between one's responses and ensuing outcomes, dyadic interaction studies would desirably employ moderately competitive play situations, where reinforcement for appropriate performance is delivered according to different contingencies.

Knowing the effects of dyad configuration and degree of uncontrollability on both the behavioral and physiological responses (such as cardiovascular and cortisol activity) of preschool children would help clarify whether precursors of the type A pattern noted in adults can be found in early childhood. In general, research efforts of this kind should permit us to better understand the emergence of Type A early in life, the individual components of this complex behavior, the role of social agents (both parents and peers) in the elicitation and maintenance of Type A behavior, and the relationship between Type A behavior and physiological responses in children and their similarity to the type A pattern that has been widely documented in adults.

REFERENCES

Burnam, M. A., Pennebaker, J. W., & Glass, D. C. (1973). Time consciousness, achievement striving and the Type A coronary-prone behavior pattern. *Journal of Abnormal Psychology, 84*, 76–79.

Carver, C. S., Coleman, A. E., & Glass, D. C. (1976). The coronary-prone behavior pattern and the suppression of fatigue on a treadmill test. *Journal of Personality and Social Psychology, 33*, 460–466.

Corrigan, S. A., & Moskowitz, D. S. (1983). Type A Behavior in preschool children: Construct Validation evidence for the MYTH. *Child Development, 54*, 1513–1524.

Dembroski, T. M., MacDougall, J. M., Shields, J. L., Petitto, J., & Lushene, R. (1978). Components of the coronary-prone behavior pattern and cardiovascular responses to psychomotor challenge. *Journal of Behavioral Medicine, 1*, 159–176.

Friedman, M., & Rosenman, R. H. (1959). Association of specific overt behavior patterns with blood and cardiovascular findings. *Journal of the A.M.A., 169*, 1286–1296.

Friedman, M., & Rosenman, R. H. (1971). Type A behavior pattern: Its association with coronary heart disease. *Annals of Clinical Research, 3(6)*, 300–312.

Friedman, M., & Rosenman, R. H. (1974). *Type A behavior and your heart*. New York: Knopf.

Glass, D. C. (1977). *Behavior patterns, stress. and coronary disease*. Hillsdale, NJ: Lawrence Erlbaum Associates.

Glass, D. C., Krakoff, L. R., Contrada, R., et al. (1980). Effect of harassment and competition upon cardiovascular and catecholaminic responses in Type A and Type B individuals. *Psychophysiology, 17,* 453–463.

Glass, D. C., & Singer, J. E. (1972). *Urban stress: Experiments on noise and social stressors.* New York: Academic Press.

Glass, D. C., Snyder, M. L., & Hollis, J. (1974). Time urgency and the Type A coronary prone behavior pattern. *Journal of Applied Social Psychology, 4,* 125–140.

Jenkins, C. D., Zyzanski, S., & Rosenman, R. (1971). Progress towards validation of a computer-scored test for the Type A coronary prone behavior pattern. *Psychosomatic Medicine, 33,* 193–202.

Krantz, D., Glass, D. C., & Snyder, M. (1974). Helplessness, stress level and the coronary prone behavior pattern. *Journal of Experimental Social Psychology, 10,* 284–300.

Manuck, S. B., & Garland, F. N. (1979). Coronary prone behavior pattern, task incentive and cardiovascular response. *Psychophysiology, 16(2),* 136–142.

Matthews, K. A. (1977). Caregiver-child interactions and the Type A coronary-prone behavior pattern. *Child Development, 48,* 1752–1756.

Matthews, K. A. (1978). Assessment and developmental antecedents of the coronary-prone behavior pattern in children. In T. M. Dembroski, S. Weiss, J. Shields, S. Haynes, & M. Feinlieb (Eds.), *Coronary prone behavior.* New York: Springer-Verlag.

Matthews, K. A. (1979). Efforts to control by children and adults with Type A coronary prone behavior pattern. *Child Development, 50,* 842–7.

Matthews, K. A. (1982). Psychological perspectives on the Type A behavior pattern. *Psychological Bulletin, 91(2),* 293–323.

Matthews, K. A., & Angulo, J. (1980). Measurement of the type A behavior pattern in children: Assessment of children's competitiveness, impatience-anger and aggression. *Child Development, 51,* 466–75.

Matthews, K. A., & Volkin, J. I. (1981). Efforts to excel and the Type A behavior pattern in children. *Child Development, 52,* 1283–89.

Myers, J. L. (1977). *Fundamentals of experimental design.* Boston: Allyn & Bacon.

Rosenman, R. H., Brank, R. J., Jenkins, C. D., Friedman, M., Straus, R., & Wurm, M. (1975). Coronary heart disease in the Western Collaborative Group Study. *Journal of the A.M.A., 233,* 872–877.

Seligman, M. (1975). *Helplessness.* San Francisco: W. H. Freeman.

Van Egeren, L. F. (1979). Social Interactions, communications, and the coronary prone behavior pattern: a psychophysiological study. Psychosomatic Medicine, 41(1), 2–18.

Williams, R. B., Kuhn, C. M., Melosh, W., White, A., & Schanberg, S. (1982). Type A behavior and elevated physiological and neuroendocrine responses to cognitive tasks. *Science, 218,* 483–485.

Whiting, C. (1981). *The role of the environment in the development of time urgent Type A behaviors in preschool children.* The Pennsylvania State University: Unpublished doctoral dissertation.

6 Coping Behaviors in Children Facing Medical Stress

Barbara G. Melamed
University of Florida, Gainesville

Lawrence J. Siegel
University of Texas Medical Branch, Galveston

Robyn Ridley-Johnson
University of Wisconsin-Milwaukee

INTRODUCTION

The experience of an acute or chronic illness is potentially stress-evoking for children and their families, providing an opportunity to study adaptation during naturally occurring stress. The primary focus of this chapter concerns a functional analysis of the specific task demands and coping behaviors in "sick" children and their families. A developmental framework is employed as children of different ages have different capacities for handling stress. A number of factors that mediate the impact of stressful medical experiences on the child and family are identified. Finally, two research approaches, one using a functional analysis of coping behaviors and one employing a microanalysis of parental influences on coping are described.

RESPONSE TO MEDICAL STRESSORS: A PROTOTYPE FOR ANXIETY MANAGEMENT

Acute Illness or Elective Surgery

Each day thousands of children undergo numerous medical and dental procedures. The natural occurrence of aversive experiences in medical and dental settings, where the child has minimal control, unfamiliar adults are involved, and

109

where brief separation from parents may occur, makes an ecological approach to the study of childhood fears possible. In the hospital, children are often restricted in movement, isolated from their peer group, and lack the information or ability to control their situation. Although the concomitant pain of illness or physical dysfunction can exacerbate the stress of a medical experience, at least some portion of children's reactions can be attributed to the aversive properties of the setting itself (Traughber & Cataldo, 1982). Medical situations provide relatively controlled environments in which stressful stimuli that elicit anxiety-related behaviors are easily identified. Children typically have repeated contact with medical and dental procedures; thus the opportunity to study the effects of repeated experience and long-term adaptability of the child is present.

Individuals facing hospitalization or an outpatient medical treatment may ordinarily function adequately, but become so anxious in response to the medical stressor that emotional equilibrium is disrupted and normal coping behaviors may be rendered ineffective. Following a hospital stay, approximately 33% of all children develop severe and long-term disturbances such as soiling, bedwetting, increased dependency, aggressiveness, excessive fear, and sleeping or eating disturbances. For some children, however, the experience may have a beneficial effect. In one study, the behavior of 25% of children was rated as improved after a hospital stay (Vernon, Foley, & Schulman, 1967). Little information exists on factors that predict coping versus maladaptive behavior among children experiencing medical stressors.

Evidence for long-term effects of stressful medical experiences is suggested by findings showing that children who had experienced early traumatic dental or medical experiences subsequently showed a greater incidence of somatic disturbances and neurotic tendencies (Cuthbert & Melamed, 1982; Sermet, 1974; Shaw, 1975). Several studies demonstrated that children who had an early negative experience with doctors or surgery later had increased dental anxiety (Martin, Shaw, & Taylor, 1977). Children have been shown to become increasingly sensitized over time to repeated dental or medical visits (Katz, Kellerman, & Siegel, 1981; Venham, Bengston, & Cipes, 1977). There is also evidence in the adult dental literature indicating that adults' dental fears may be learned in childhood (Kleinknecht, Klepac, & Alexander, 1973). In addition, adults with high dental anxiety were found to have high scores on the Neuroticism dimension of the Eysenck's Personality Inventory (Lautch, 1971).

Family System

It is important to view illness within the family system. The process of becoming a medical patient has many aspects of a life crisis for the parent of the sick child, and healthy siblings (Auerbach, 1980; Melamed & Bush, 1984). Although there are few empirical studies of siblings of acutely ill children, studies of siblings of chronically ill children do show them to be at higher risk for adjustment problems (Breslau, Weitzman, & Messenger, 1981; Travis, 1976; Vance, Fazan, Satterwhite, & Pless, 1980). For the parent, there are an array of concerns that have to do with the seriousness of the problem, physical burdens of illness, special diets or regimens, management of their other roles, and financial strain. Often parents must cope with their uncertainty about outcome, try to mitigate the child's fears, pains, and discomforts, and juggle their own expectations and past experiences in addition to maintaining their continuing familial, occupational, marital, and personal roles (Melamed, Robbins, & Fernandez, 1982).

The influence of the parent as a mediator of anxiety effects in medical settings has also been documented. However, this influence can be both positive or negative. Studies of emotional contagion (Escalona, 1953) consistently document that anxious mothers have children who are also anxious in the face of hospitalization or medical procedures. The data on the influence of mother's absence or presence on children's maladaptive behavior in face of invasive medical procedures has been much less consistent. Although the literature on preparation of parents and their children for hospitalization and stressful medical and dental procedures was based on the assumption that reducing maternal anxiety would reduce their children's stress, the mechanism of change was never well specified. Interventions consisted of general psychological packages of coping skills for the child, such as relaxation or cognitive distractions, but few studies observed what the mothers or fathers actually did in facilitating their children's coping. In fact, two recent studies suggested that parent presence in the doctor's treatment room during the venipuncture procedure led to more intense and longer lasting crying in children, particularly for those children under the age of 5 (Gross, Stern, Levin, Dale, & Wojnilower, 1983; Shaw & Routh, 1982). Although the younger children exhibited aggression, resistance, and crying whether the mothers were present or absent, older children showed more crying immediately prior to the initiation of the blood test when their mothers were present rather than absent. The investigators interpreted this behavior as a form of protest since the child may have the belief that the parent will emit comforting responses at the signal of distress. Identifying those interactive patterns that enhance emotional distress during outpatient treatment or hospitalization may pinpoint those families with members who could benefit from stress management training.

Chronic Illness

The study of children with chronic illness provides an opportunity to investigate the course of long-term adaptation over several developmental phases. Children with chronic illness and their families are exposed to aversive events and experiences that are highly stressful, but which occur over an extended period of time. Mattson (1972) has defined a chronic illness as "a disorder with a protracted course which can be fatal or associated with a relatively normal life span despite impaired physical or mental functioning"(p. 801). Pless and Rogham (1971) estimate that 10% of children will experience one or more chronic illnesses by age 15, and as many as 30% of these children may be handicapped by secondary social and psychological problems. Recent advances in medical care have changed the pattern of childhood morbidity, especially in illnesses such as cancer, cystic fibrosis, diabetes, and renal failure, resulting in an increased number of these children reaching adolescence and/or adulthood.

Chronic physical illness in children is commonly thought to be a major life stressor. These children must cope with frequent invasive medical procedures, repeated hospitalizations, periodic and unpredictable exacerbation of symptoms, physical discomfort and bodily disfigurement, side effects of medication, and the potential for shortened life expectancy (Travis, 1976). The early literature in this area, based primarily on anecdotal evidence and uncontrolled investigations, tended to suggest that the presence of a chronic illness rendered a child different from his or her physically healthy peer group, placing the child at risk for normal psychological adjustment. However, recent more well-designed studies indicate that children with chronic illnesses are considerably less deviant when compared to normative groups than the early literature supposed (Drotar, Owens, & Gotthold, 1980; Gayton, Friedman, Tavormina, & Tucker, 1977; Kellerman, Zeltzer, Ellenberg, Dash, & Rigler, 1980; Tavormina, Kastner, Slater, & Watt, 1976).

Current research supports the conclusion that although chronic illness can be a life stressor for children, the disease process itself does not appear to be the primary cause of behavioral adjustment problems for the chronically ill child. Most children show surprising resilience and regain a level of adaptive coping with minimal psychological intervention. On the other hand, a protracted retreat from age-appropriate development tasks, particularly in a child with mild physical disease, can signal a more ominous disturbance requiring more intensive intervention (Drotar, 1981). The impact of the illness depends on a number of factors including: (1) features unique to the illness such as its course and severity, its visibility, and the degree of handicap it imposes; (2) specific attributes of the child such as age of onset of the illness, intellectual and cognitive abilities, and social and emotional adjustment; (3) family resources such as problem-solving skills, level of cohesion, and adaptability to change, openness of communication patterns, etc.; and (4) the support systems that are available to the child and his or her family including extended family networks, friends and community resources (Drotar, 1981; Sperling, 1978; Willis, Elliot, & Jay, 1982). This chapter focuses on the individual child attributes and family resources as influencing factors on coping with medical events.

ILLNESS AND MEDICAL CONCERNS

Many factor-analytic studies (Lapouse & Monk, 1959; Miller, Barrett, & Hampe, 1974) revealed that children's fears of physical injury, doctors, dentists, and having an operation, remain over a wide range of developmental periods. Fear of strangers is more characteristic of younger children, and the separation from parents due to hospitalization would be a greater concern for younger children aged 6 and under. Following a routine hospital experience, 10% to 92% of all children show regressive behaviors such as increased dependency, loss of toilet training, excessive fears, and sleeping or eating disturbances. In 33% of these children these fears persist and require psychological intervention. In an attempt to understand why some children do not cope as well as others in face of illness or hospitalization, we turned to the basic learning theory approaches to the development and maintenance of fear.

THEORIES OF THE DEVELOPMENT OF FEAR

From the learning viewpoint, sampling how the child behaves within a particular setting and in the presence of repeated stress-related stimuli is important in understanding the development of children's fears. Operant conditioning of fear may occur by direct reinforcement of the behavior or observational learning processes (Morris & Kratochwill, 1983). Observational learning of fears from parents and siblings has been well documented (Bandura, 1969). A number of studies support the contributing influence of modeling in the development of children's fears. Children often experience the same kind and number of fears as their mothers (Hagman, 1932). Solyom, Beck, Solyom, and Hugel (1974) noted that 30% of the mothers of phobic patients and 3% of their fathers were also phobic. Similar findings have been reported by Bandura and Menlove (1968), who reported that 35% of dog phobic children had parents who were also fearful.

Parents may contribute to children's fearful behavior in other ways as well. Maternal anxiety has been related to children's stress reactions in dental or medical settings (Heffernan & Azarnoff, 1971; Shaw, 1975; Wright & Alpern, 1971; Wright, Alpern, & Leake, 1973). In addition to modeling anxious behavior, anxious mothers may influence the development of maladaptive or overwhelming anxiety in their children by genetic transmission to condition anxiety, or by dysfunctional parenting behavior. The importance of studying actual parenting behavior in stressful situations is predicated on findings such as reported by Weissman (1985), who found that children of phobic mothers also show concurrent anxiety disorders. Children between the ages of 6 and 17 whose mothers had been diagnosed as depressed and as either agoraphobic or manifesting panic disorder were themselves diagnosed as having high rates of depression, separation anxiety, and other categories of anxiety disorders. These ratings, however, were not blind with respect to parental pathology.

The understanding of children's fears may have preventive implications. Many retrospective studies have found that adult anxiety disorders may have had their roots in childhood or early adulthood (Agras, Chapin, & Oliveau, 1972;

Berg, 1976; Buglass, Clarke, Henderson, Krietman, & Presley, 1977; Klein, 1964; Roth, 1960; Tyrer & Tyrer, 1974). Weissman (1985) also reported that women with agoraphobia had significantly more reports of separation anxiety in childhood and that a large proportion of them had not separated from their parents for normal childhood experiences like going to camp, staying overnight at a friends, etc. Berg and his colleagues (Berg, Marks, McGuire, & Sipsedge, 1974) found that outpatient agoraphobics with a childhood history of separation anxiety rated themselves as more fearful and as being more impaired as adults and having an earlier onset of symptoms. Yet as Weissman points out, there are no prospective longitudinal studies to elucidate the clinical significance of childhood anxiety and its relationship, if any, to anxiety disorders in adulthood.

Maternal-Child Attachment in the Development of Anxiety or Dependency

The medical situation is an ideal environment to study maternal-child attachment. Some important implications from the maternal deprivation studies stemming from Bowlby (1973), Spitz (1950), and Bretherton and Ainsworth's (1974) stranger approach situations relate to the quality of bonding of the parent and child (Michels, Frances, & Shear, 1984). Early relationships between parent and child may lead to the development of later emotional disorders in children (distress syndrome, affectionless character). Few investigators, however, have applied this notion to children above 3-years-of-age (Rutter, 1981).

Maternal overprotectiveness, common in parents with sick children, which is defined as encouraging dependent behavior by consistently assisting the child or displaying excessive concern when the child becomes upset or stressed, has been shown to be associated with dependency in children (Kagan & Moss, 1962; Levy, 1943). Martin (1975) has explained the mechanism by which overly protective mothers foster the development of dependent behaviors in their children as follows:

> separate tendencies on the part of the child may be experienced as aversive by the mother, and her attempts to restore the closeness may be reinforced by the reduction of 'her' distress. The child, at the same time, may also experience forced separation as aversive, and returning to the mother may be reinforced by the reduction of his distress . . . When (this) system becomes especially strong and the negative affect associated with separation behavior becomes intense, . . . phenomena such as school phobia may appear. (p. 487)

Lewis and Michalson (1981) studied very young children from 3 months to 3 years who were rated on five affective states including fear, anger, happiness, competence, and attachment/dependency. The children were observed across a wide range of situations. One finding particularly relevant to the topic of this chapter was that fearful behavior was significantly related to attachment/dependence and competence in these children. Highly fearful children were rated high on attachment/dependence and low on competence (defined as success in meeting the task demands of a day care program).

There is data suggesting that these early experiences between mothers and their children have long-term implications. Kagan and Moss (1962) investigated the long-term effects of maternal overprotectiveness in 54 adults who had been observed in the home, school, and summer camp between the ages of 3 and 10 years. As children, the subjects were observed in terms of behavioral dimensions such as passivity, seeking nurturance, and seeking reassurance. In addition, the mothers were observed interacting with their children; mothers were interviewed regarding their attitudes toward their children and child rearing. As adults, the subjects were interviewed regarding their dependent behaviors such as seeking support and nurturance from significant others. Kagan and Moss found that girls who had been highly protected as children tended to withdraw from stressful or challenging situations as adults. For boys, maternal protectiveness was positively related with the boy's passivity and dependence throughout childhood.

Maccoby and Masters (1970) have written about the means by which parental restrictiveness is associated with a child's emotional dependency: ". . . restrictiveness will prevent the child from acquiring autonomous skills for coping with his needs, and will therefore be associated with continued high dependency on parents and other adults'' (p. 143). Restrictiveness resulting from maternal overprotectiveness, therefore, may impede the child from developing coping skills. In turn, a lack of coping skills in the face of a stressful experience may be associated with greater fear and distress in response to the stressor.

In a recent prospective, longitudinal study by Lewis and his colleagues (Lewis, Feiring,McGuffog, & Jaskir, 1984) the relationship between the quality of the early attachment relationships and later psychopathology was demonstrated for 6-year-old boys. This excellent study found that 40% of the boys who as 1-year-olds had been classified as insecurely attached (avoidant and ambivalent) on the modified Ainsworth-Wittig (1969) Strange Situation, exhibited signs of psychopathology on a mother's report of Children's Behavior Problems (Achenbach, 1979), a widely used clinical instrument with both normative and clinical norms. This study also included environmental measures thought capable of mediating these effects, namely social network and life events stress. The results suggested that an early secure attachment for boys makes them somewhat impervious to the effects of stress and places them at low risk for psychopathology. These results thus provide evidence for the influence of the early mother-child relationship upon the child's ongoing emotional development. The limitations of the study were that the sample included only middle and upperclass white intact families and there was not an equal distribution of children in each class facing equivalent environmental stress.

PARENTING BEHAVIORS IN STRESSFUL
MEDICAL SETTINGS

Given the importance of the mother-child relationship, supported by both theory and data, for children's emotional development in general, and specifically for the development of coping skills, mother-child interaction should be an important factor influencing children's anxiety and coping responses in stressful medical situations. The relevance of the medical situation as a place to study patterns of parenting and their influence on child behavior has, however, often been overlooked.

Separation from parents is frequently cited as a source of stress for hospitalized children (Nasera, 1978). The dental and medical situation often evokes anxiety because of separation from mothers during aversive procedures. Even when the parents are allowed to be present, aversive procedures are often carried out by unfamiliar adults. Thus, this situation may be analagous to anxiety elicited by stranger approach. Parents' behaviors as they assist in the comfort of their children may reveal patterns facilitating or inhibiting good coping skills. For instance, Hannallah and Rosales (1983) have demonstrated that when mothers elected to accompany their preschool children during short hospitalization or anesthesia induction, the youngsters were less disturbed. This study has serious limitations, though, since the groups of children were not matched for ailment or length of stay, and the only outcome measures were based on mother's report. Also, mothers who elected to stay may have had better relationships with their children, and patterns of mother-child interaction were not studied.

There are some additional compelling reasons to see medical contexts as a naturalistic laboratory for the study of transmission of adaptive coping or maladaptive anxiety. Data reported by Mechanic (1964) suggested the influence of maternal anxiety as a primary factor in bringing children to physicians. In his study of 350 mothers, he found that it was more likely that psychologically distressed mothers defined their children as ill and requiring medical attention.

Mothers' reports of their disciplinary styles have also been found to be related to how well their children coped with dental and medical situations (Venham, Murray, & Gaulin-Kremer, 1979; Zabin & Melamed, 1980). Mothers who reported that they dealt with their children's fear-related behaviors across a wide range of separation and fear-eliciting situations with reassurance and modeling of approach behaviors had children who coped more effectively with hospitalization and dental restorative treatments. Children whose mothers reported reinforcing dependency or forcing approach behavior or punishing avoidance behaviors coped less effectively. Fathers who reported the use of threat of punishment in order to prevent the child from avoiding a feared situation also had children who could not cope well with hospitalization (Zabin & Melamed, 1980). In one of the few studies in which actual observations were made of children and concurrent mothers' reports of childrearing obtained, Venham et al. (1979) found that children who were more anxious during dental treatment had mothers who reported that they tended to avoid the use of reward and punishment whereas low-child anxiety during treatment was related to maternal responsivity and the organization of the home environment. Children whose parents tended to use nonintervention were unable to tolerate stress. On the other hand, too much restrictiveness has also resulted in poorer coping. Heffernan and Azarnoff (1971) found a significant interaction between children's previous anxiety about medical examinations (as reported retrospectively by mothers) and mothers' suppressiveness of the child's crying when frightened. Among children rated by their mother as previously nonfearful, those with suppressive mothers reported high anxiety, while those with nonsuppressive mothers reported low anxiety about the impending examination. Children of suppressive mothers reported greater anticipatory anxiety regardless of maternally reported child anxiety on previous visits.

Several methodological problems exist in the studies discussed where the influence of parenting in the medical setting was of interest. Selective report, problems in recall, and social desirability may have biased these results. Definitions of parental disciplinary behavior differed across studies and may account for inconsistencies in the findings. Most important, in none of the studies reported was actual parenting behavior observed in these situations. In the final section we share our current approach to overcome these problems.

FACTORS WHICH MEDIATE THE IMPACT OF MEDICAL EXPERIENCES

The effects of medical experiences are far from uniform and depend on a multitude of factors including: (a) those that involve the psychosocial aspects of the family, and (b) those that are related to the illness itself. There is not a consistent one-to-one relationship between the severity of an illness and the response to it. The children's temperament and age, as well as their cognitive and behavioral styles, mediate their response to the medical experience. The degree to which the child and the family perceive that they can control the illness-related stressors is another factor to be considered. This perception of controllability/predictability may be influenced by previous experience. The appraisal of one's ability to cope with current stressful events may also be influenced by prior success or failure in coping (Bandura, 1977, 1982; Lazarus & Launier, 1978). Finally, the family relationship may also affect the manner in which the child adapts to hospitalization or illness.

Temperament

Certain individual temperamental traits or behavioral styles may place a child at risk for developing behavior problems. Temperament is defined as the child's behavioral style or emotional reactivity as he or she interacts with the environment (Willis, Swanson, & Walker, 1983). There is some evidence that these temperamental characteristics are innate and identifiable at the time of birth (Thomas & Chess, 1977).

The longitudinal research by Thomas, Chess, and Birch (1968) demonstrated that a child's temperament is an important variable that relates to later behavioral adjustment. They identified nine dimensions of temperament including: (1) level and extent of motor activity; (2) rhythmicity or degree of regularity of functions (i.e., sleep-wake cycle, hunger, etc); (3) approach or withdrawal in response to new stimuli; (4) adaptability to new or altered situations; (5) threshold or responsiveness to stimulation; (6) intensity of reactions; (7) quality of mood; (8) distractibility; and (9) length of attention span and persistence. Five of these dimensions were found to cluster together to determine three general classes of temperament. "Difficult" children are described as displaying irregularity in biological functions, negative withdrawal responses to new stimuli, slow adaptability to change, and intense mood expressions which are generally negative. "Easy" children, on the other hand, are characterized by regularity in biological functions, positive approach responses to new stimuli, high adaptability to change, and mild or moderately intense moods which are usually positive in nature. The "slow-to-warm-up" child displays a combination of negative responses of mild intensity to new stimuli with slow adaptability after repeated contact. Furthermore, this child shows a mild intensity of reactions, whether positive or negative, and less tendency to exhibit irregularity of biological functions. Thomas et al. (1968) found that 70% of the children classified as difficult developed a variety of behavior problems at some later point, while only 18% of those children identified as "easy" developed such problems. Studying children during a hospital experience would allow one to pinpoint temperament factors as they modulate adjustment since a hospital experience often involves an unfamiliar setting and often frequent night wakings and occasional ureter catheterization which may interfere with regularity of biological functioning.

Age

Younger children are more vulnerable to separation from adults (Rutter, 1981). Medical situations often require physical or psychological separation of mother and child, while an unfamiliar adult (doctor or nurse) may administer unpleasant procedures.

It is known that children's awareness and knowledge of health, illness, and hospitalization increases as the child gets older (Neuhauser, Amsterdam, Hines, & Steward, 1978). There is evidence, for example, that children of different ages have different conceptions of illness causality (Campbell, 1975; Peters, 1978; Simeonsson, Buckley, & Monson, 1979). Younger children fear immediate and concrete events such as *shots* and *physical restraint*, whereas older children who have a capacity for abstract reasoning may fear the symbolic and long-term aspects of illness such as contagion or disfigurement. In younger children, the meaning of an illness is often misinterpreted as punishment for bad behavior. These differences in ability to abstract information may underlie the age differences found in preparation studies.

Children under the age of 7 are usually less able to profit from psychological preparations which focus on providing information about how to cope with medical procedures. They require a more concrete preparation close in time to the events that they must handle. There is some recent evidence (Melamed, Dearborn, & Hermecz, 1983) that children who are under the age of 8 and have had a previous surgery experience are most vulnerable and may even be sensitized by receiving information about impending events.

Controllability-Predictability

Although much data exists in the animal literature and the adult human literature on the psychobiological effects of predictability and uncontrollability in response to an aversive stimulus (Mineka et al., 1984), Traughber and Cataldo (1982) pointed out that this research has not been applied to the understanding of pediatric hospitalization. The tendency to give information packages prior to enduring hospitalization has not considered the influence of whether the impending situation is predictable or controllable. However, the nature of the stressor as well as the individual characteristics of the patient, i.e., preference for information or denial, must be considered.

Animal studies have consistently demonstrated a preference for signaled versus unsignaled shock even if inescapable (Badia & Culbertson, 1972; Badia, Culbertson, & Harsh, 1973). Conditions mitigating the effects of aversive stimulation include presenting of competing positive events (Pavlov, 1927) or making the aversive stimulus more predictable (Brady, 1955). However, human research suggests that suppression of behavior occurs as the individual learns that his responses and the aversive event are independent (Seligman, 1975). In pediatric intensive care settings, Cataldo and his colleagues (Cataldo, Bessman, Parker, Pearson, & Rogers, 1979) noted extreme apathy and social withdrawal in children whose activity and movement were restricted during medical treatment. Katz, Kellerman, and Siegel (1981) found behavioral withdrawal, increased muscle tension, and other signs of anxiety and disruption in 97% of all children during bone marrow aspirations regardless of the number of procedures the children had undergone previously. Given lack of control over repeated aversive tasks, predictability does not reduce the stress. Katz, Sharp, Kellerman, Marston, Hershman, and Siegel (1982) showed increased Beta-endorphin release associated with behavior distress (nurses' ratings) in children with acute leukemia during repeated experience with lumbar punctures and bone marrow aspiration. Melamed and her colleagues (Melamed et al., 1983; Melamed & Siegel, 1980) found that information in advance of a repeated hospitalization for elective surgery could even sensitize children under 8-years-of-age.

When the adult literature is reviewed (Auerbach, Martelli, & Mercuri, 1983; Miller, S., 1983), it becomes clear that adults have preferred cognitive styles of processing information about impending stressful events. The evidence suggests that individual differences in information seeking preferences moderate the effects of stress. Recent studies (Miller, 1983) have identified a blunter versus monitor mode. "Monitoring" involves being alert for and sensitized to the negative aspects of experience. "Blunting" involves distraction from and cognitively shielding oneself from objective sources of danger. When an aversive event is controllable, monitoring is the main coping modality. Although monitoring heightens arousal, it enables the individual to initiate controlling behaviors to attempt to manage the stress. When an aversive event is uncontrollable, monitoring has little instrumental value. Then blunting or tuning out information by engaging in distraction and similar psychological strategies is more adaptive. Miller (1983) postulates that inflexibility or inability to turn off the "monitoring" mode for threat relevant cues when there is inescapable pain may underlie susceptibility to anxiety disorders.

> Since anxiety appears in part, to be a function of being in the psycholgoical presence of arousing danger signals (even when these are objectively absent), those who constantly monitor for threatening cues may be prone to chronic anxiety (e.g., by misinterpreting neutral cues as danger signals or by not detecting signals of safety. (p. 77)

Thus, inflexibility in self-regulatory patterns may be the hallmark of maladaptive coping.

In the area of surgery preparation, a critical review (Auerbach & Kilman, 1977) has indicated that sensitizers who are vigilant about what will happen do better with specific information, whereas avoiders given specific information make more complaints postoperatively than those who had only received general information.

Little parallel research exists in the area of children's coping styles. Burstein and Meichenbaum (1979) did find that children who tended to avoid playing with hospital-related toys 1 week before surgery were more anxious about hospitalization than those who chose to play with such toys. Unger (1982) found that children who tended to deny worry actually obtained less information from videotaped models in face of impending dental procedures and showed more behavioral disruption than those who were low on denial. Knight, Atkins, Eagle, Evans, Finklestein, Fukushima, Katz, and Weiner (1979) found that stress hormones were more adaptive (i.e., lower cortisol production) in children who wanted to know about the upcoming hospital experience and who used flexible defenses of intellectualization and isolation. The children who used either denial, denial with isolation, displacement, or projection regarding the upcoming hospital experience showed maladaptive stress physiology reflected in increased cortisol production rates on the day after hospital admission.

A recent study (Peterson & Toler, 1986) found that children rated as information-seeking by their mother's asked more questions during the blood test and recovery from surgery. High information seekers also showed more adaptive responses prior to the blood test.

Therefore, simply providing children with increased information about an upcoming aversive hospital or dental procedure is probably not an effective stress-reducing strategy. Studies are not uniform in providing evidence that information without behavioral rehearsal helps children to reduce their anxiety relative to unprepared children. Exposure to either puppet or filmed peer modeling is a more effective means of alleviating anxiety if it induces them to engage in muscle relaxation and pleasant imagery or provides them with sensory information (Cassell, 1965; Johnson & Stockdale, 1975; Melamed, Yurcheson, Fleece, Hutcherson, & Hawes, 1978; Siegel & Peterson, 1980, 1981). Information may not be assimilated or may fail to instigate useful coping strategies. Information may sensitize young children with previous surgeries (Melamed et al., 1983; Siegel & Harkevy, in press). We found that children who were to receive elective surgery directly from the emergency room were actually less anxious after viewing a distracting film than those who saw hospital-relevant information (Faust & Melamed, 1984). Thus, if the situation does not allow for controllability, information may have negative value and/or heighten arousal particularly if there is not any opportunity to practice new or adaptive responses.

On the other hand, when children with high injection fears were encouraged to practice along with the peer model who demonstrated coping strategies, then exposure to a coping videotape prior to restorative treatment effectively reduced anxiety and improved cooperative behavior (Klingman, Melamed, Cuthbert, & Hermecz, 1984). In addition, those youngsters who had reported a more varied range of self-mastery skills made better use of the participant modeling preparation.

Thus, studies are needed which take into account the controllability of the aversive stimulation as well as the information processing abilities of the child. These factors need to be considered prior to providing preparatory strategies or information about the nature of impending procedures.

Previous Experience

Children's previous experience affects their expectancies regarding their ability to cope as well as provide information about controllability or lack of controllability of a given aversive situation. Prior experience also affects the parent's perception of how well the child will cope with the present stressor. Several of the information packages shown to children and their parents during the hospital preparation are geared toward correcting misinformation and explaining what sensations will accompany the procedures. If the upcoming event is familiar and has been successfully handled in the past, it is unlikely that additional information will add much to the child's coping repertoire. Melamed et al. (1978) and Klorman, Hilpert, Michael, LaGana, and Sveen (1980) demonstrated that children with previous experience do not benefit from peer-relevant modeling as compared to a simple reminder of what to expect in the situation of routine dental treatment. However, when the procedures are more demanding and the child's experience more negative, the presentation of information might even lead to a conditioned emotional response which interferes with adaptive functioning.

This section examines those studies in which previous experience has led to maladaptive behavioral problems when children are faced with repeated medical events. Siegel and Harkavy (personal communication) found an increase in physiological arousal and maladaptive behavior in children facing a second surgery if they were exposed to information about the impending stressors. Melamed et al. (1983) also demonstrated that children who were shown a hospital-relevant slide-audiotape who were under 8-years-of-age and had one surgery (over the age of 3) actually reported an increase in medical concerns and showed more behavioral disruptiveness during the procedures than a matched control group who viewed an unrelated film. It would appear that the exposure re-invoked those feelings of discomfort that had previously been conditioned to situations similarly depicted. In fact, when children were faced with repeated aversive procedures, such as bone marrow aspirations, lumbar punctures, and chemotherapy, some developed phobic symptoms such as conditioned nausea (Redd & Andrykowsky, 1982). This may be generalized and may occur not only during the procedure itself, but as the child approaches the hospital, whenever medical personnel are seen, or even if the child merely thinks about these procedures as well.

The degree of cortisol production and Beta-endorphin production has been related to repeated experience with medical stressors (Katz et al., 1982; Knight et al., 1979). Children who use effective defenses as based on interview data and Rorschach responses have been shown to be less likely to produce cortisol the day before surgery than children using ineffective defenses. This relationship is lost if the measures are taken 2 weeks prior to the actual hospitalization. Therefore, before presenting information one must pay attention to the degree and manner in which a child normally copes with stimuli in his environment.

It would be useful to evaluate the children's success in dealing with previous noxious experiences. Naturalistic studies suggest that those children who use flexible coping strategies and can verbalize many coping techniques do better than those who have only a few at hand (Siegel, 1983). This appears to be a fruitful area for further study.

Developmental Differences in Child Coping

If one is interested in assessing the degree of coping capability, it is important to conduct longitudinal research so that the children's adaptation can be assessed as the demands of the situation change and as the developmental level varies. Very few longitudinal studies of children having repeated medical procedures have been undertaken. In these studies, developmental factors have been found to play an important role. Thus, Katz et al. (1982) found that whereas younger children have been found to cry more and exhibit protest behaviors older children undergoing repeated bone marrows showed their anxiety by social withdrawal and muscular tension.

Venham et al. (1977) found that with repeated experience in dental procedures, children showed increased anxiety and heart rate in a discriminative fashion. They were likely to be rated as more anxious and show an increase in heart rate only immediately prior to the novocaine injections.

In a cross-sectional study of children between 6 months and 16-months-of-age, developmental trends in emotional responses and coping mechanisms before, during, and after routine medical examinations were evaluated (Hyson, 1983). Negative emotional responses were found to decrease with age and to be greater during the examination than before or after. Information seeking was the most commonly observed coping behavior, particularly during the preexamination period, whereas autonomy seeking was found to increase during and after the exam. Older children engaged in autonomy-seeking during the preexamination period, which was generally instrumental. However, they too, exhibited expressive behavior (e.g., crying, verbal protest) during the exam. The ratio of instrumental to expressive autonomy seeking was also found to increase with age. Younger children are more threatened by concrete events, such as being touched by instruments, whereas older children are concerned with symbolic events, fear of bodily injury and being different. Thus, with increasing age, fear responses and coping behaviors were found to be more realistic, more anticipatory, and goal-directed.

The developmental differences in coping behavior reported by Hyson (1983) underscore the importance of evaluating coping behavior within the context of the developmental status of the child. For example, the measures of anxiety in younger children tend to show more upset behaviors in both the verbal and motor systems, while older children are less likely to exhibit distress motorically. Older children may sit still and appear to cooperate with procedures although they are actually under great distress. Measures such as cortisol and Beta-endorphin may more accurately reflect the degree of stress experienced by these children. Possible developmental differences in children's anxiety and coping responses is an important factor to consider in developing research designs.

NEW APPROACHES TO STUDYING CHILDREN'S FEARS

Global Trait-Approach to Stress Adaptation

Much of the research on the impact of illness on children has taken a ''shotgun'' approach to investigating children's responses to a presumed life stressor. The typical approach has been to give children a number of global measures of "psychological adjustment" with the assumption that these measures will pinpoint some of the differences between the children with various illnesses and their physically healthy peers. Drotar (1981) has noted in this regard that:

> research in chronic illness has been dominated by a personality-focused paradigm associated with a counterproductive focus on differences between chronically ill and physically healthy children and a neglect of factors which contribute to successful coping in family, school, and social relationships. (p. 211)

Based on a considerable body of literature a number of writers have admonished researchers in this area for using this global trait approach, since it has not proven useful as a means of understanding why some individuals show satisfactory adaptation to their illness while others do not (Cohen & Lazarus, 1979; Moos & Tsu, 1977). Instead, it has been proposed that a competency-based model, which focuses on the coping tasks and strategies which individuals use to manage their illness should be the guiding framework for research in this area. Coping has received much recent attention in literature on stress, but it remains an elusive concept that has not been clearly operationalized. Lazarus and Launier (1978) have offered a useful definition of coping which they regard as a:

> wide range of problem-solving efforts, both action-oriented and intrapsychic to manage, master, tolerate, reduce, or minimize environmental and internal demands and conflicts among them, which tax or exceed a person's resources. (p. 311)

Coping is, within this framework, an *ongoing* rather than a static process which can be understood only by studying the individual as he or she interacts with the environment. Specifically, Lazarus notes the importance of understanding what the children and their families *do* and *think* in specific situations in order to learn about their coping efforts with their illness. There have been few attempts to investigate specific coping behaviors in children. The approaches for assessing coping strategies in physically healthy children as represented in the work of Murphy and Moriarty (1976) and Zeitlin (1980) are useful contributions in this area.

Mattson (1972) reports one of the first attempts at studying children who were coping effectively with their chronic illness. He identified several coping mechanisms that were associated with children who were judged to be adapting well to their illness, including the use of cognitive skills to accept the limitations imposed by their illness, participation in compensatory activities, use of family members for support, and the ability to express negative emotion in an appropriate manner. More recent efforts at investigating specific coping efforts in children with physical illness include the identification of coping strategies of children with cancer (Spinetta & Maloney, 1978) and the study of cognitive and behavioral coping strategies of children hospitalized for surgery (Siegel, 1983).

Functional Analysis of Coping Behavior

As with other stressful life experiences, children's reactions to chronic illness range from adaptive coping efforts to severe maladjustment. A number of factors, as noted earlier, may mediate the impact of the illness on a particular child. Among these factors, the coping skills that children use in their attempts to manage the potential stresses imposed by their illness have received little attention in the research literature. The coping skills in a child's repertoire are an important focus of study in our understanding of the individual differences observed in children's response to their illness in the face of comparable degrees of severity and type of illness.

The initial step in this area must be the identification of situations or tasks with which the physically ill child needs to cope across a comprehensive set of adaptive contexts. Although his work has been primarily with adults, Moos (1982) has provided a useful framework for conceptualizing the tasks that the physically ill patient has to confront. He has identified a set of major adaptive tasks or challenges with which patients must cope in acute health-related situations. The first group of tasks is primarily illness-related and includes the management of pain and other symptoms, coping with the hospital and treatment procedures, and developing and maintaining satisfactory relationships with the medical personnel. In the second group of tasks, Moos has outlined more general experiences that he suggests are applicable to most stressful life events. This latter group of tasks include maintaining emotional balance such as moderating anxiety, maintaining a sense of self-worth and competence, maintaining satisfactory relationships with significant others, and preparing for possible impairment or loss of functioning as a result of illness.

Drotar (1981) has noted that coping behavior in chronically ill children and their families is "best studied from an ipsative and/or developmental perspective . . . over time . . . with measures which link coping processes to adaptive outcome in life situations" (p. 219). Using an approach similar to that outlined above by Moos (1982), coping strategies in chronically ill children need to be evaluated from two perspectives. First, one must study how children negotiate the normal tasks of childhood and adolescence (Table 6.1). Whether or not a child is physically ill, adaptation and coping must be assessed within the context of age-appropriate developmental tasks that must be accomplished by all children

TABLE 6.1
Tasks of Childhood and Adolescence

School attendance
Academic achievement
Establish career/occupational interests
Establish and maintain peer relationships/acceptance
Establish and maintain heterosexual relationships
Self-Acceptance (physical, sexual identity)
Maintain an integral role in the family system
Develop skills/competence for independence

TABLE 6.2
Tasks of Patients With Sickle Cell Disease

```
Vaso-occlusive (painful) crises
Medication compliance (antibiotics)
Blood transfusions
Hospitalizations
Frequent clinic visits
Frequent fluid intake
Adjustment to growth retardation
Adjustment to delayed sexual maturation
Adjustment to fatigability
Adjustment to neurological problems (headache/stroke)
Adjustment to urinary-genital problems (bed-wetting, impotence)
```

(Willis et al., 1982). Physical illness may or may not increase the difficulty of a child mastering each developmental task.

The second level of assessment of coping in children with physical illness must also focus on disease-related tasks that are unique to the child's particular illness such as compliance with a specific medication regimen or tolerating invasive medical procedures. For example, the specific tasks with which children with sickle cell disease typically must cope are presented in Table 6.2.

Based on these task situations, a structured interview was developed to identify specific behaviors and cognitions associated with the child's attempts to meet the challenges and demands which are imposed by these various developmental and disease-related tasks. Interviews were conducted every 4 months in order to sign. The interviews were focused on the child's specific actions in which they engaged in order to respond to the various tasks. In addition, the interviews engaged in response to the various tasks. In addition, the interviews explored the metacognitive activities of the children during specific events or activities.

In addition to the interviews, observations and ratings of the child's behavior were obtained relative to the tasks described earlier. It will then be possible to look at the relationship between the child's behvaior in the specific situations and his or her own coping strategies as obtained from the interviews.

In a recent study, Siegel (1983) conducted an ecological assessment of self-generated coping strategies used by hospitalized children to evaluate whether children who make an optimal adjustment to hospitalization for illness use different coping strategies from those children who make less satisfactory adjustments to the experience. The primary focus of the research was on the assessment of cognitive and behavioral coping behaviors in which children engaged during stressful and painful medical procedures. A multi-dimensional assessment approach was used to to evaluate the anxiety level and response to pain of 80 children 8- to 14-years-old who were hospitalized for various medical illnesses including sickle cell disease, cancer, cystic fibrosis, and chronic renal failure. A structured interview was conducted with the children to evaluate, among other things, the typical coping responses to painful and anxiety-provoking experiences in the hospital.

Children were classified as successful copers if they were consistently rated by a nurse and physician as being cooperative with the procedures, showed low anxiety, and manifested high tolerance for discomfort. The results indicated that successful copers had more accurate information about why they were in the hospital and reported using more different strategies for managing stressful and painful experiences. Unsuccessful copers, on the other hand, reported using significantly more negative self-statements regarding their ability to tolerate discomfort and reported thinking more often about past experiences where they were unable to effectively tolerate painful procedures similar to those encountered in the hospital.

Using this approach, we hope to determine whether chronically ill children differ from their physically healthy peers both in terms of their accomplishing the developmental tasks and their use of coping strategies. We also plan to assess whether children with different disease-related tasks show different levels of adjustment based on their use of particular coping strategies. Eventually we hope that this research program will enable us to systematically identify adaptive coping strategies so as to develop more effective intervention programs for chronically ill children. By building on the coping skills that are already in the child's repertoire, interventions can be tailored to a particular child's specific needs to assist him or her [in their efforts] to negotiate key developmental [tasks] and disease-related tasks.

Emotional Contagion in Parent-Child Interactions

In order to identify dysfunctional patterns of interaction between mothers and their children during medical stressors, a Dyadic Prestressor interaction scale (DPIS) (Table 6.3) was derived from theoretical positions involving emotional contagion (Escalona 1953; Vanderveer 1949), crisis parenting (Kaplan, Smith, Grobstein, & Fischman, 1973; Melamed & Bush, 1986), and earlier work on attachment behavior and stranger approach (Bretherton & Ainsworth, 1974).

The emotional contagion hypothesis states that parental anxiety is communicated to the child bv nonverbal as well as verbal means and that this in turn increases the child's anxiety level. It is nonspecific as to exactly how or why the parental anxiety elicits child anxiety. It does have empirical support in studies correlating parental and child state anxiety in medical situations (Bailey, Talbot, & Taylor, 1973; Sides, 1977).

The crisis-parenting model is more specific and emphasizes the increased importance of parenting when children face stressors. Vernon et al. (1967) found that maternal presence had a calming effect on children's (2- to 6-years-old) distress during anesthesia induction but made little difference during a nonstressful procedure such as admission. High parental anxiety at such times is

TABLE 6.3
Dyadic Prestressor Interaction Scale: Functional Definitions

CHILD BEHAVIOR CATEGORIES

Attachment

Look at parent: child looking at parent
Approach parent: child motorically approaching parent
Touch parent: child physically touching parent
Verbal concern: child verbalizing concern with the parent's
    continuing presence throughout the procedures

Distress

Crying: child's eyes watering and/or the child is making
    crying sounds
Diffuse motor: child running around, pacing, flailing arms,
    kicking, arching, engaging in repetitive fine motor activity,
    and so forth
Verbal unease: child verbalizing fear, distress, anger, anxiety,
    and so forth
Withdrawal: child silent and immobile, no eye contact with
    parent, in curled-up position

Exploration

Motoric exploration: child locomoting around room, visually
    examining
Physical manipulation: child handling objects in room
Questions parent: child asking parent a question related to
    doctors, hospitals, and so forth
Interaction with observer: child attempting to engage in verbal
    or other interaction with observer

Prosocial

Looking at book: child is quietly reading a book or magazine
    unrelated to medicine or looking at its pictures
Other verbal interaction: child is verbally interacting with
    parent on topic unrelated to medicine
Other play: child playing with parent, not involving medical
    objects or topics
Solitary play: child playing alone with object brought into
    room, unrelated to medicine

PARENT BEHAVIOR CATEGORIES

Ignoring

Eyes shut: parent sleeping or has eyes shut
Reads to self: parent reading quietly
Sitting quietly: parent sitting quietly, not making eye con-
    tact with child
Other noninteractive: parent engaging in other medically
    unrelated solitary activity

Reassurance

Verbal reassurance: parent telling child not to worry, that
    the child can tolerate the procedures, that it will not be
    bad, and so forth
Verbal empathy: parent telling child he or she understands
    the child's feelings, thoughts, situation; questions child
    for feelings

(continued)

(continued)

Verbal praise: parent telling child that the child is mature,
    strong, brave, capable, doing fine, and so forth
Physical stroking: parent petting, stroking, rubbing, hugging,
    kissing child

Distraction

Nonrelated conversation: parent engaging in conversation with
    child on unrelated topic
Nonrelated play: parent engaging in play interaction with child
    unrelated to medicine
Visual redirection: parent attempting to attract child's atten-
    tion away from medically related object(s) in the room
Verbal exhortation: parent telling child not to think about or
    pay attention to medically related concerns or objects

Restraint

Physical pulling: parent physically pulling child away from an
    object in the room
Verbal order: parent verbally ordering child to change the
    child's current activity
Reprimand, glare, swat: parent verbally chastising, glaring at,
    and/or physically striking child
Physically holds: parent physically holding child in place,
    despite resistance

Agitation

Gross motor: parent pacing, flailing arms, pounding fists, stomp-
    ing feet, and so forth
Fine motor: parent drumming fingers, tapping foot, chewing fingers,
    and so forth
Verbal anger: parent verbally expressing anger, dismay, fear, un-
    ease, and so forth
Crying: parent's eyes watering, verbal whimpering, sobbing, wailing

Informing

Answers questions: parent attempting to answer child's medically
    relevant/situationally relevant questions
Joint exploration: parent joining with child in exploring the room
Gives information: parent attempting to impart information, un-
    solicited by child, relevant to medicine/the current situation,
    to the child
Prescribes behavior: parent attempting to describe to the child
    appropriate behavior for the examination session

thought to lead to impaired parental functioning (Duffy, 1972; Skipper, Leonard, & Rhymes, 1968) and consequently to less adequate support for the child's coping efforts. Supportive of this hypothesis, Robinson (1968) found that more fearful mothers of hospitalized children were likely to spend less time visiting, less frequently entered into conversations with the child's surgeon, and were less likely to complain or criticize aspects of their children's hospitalizations.

There are many correlative studies that demonstrate that parental anxiety has a negative effect on children's adjustment to medical procedures. This relationship is stronger in preschool than in older children. Bailey et al. found that children's Manifest Anxiety Scale scores correlated positively with mothers' Taylor Manifest Anxiety Scale scores for 9- to 10-year-olds but not for 11- to 12-year-olds

(Bailey et al., 1973). Many of these correlations were found for a first dental visit but not during repeated visits (Koenigsberg & Johnson, 1972). The mother-child relationship prior to hospitalization is also important to consider. Brown (1979) found that children with closer relationships with their mothers were likely to show more distress and withdrawal in the hospital, especially with anxious mothers, than those with poorer quality relationships. These anxious mothers were also more likely to be accepting of the hospital procedures without question.

The crisis parenting hypothesis takes a closer look at the specific parenting strategies in effect during the crisis. Parental anxiety at such times may have a disorganizing influence on effective parenting behaviors. Therefore, in our research approach, we have undertaken an ecological approach to defining dyadic interactions.

Functional Analysis of Specific Parent-Child Interactions

A scale (Table 6.3), the Dyadic Prestressor Interaction Scale (DPIS) was devised out of the theoretical work on children in a stranger approach situation in order to operationalize maternal-child interactions in the medical setting (Melamed & Bush, 1984). Four categories were used to describe children's behavior: Distress, Attachment, Exploration and Social-Affiliative behaviors. Functional definitions were derived that would be suitable across a wide range of ages 4 to 12 years. Another six categories of parenting behaviors were derived from the parenting literature with a specific focus on the surgery preparation literature: Agitation, Ignoring, Reassurance, Information Provision, Distraction, and Restraint. All of the categories except Restraint meet acceptable reliability.

Children and their mothers were observed, using the DPIS, in pediatric clinics during the waiting period prior to children's medical examinations. In order to investigate combinations of parenting behavior and their relationship to the children's distress and attachment in the medical setting, canonical correlations were undertaken. It was found that observations of the mother's behavior accounted for 49% of the observed child categories, and knowledge about the children's behaviors accounted for 36% of the variance of the parenting behaviors. All four canonicals were significant beyond the .05 level. Age, sex, type, and severity of the diagnosis did not correlate with the categories on this Dyadic Prestressor Interaction Scale.

The investigation (Bush, Melamed, Sheras, & Greenbaum, 1986) of the mother-child interaction patterns revealed that the same strategies of information provision or distraction used by the mothers could lead to different patterns of children's behaviors depending upon other indices of maternal affect, i.e., agitation, reassurance, and ignoring. Mothers who were calm and interactive with their children, providing them with information about what to expect, were more likely to have less distressed children than mothers employing the same strategies, but who were also seen to be agitated or ignoring of their children. Mothers who had reported higher state anxiety on the Spielberger STAIT Questionnaire were more likely to ignore their children ($r = .35, p < .01$). This had a more detrimental effect on 4- to 6-year-old children than on 7- to 10-year-olds.

The effects of maternal reassurance also depended upon whether or not the mother was using any other parenting strategies to help her child cope with the medical visit. When reassurance was used in the absence of other strategies, children exhibited a high frequency of all behaviors, including distress, attachment, exploring, and social-affiliative behaviors. Again, younger children were more likely to exhibit attachment behavior in this condition. If, on the other hand, mothers of these young children provided them with information and were not overly reassuring, their youngsters showed more exploration of the examination room.

Thus, in terms of the emotional contagion theory (Escalona, 1953), it was found that agitated mothers were likely to have distressed children who were showing inhibition of attachment behaviors. These findings are similar to those reported by Bretherton and Ainsworth (1974) with younger children in the stranger approach situation. The results, furthermore, are consistent with crisis parenting model, in that the behaviors of mothers who are agitated tended to be dysfunctional in the time of stress. Agitated mothers provided their children with less information relevant to the medical situation and tended to ignore them more. Mothers who used informing without agitation had children who explored the medical environment.

Physicians' ratings of maternal anxiety were also obtained. It is interesting that the physicians' ratings of mothers' anxiety tended to influence how much information they provided to the mothers. Anxious mothers were given more information but were asked fewer questions. In addition, these anxious mothers were rated as less helpful in achieving their children's cooperation with medical procedures.

The patterns of mother-child interaction identified in our clinic observations have encouraged a more sophisticated sequential analysis that might pinpoint the direction of influence in addressing the children's ability to cope with medical examinations. We plan to analyze the mother-child interaction as it predicts the child's cooperation and distress during the actual medical examination. Interestingly, another scale has been developed (Jay, Ozolins, Elliott, & Caldwell, 1983) that is similar in design to the DPIS, to assess mother-child dyadic interaction in stressful medical situations. As with the DPIS, sequential analysis can be used with the Expressive Pain Interaction Coding System to analyze parent responses to child behaviors and to indentify behavioral contingencies in the mother-child interaction. These current efforts to examine parenting and child behavior in the medical setting promise to yield important information regarding parental influences on children's distress and coping responses to stressors.

SUMMARY AND CONCLUSIONS

This chapter has argued for the use of medical settings as a prototype for the study of the development of coping behaviors in children. Theoretical support for this approach was derived from a learning theory model which emphasizes both conditioned fear and observational learning as the basis of phobia development. The existing literature was reviewed and found to be inadequate in predicting vulnerability to anxiety in children facing medical procedures. Therefore, the use of an ipsative approach was recommended. This framework takes into account individual differences of the child relative to the task demands as well as to the social context. Suggestions for future research directions emphasize the importance of a longitudinal approach which allows for the study of developmental changes in the coping behaviors of children. In addition, the importance of considering the family system as an indicator of the functional or dysfunctional coping behaviors of the child has received support from exploratory investigations.

ACKNOWLEDGMENTS

The authors wish to acknowledge the support of the National Institute of Dental Research Funding provided the first author through Grant No. RO1-DE05305 and to NIDR Behavioral Research Training Grant No. 5T32 DE07133 which provided postdoctoral fellowship support to the third author.

REFERENCES

Achenbach, T. M. (1979). The child behavior profile: An empirically-based system for assessing children's behavior problems and competencies. *International Journal of Mental Health, 7,* 24–42.

Agras, W. S., Chapin, H., & Oliveau, D. (1972). The natural history of phobia. *Archives of General Psychiatry, 26,* 315–317.

Ainsworth, M. D. S., & Wittig, B. A. (1969). Attachment and exploratory behavior of one-year-olds in a strange situation. In. B. M. Foss (Ed.), *Determinants of infant behavior IV.* London: Methuen.

Auerbach, S. M. (1980). Surgery-induced stress. In R. H. Woody (Ed.), *Encyclopedia of clinical assessment* (Vol. II). San Francisco: Jossey-Bass.

Auerbach, S. M., & Kilman, P. R. (1977). Crisis intervention: A review of outcome research. *Psychological Bulletin, 84*(6), 1189–1217.

Auerbach, S. M., Martelli, M. F., & Mercuri, L. G. (1983). Anxiety, information, interpersonal impacts, and adjustment to a stressful health care situation. *Journal of Personality and Social Psychology, 44,* 1284–1296.

Badia, P., & Culbertson, S. (1972). The relative aversiveness of signaled versus unsignaled escapable and inescapable shock. *Journal of the Experimental Analysis of Behavior, 17,* 463–471.

Badia, P., Culbertson, S., & Harsh, J. (1973). Choice of longer or stronger signaled shock over shorter or weaker unsignaled shock. *Journal of Experimental Analysis of Behavior, 19,* 25–32.

Bailey, P. M., Talbot, A., & Taylor, P. P. (1973). A comparison of maternal anxiety levels with anxiety levels manifested in the child dental patient. *Journal of Dentistry for Children, 40,* 277–284.

Bandura, A. (1969). *Principles of behavior modification.* New York: Holt, Rinehart & Winston.

Bandura, A., (1977). Self-efficacy: Toward a unifying theory of behavioral change. *Psychological Review, 84,* 191–215.

Bandura, A. (1982). Self-efficacy mechanism in human agency. *American Psychologist, 37,* 122–147.

Bandura, A., & Menlove, F. (1968). Factors determining vicarious extinction of avoidance behavior through symbolic modeling. *Journal of Personality and Social Psychology, 8,* 99–108.

Berg, I. (1976). School phobia in the children of agoraphobic women. *British Journal of Psychiatry, 128,* 86–89.

Berg, I., Marks, I., McGuire, R., & Sipsedge, M. (1974). School phobia and agoraphobia. *Psychological Medicine, 4,* 428–434.

Bowlby, J. (1973). *Attachment and Loss. Vol. 2: Separation and Anger.* New York: Basic Books.

Brady, J. V. (1955). Extinction of a conditioned "fear" response as a function of reinforcement schedules for competing behavior. *Journal of Psychology, 40,* 25–34.

Breslau, N., Weitzman, M., & Messenger, K. (1981). Psychological functioning of siblings of disabled children. *Pediatrics, 67*(3), 344–353.

Bretherton, I., & Ainsworth, M. (1974). Responses of one-year-olds to a stranger in a strange situation. In M. Lewis & L. A. Rosenblum (Eds.), *The origins of fear.* New York: Wiley.

Brown, B. (1979). Beyond separation. In D. Hall & M. Stacey (Eds.), *Beyond separation.* London: Routledge and Kegan Paul.

Buglass, D., Clarke, J., Henderson, A. S., Krietman, N., & Presley, A. S. (1977). A study of agoraphobic housewives. *Psychological Medicine, 7,* 73–86.

Burstein, S., & Meichenbaum, D. (1979). The work of worrying in children undergoing surgery. *Journal of Abnormal Child Psychology, 7*(2), 121–132.

Bush, J. P., Melamed, B. G., Sheras, P. L., & Greenbaum, P. E. (1986). Mother-child patterns of coping with anticipatory medical stress. *Health Psychology, 5,* 137–157.

Campbell, J. D. (1975). Illness is a point of view: The development of children's concepts of illness. *Child Development, 46,* 92–100.

Cassell, S. (1965). Effects of brief puppet therapy upon the emotional responses of children undergoing cardiac catheterization. *Journal of Consulting Psychology, 29,* 1–8.

Cataldo, M. F., Bessman, G. A., Parker, L. H., Pearson, J. E. R., & Rogers, M. C. (1979). Behavioral assessment of pediatric intensive care units. *Journal of Applied Behavior Analysis, 12,* 83–97.

Cohen F., & Lazarus, R. S. (1979). Coping with the stress of illness. In G. C. Stone, F. Cohen & N. E. Adler (Eds.), *Health psychology: A handbook.* San Francisco: Jossey-Bass.

Cuthbert, M., & Melamed, B. G. (1982). A screening device: Children at risk for dental fears and management problems. *Journal of Dentistry for Children, 49,* 432–436.

Drotar, D. (1981). Psychological perspectives in chronic childhood illness. *Journal of Pediatric Psychology, 6,* 211–228.

Drotar, D., Owens, R., & Gotthold, J. (1980). Personality adjustment of children and adolescents with hypopituitarism. *Child Psychiatry and Human Development, 11,* 59–66.

Duffy, J. C. (1972). Emotional reactions of children to hospitalization. *Minnesota Medicine, 55,* 1168–1170.

Escalona, S. (1953). Emotional development in the first year of life. In M. J. Senn (Ed.), *Problems of infancy and childhood.* Mineola New Jersey: Foundation Press.

Faust, J., & Melamed, B. G. (1984). The influence of arousal, previous experience, and age on surgery preparation of ambulatory and in-hospital patients. *Journal of Consulting and Clinical Psychology, 52,* 359–365.

Gayton, W. F., Friedman, S. B., Tavormina, J. F., & Tucker, F. (1977). Children with cystic fibrosis: 1. Psychological test findings of patients, siblings, and parents. *Pediatrics, 59,* 888–894.

Gittelman, R., & Klein, D. F. (1985). Childhood separation anxiety disorder and adult agoraphobia. In A. M. Tuma & J. Maser (Eds.) *Anxiety and the anxiety disorders.* (pp. 389–402). Hillsdale, NJ: Lawrence Erlbaum Associates.

Hagman, E. (1932). A study of fears of children of pre-school age. *Journal of Experimental Education, 1,* 110–130.

Gross, A. M., Stern, R. M., Levin, R. B., Dale, J., & Wojnilower, D. A. (1983). The effect of mother-child separation on the behavior of children experiencing a diagnostic medical procedure. *Journal of Consulting and Clinical Psychology, 51,* 783–785.

Hannallah, R. S., & Rosales, J. K. (1983). Experience with parents' presence during anesthesia induction in children. *Canadian Anesthesiology Society Journal, 30,* 286–289.

Heffernan, M., & Azarnoff, P. (1971). Factors in reducing children's anxiety about clinical visits. *HSMHA Health Reports, 86*(12), 1131–1135.

Hyson, M. C. (1983). Going to the doctor: A developmental study of stress and coping. *Journal of Child Psychology and Psychiatrv, 24*(2), 247–259.

Jay, S. M., Ozolins, M., Elliott, C. H., & Caldwell, S. (1983). Assessment of children's distress during painful medical procedures. *Health Psychology, 2,* 133–147.

Johnson, P., & Stockdale, D. (1975). Effects of puppet therapy on palmar sweating of hospitalized children. *Johns Hopkins Medical Journal, 137,* 1–5.

Kagan, J., & Moss, H. A. (1962). *Birth to maturity.* New York: Wiley.

Kaplan, P. M., Smith, A., Grobstein, R., & Fischman, S. E. (1973). Family mediation of stress. *Social Work, 18,* 60–69.

Katz, E. R., Kellerman, J., & Siegel, S. E. (1981). Anxiety as an effective focus in the clinical study of acute behavioral distress: A reply to Shacham and Daut. *Journal of Consulting and Clinical Psychology, 49,* 470–471.

Katz, E. R., Sharp, B., Kellerman, J. Marston, A. R., Hershman, I. H., & Siegel, S. (1982). B-endorphin immonoreactivity and acute behavioral distress in children with leukemia. *Journal of Nervous and Mental Diseases, 170,* 72–77.

Kellerman, J., Zeltzer, L., Ellenberg, L., Dash, J., & Rigler, D. (1980). Psychological effects of illness in adolescence: Anxiety, self-esteem and the perception of control (Part 1). *Journal of Pediatrics, 97,* 126–131.

Klein, D. F. (1964). Delineation of two drug-responsive anxiety syndromes. *Psychopharmocologiea, 5,* 397–408.

Kleinknecht, R., Klepac, R., & Alexander, L. (1973). Origins and characteristics of fear of dentistry. *Journal of the American Dental Association, 86,* 842–848.

Klingman, A., Melamed, B. G., Cuthbert, M. I., & Hermecz, D. A. (1984). Effects of particpant modeling on information acquisition and skill utilization. *Journal of Consulting and Clinical Psychology, 52,* 414–422.

Klorman, R., Hilpert, P., Michael, R., LaGana, C., & Sveen, O. (1980). Effects of coping and mastery modeling on experienced and inexperienced pedodontic patients' disruptiveness. *Behavior Therapy, 11,* 156–168.

Knight, R., Atkins, A., Eagle, C., Evans, N., Finklestein, J. W., Fukushima, D., Katz, J., & Weiner, H. (1979). Psychological stress, ego defenses, and cortisol production in children hospitalized for elective surgery. *Psychosomatic Medicine, 41,* 40–49.

Koenigsberg, S., & Johnson, R. (1972). Child behavior during sequential dental visits. *Journal of the American Dental Association, 85,* 128–132.

Lapouse, R., & Monk, M. A. (1959). Fears and worries in a representative sample of children. *American Journal of Orthopsychiatry, 29,* 803–819.

Lautch, H., (1971). Dental phobia. *British Journal of Psychiatry, 119,* 151–158.

Lazarus, R. S., & Launier, R. (1978). Stress-related transactions between person and environment. In L. A. Pervin & M. Lewis (Eds.), *Perspectives in interactional psychology,* New York: Plenum.

Levy, D. M. (1943). *Maternal overprotection.* New York: Columbia University Press.

Lewis, M., Feiring, C., McGuffog, C., & Jaskir, J. (1984). Predicting psychopathology in six-year-olds from early social relations. *Child Development, 55,* 123–136.

Lewis, M., & Michalson, L. (1981). The measurement of emotional states. In C. Izard (Ed.), *Measurement of emotion in infants and children.* New York: Cambridge University Press.

Maccoby, E., & Masters, J. C. (1970). Attachment and dependency. In P. H. Mussen (Ed.), *Charmichael's manual of child psychology* (Vol. 2). New York: Wiley.

Martin, B. (1975). Parent-child relations. In F. D. Horwitz (Ed.), *Review of child development research* (Vol. 4). Chicago: University of Chicago Press.

Martin, R. B., Shaw, M. A., & Taylor, P. P. (1977). The influence of prior surgical experience on the child's behavior at the initial dental visit. *Journal of Dentistry for Children, 44,* 35–39.

Mattson, A. (1972). Long-term physical illness in childhood: A challenge to psychosocial adjustment. *Pediatrics, 50,* 801–810.

Mechanic, D. (1964). The influence of mothers on their children's health attitudes and behavior. *Pediatrics, 3,* 444–453.

Melamed, B. G., & Bush, J. P. (1986). Family factors in children with acute illness. In S. Auerbach & A. Stolberg (Eds.), *Crisis intervention with children and families.* Wash. D.C.: Hemisphere.

Melamed, B. G., Dearborn, M., & Hermecz, D. (1983). Necessary considerations for surgery preparation: Age and previous experience. *Psychosomatic Medicine, 45*(6), 517–525.

Melamed, B. G., Robbins, R. L., & Fernandez, J. (1982). Factors to be considered in psychological preparation for surgery. In D. Routh & M. Wolraich (Eds.), *Advances in behavioral pediatrics.* Greenwich, CT: JAI Press.

Melamed, B. G., & Siegel, L. (1980). *Behavioral medicine: Practical applications in health care.* New York: Springer Publishing Company.

Melamed, B., Yurcheson, R., Fleece, L., Hutcherson, S., & Hawes, R. (1978). Effects of filmed modeling on the reduction of anxiety-related behaviors in individuals varying in level of previous experience in the stress situation. *Journal of Consulting and Clinical Psychology, 46,* 1357–1367.

Michels, R., Frances, A., & Shear, M. K. (1984). Psychodynamic models of anxiety. In A. H. Tuma & J. Maser (Eds.), *Anxiety and the anxiety disorders.* Hillsdale, NJ: Lawrence Erlbaum Associates.

Miller, L. C. (1983). Fears and anxiety in children. In C. E. Walker & M. C. Roberts (Eds.), *Handbook of clinical child psychology.* New York: Wiley.

Miller, L. C., Barrett, C. L., & Hampe, E. (1974). Phobias of childhood in a prescientific era. In A. Davids (Ed.), *Child personality and psychopathology* (Vol. 1). New York: Wiley.

Miller, S. M. (1981). Predictability and human stress: Towards a clarification of evidence and theory. In L. Berkowitz (Eds.), *Advances in experimental social psychology* (Vol. 14). New York: Plenum Press.

Mineka, S., Davidson, M., Cook, M., & Keir, R. (1984). Observational conditioning of snake fear in Rhesus monkeys. *Journal of Abnormal Psychology, 93,* 355–372.

Moos, R. H. (1982). Coping with acute health crises. In T. Millon, C. Green, & R. Meagber (Eds.), *Handbook of clinical health psychology.* New York: Plenum.

Moos, R. H., & Tsu, V. D. (1977). The crisis of physical illness: An overview. *Coping with physical illness.* New York: Plenum.

Morris, R. J., & Kratochwill, T. R. (1983). *Treating children's fears and phobias: A behavioral approach.* New York: Pergamon Press.

Murphy, L. B., & Moriarty, A. E. (1976). *Vulnerability, coping & growth from infancy to adolescence.* London: Yale University Press.

Nasera, H. (1978). Children's reactions to hospitalization and illness. *Child Psychiatry and Human Development, 9,* 3–19.

Neuhauser, C., Amsterdam, B., Hines, P., & Steward, M. (1978). Children's concepts of healing: Cognitive development and locus of control factors, *American Journal of Orthopsychiatry, 48,* 335–341.

Pavlov, I. P. (1927). Conditioned reflexes. London: Oxford University Press.

Peters, B. M. (1978). School-aged children's beliefs about causality of illness: A review of the literature. *Maternal Child Nursing Journal, 7,* 143–154.

Peterson, L. & Ridley-Johnson, R. (1980). Pediatric hospital responses to survey on pre-hospital preparation for children. *Journal of Pediatric Psychology, 5,* 1–7.

Peterson, L., & Toler, S. M. (1986). An information seeking disposition in child surgery patients. *Health Psychology, 5,* 343–358.

Pless, I. B., & Rogham, K. J. (1971). Chronic illness and its consequences: Observations based on three epidemiologic surveys. *The Journal of Pediatrics, 79,* 351–359.

Redd, W. H., & Andrykowsky, M. A. (1982). Behavioral intervention in cancer treatment: Controlling aversion reactions to chemotherapy. *Journal of Consulting and Clinical Psychology, 50,* 1018–1029.

Robinson, D. (1968). Mothers' fear, their children's well-being in hospital, and the study of illness behavior. *British Journal of Preventive Social Medicine, 22,* 228–233.

Roth, M. (1960). The phobic anxiety-depersonalization syndromes and some general etiological problems in psychiatry. *Journal of Neuropsychiatry, 1,* 293–306.

Rutter, M. (1981). *Maternal deprivation reassessed* (2nd Ed.). New York: Penguin Books.

Seligman, M. E. (1975). *Helplessness: On depression, development, and death.* San Francisco: W. H. Freeman.

Sermet, O. (1974). Emotional and medical factors in child dental anxiety. *Journal of Child Psychology and Psychiatry, 15,* 313–321.

Shaw, E. G., & Routh, D. K. (1982). Effects of mothers' presence on children's reactions to aversive procedures. *Journal of Pediatric Psychology, 7,* 33–42.

Shaw, O. (1975). Dental anxiety in children. *British Dental Journal, 139,* 134–139.

Sides, J. P. (1977). Emotional responses of children to physical illness and hospitalization. *Dissertation Abstracts International, 38B,* 917–B.

Siegel, L. J. (1983). Hospitalization and medical care of children. In C. E. Walker & M. C. Roberts (Eds.), *Handbook of clinical child psychology.* New York: Wiley.

Siegel, L. J., & Harkavy, J. (in press). The effects of filmed modeling as a prehospital preparatory on children with previous hospital experience. *Journal of Consulting and Clinical Psychology.*

Siegel, L. J., & Peterson, L. (1980). Stress reduction in young dental patients through coping skills and sensory information. *Journal of Consulting and Clinical Psychology, 48,* 785–778.

Siegel, L. J., & Peterson, L. (1981). Maintenance effects of coping skills and sensory information on young children's response to repeated dental procedures. *Behavior Therapy, 12,* 530–535.

Simeonsson, R. J., Buckley, L., & Monson, L. (1979). Conceptions of illness causality in hospitalized children. *Journal of Pediatric Psychology, 4,* 77–84.

Skipper, J. K., Jr., Leonard, R. G., & Rhymes, J. (1968). Child hospitalization and social interaction: An experimental study of mothers' feelings of stress, adaptation, and satisfaction. *Medical Care, 6*(6), 496–506.

Solyom, I., Beck, P., Solyom, C., & Hugel, R. (1974). Some etiological factors in phobic neurosis. *Canadian Psychiatric Association Journal, 19,* 69–78.

Sperling, E. (1978). Psychological issues in physical illness and handicap. In E. Geller (Ed.), *Psychosocial aspects of pediatric care.* New York: Grune and Stratton.

Spitz, R. A. (1950). Anxiety in infancy: A Study of manifestations in the first year of life. *International Journal of Psychoanalysis, 31,* 138–143.

Spinetta, J. J., & Maloney, L. J. (1978). Child with cancer: Patterns of communications and denial. *Journal of Consulting and Clinical, 48,* 1540–1541.

Tavormina, J. B., Kastner, L. S., Slater, P. M., & Watt, S. L. (1976). Chronically ill children: A psychologically and emotionally deviant population. *Journal of Abnormal Child Psychology, 4,* 99–110.

Thomas, A., & Chess, S. (1977). *Temperament and development.* New York: Brunner/Mazel.

Thomas, A., Chess, S., & Birch, H. G. (1968). *Temperament and behavior disorders in children.* New York: New York University Press.

Traughber, B., & Cataldo, M. (1982). Biobehavioral effects of pediatric hospitalization. In J. Tuma (Ed.), *Handbook for the practice of pediatric psychology.* New York: Wiley.

Travis, G. (1976). Chronic illness in children. California: Stanford University Press.

Tyrer, P., & Tyrer, S. (1974). School refusal, truancy, and adult neurotic illness. *Psychological Medicine, 4,* 416–421.

Unger, M. (1982). *Defensiveness in children as it influences acquisition of fear-relevant information.* Unpublished masters thesis, University of Florida.

Vance, J. C., Fazan, L. E., Satterwhite, B., & Pless, I. B. (1980). The effects of nephrotic syndrome on the family: A controlled study. *Pediatrics, 65,* 948–955.

Vanderveer, A. H. (1949). The psychopathology of physical illness and hospital residence. *Quarterly Journal of Child Behavior, 1,* 55–71.

Venham, L., Bengston, D., & Cipes, M. (1977). Parents' presence and the child's response to dental stress. *Journal of Dentistry for Children, 45,* 213–217.

Venham, L. L., Murray, P., & Gaulin-Kremer, E. (1979). Child-rearing variables affecting the preschool child's response to dental stress. *Journal of Dental Research, 58,* 2042–2045.

Vernon, D. T. A., Foley, J., & Schulman, J. (1967). Effect of mother-child separation and birth order on young children's responses to two potentially stressful experiences. *Journal of Personality and Social Psychology, 5*(2), 162–164.

Weissman, M. N. (1985). The epidemiology of anxiety disorders: Rates, risks, and familial patterns. In A. H. Tuma & J. Maser (Eds.), *Anxiety and the anxiety disorders.* Hillsdale, NJ: Lawrence Erlbaum Associates.

Willis, D. J., Elliot, C. H., & Jay, S. M. (1982). Psychological effects of physical illness and its concommitants. In J. Tuma (Ed.), *Handbook for the practice of pediatric psychology.* New York: Wiley.

Willis, D. J., Swanson, B. M., & Walker, C. E. (1983). Etiological factors. In T. H. Ollendick & M. Hersen (Eds.), *Handbook of child psychopathology.* New York: Plenum.

Wright, G. Z., & Alpern, G. D., (1971). Variables influencing children's cooperative behavior at the first dental visit. *Journal of Dentistry for Children, 40,* 265–271.

Wright, G. Z., Alpern, G. D., & Leake, J. L. (1973). The modifiability of maternal anxiety as it relates to children's cooperative dental behavior. *Journal of Dentistry for Children, 40,* 265–271.

Zabin, M. A., & Melamed, B. G. (1980). The relationship between parental discipline and children's ability to cope with stress. *Journal of Behavioral Assessment, 2,* 17–38.

Zeitlin, S. (1980). Assessing coping behavior. *American Journal of Orthopsychiatry, 50,* 139–144.

7 Children with Diabetes and their Families: Coping and Disease Management

Annette M. La Greca
University of Miami

Recently, tremendous interest has emerged in investigating factors related to treatment compliance and glycemic control in children and adolescents with diabetes. Diabetes is a chronic disease, with a very difficult treatment regimen, and very serious, aversive health consequences for poor self-care. Understanding the kinds of difficulties encountered by children and parents in coping with diabetes may facilitate the development of suitable interventions for improving treatment adherence and metabolic functioning and, as a result, improve the health outlook for youngsters affected by this disease.

This chapter describes the status of current research on coping and disease management in childhood diabetes and delineates future research directions. In order to provide a framework for understanding some of the difficulties encountered by youngsters with diabetes, a brief overview of diabetes care is first presented.

OVERVIEW OF DIABETES

Description of the Disease

Juvenile-onset diabetes, referred to as insulin-dependent diabetes mellitus (IDDM), is the most common endocrine disorder of childhood, affecting some 100,000 children and adolescents in the United States (Johnson, 1980; Waife, 1979). This type of diabetes is differentiated from the more common adult-onset form of diabetes (non-insulin-dependent diabetes mellitus or NIDDM), in that, for children no insulin is produced endogenously. Insulin is essential for survival, as the body needs this hormone to convert glucose into a usable energy source; without insulin, there is a breakdown of fatty tissue, depletion of energy reserves, and eventually death (Travis, 1969). Consequently, for children with IDDM, survival depends on exogenous insulin administration, and a very complex daily regimen to balance the insulin intake. In the adult-onset form, which is often associated with obesity, insulin is produced endogenously, but problems with the availability of insulin, insulin receptors and/or defects in insulin action produce unacceptably high plasma glucose levels (Olefsky & Kolterman, 1981). With the adult-onset type, diet and exercise may be sufficient to control the disease. This is never the case with children.

Perhaps the most unsettling aspect of diabetes is the aversive health complications that can result from this disease, especially for those with IDDM. The most common health complications are: retinopathy, neuropathy, renal disease, hypertension, microvascular difficulties and, related to these complications, a shortened life expectancy (Waife, 1979). Diabetic complications are quite serious and prevalent; for example, diabetic retinopathy is the leading cause of blindness in adults between 20- and 65-years-of-age (Skyler & Cahill, 1981). Retinitis, one of the early signs of diabetic retinopathy, occurs fairly early in the young adult's life (in the 20s), and affects a very high proportion of individuals with IDDM (Waife, 1979; White, 1960).

There is mounting evidence to suggest that persistently high levels of blood glucose (or hyperglycemia) in individuals with diabetes may hasten the development of health complications (Jovanovic & Peterson, 1981). Although more controversial, it appears that some diabetes complications may be prevented or forestalled by extremely good glycemic control (see Tattersall & Gale, 1981). As a result, there has been considerable medical emphasis on the importance of maintaining adequate and, if possible, near-normal levels of glycemic control. This is a very difficult task, particularly for children and adolescents, as we shall see.

Management of Diabetes in Children

The management of diabetes in children and adolescents requires a very complicated multicomponent treatment regimen that typically includes: twice daily insulin administration, multiple daily glucose tests, dietary regulation, strict timing of meals and snacks, and careful monitoring of physical activities.

First of all, multiple daily measures of glucose levels are needed to determine insulin requirements. Most children test for urine glucose using the two-drop clinitest tablet method (Travis, 1969), and then compare the color of the test fluid to a color chart to obtain a gross estimate of their glucose levels. Methods for home monitoring of blood glucose levels also have become available recently (Tattersall, 1979). Although they provide much more accurate estimates of plasma glucose levels than urine analyses, they are also more expensive and difficult to use.

Children usually are advised to test for glucose four times per day—before each meal and before bedtime. The results are recorded on a log form along with each insulin dose, so one can determine whether glucose levels are too high or too low, and if insulin adjustments are needed. When high levels of glucose are present, youngsters must also test for the presence of ketones to determine the extent to which the body is converting fatty tissue to energy. The presence of ketones represent an early sign of diabetic ketoacidosis, a serious and potentially fatal consequence of persistent and extreme hyperglycemia (Skyler & Cahill, 1981).

The goal of insulin therapy is to mimic the pattern of insulin secretion in nondiabetic individuals (Tattersall & Gale, 1981). To this end, insulin is usually administered twice daily—before breakfast and before dinner. Each injection is generally a combination of regular (or fast acting) and lente (or slow acting) insulin. Regular insulin peaks shortly after administration, whereas the lente insulin peaks several hours after injection. Insulin should be taken at about the same time each day and meals must follow at regular, fixed intervals in synchrony with the insulin effect. For example, breakfast must be eaten within 30 to 60 minutes after morning insulin administration, otherwise there is a danger of having a hypoglycemic (low blood sugar) reaction. In addition, the insulin injection site must be regularly rotated so that tissue atrophy is minimized.

The amount of insulin and food intake need to be balanced so that hyperglycemia and hypoglycemia are avoided. This means keeping the food intake fairly constant, from day to day.

In addition to eating at regular, fixed intervals, and eating about the same quantity of food, regardless of appetite, the types of food the youngster consumes are also critical. The typical diet is low in fats, high in carbohydrates, and eliminates most or all sweets or "fast-acting" sugars (e.g., candy, soda, etc.) (American Diabetes Association, 1984). The diet is usually prescribed in terms of food exchanges and, at each meal or snack, a certain "mix" of exchanges is allowed. For instance, breakfast might consist of one milk, one fat, two breads, one protein, and two fruit exchanges, and appropriate foods are selected from each exchange list. Certain foods count in more than one exchange category. Consequently, a fairly sophisticated grasp of nutrition is required to maintain this meal plan, as well as considerable self-discipline.

To complicate matters further, exercise or energy expenditure must also be taken into account. Exercise facilitates insulin absorption and utilization, and regimen adjustments must be made by either eating more food than usual or taking less insulin. The reverse is true for an unusually inactive day—more insulin or less food is required. Clearly, exercise is easiest to accomodate if it is a regular part of the daily routine.

As should be apparent from the foregoing description, it is very difficult to strike just the right balance between insulin and glucose levels. Attempts to maintain blood glucose on the low side, to approximate normal levels, increase the risk of hypoglycemia. When this occurs, the individual needs to be treated immediately with some "fast acting sugar," such as candy, sugar cubes, honey, or orange juice, to raise plasma glucose to normal levels, otherwise a loss of consciousness, coma, and convulsions may eventually ensue (Travis, 1969).

A youngster must learn how to recognize the signs of hypoglycemia so that it may be treated promptly. However, the symptoms of hypoglycemia have been found to vary considerably from one person to the next, so that the individual must learn to recognize his or her own typical response.

The preceding discussion represents a somewhat simplified version of the typical regimen for children and adolescents with diabetes. Nevertheless, it is apparent that diabetes care is difficult and complex, requires a high degree of self-regulation, and often necessitates a change in lifestyle for the child and for the family. There are no immediate consequences for poor adherence. (Children don't usually feel any different if they eat something that's *forbidden* or neglect to test their urine.) In fact, the most immediate, negative consequence of diabetes care may be having a hypoglycemic reaction, which is most common when one is striving for excellent or near-normal glycemic control.

PSYCHOSOCIAL ASPECTS OF TREATMENT ADHERENCE AND GLYCEMIC CONTROL

Until very recently, research on psychosocial factors related to treatment adherence and glycemic control for youngsters with IDDM was virtually nonexistent. Psychosocial investigations had been heavily focused on personality comparisons between diabetic and nondiabetic youth, which for the most part, and not surprisingly, produced few conclusive findings (see Dunn & Turtle, 1981, and Johnson, 1980, for reviews). However, renewed interest in psychosocial aspects of diabetes management (e.g., Fisher, Delamater, Bertelson, & Kirkley 1982; Surwit, Scovern, & Feinglos, 1982) coupled with increased recognition of the difficulties associated with managing chronic illness (e.g., Epstein & Cluss, 1982) have spurred new efforts to examine social, behavioral, and psychological factors related to treatment adherence and metabolic control in youngsters with diabetes.

Although still in its infancy, psychosocial-diabetes research has been limited by a tendency to examine a multitude of variables, and their relationship to either treatment adherence or diabetic control, in univariate fashion. A host of psychological and behavioral variables have been found to correlate with adherence or control, however, the magnitude of the relationships generally have been very modest. The glaring absence of a model or framework for understanding and integrating various research findings contributes to this shot-gun approach to diabetes research. Thus, prior to reviewing some current research directions, a potential framework for organizing psychosocial findings is presented.

Framework for Investigating Adherence and Control in IDDM

Figure 7.1 depicts a framework for examining adherence and glycemic control in children and adolescents with diabetes. Each of the key "elements" or factors is either theoretically or empirically linked with metabolic control. Moreover, each factor is multivariate and complex in its own right, as discussed shortly, and is presented in simplified form here for illustrative purposes.

The psychosocial factors are organized into levels, with the most specific or basic preceding the more complex. All might be considered to be necessary, but not sufficient conditions, for good metabolic control.

Factors at each level may affect or interact with factors at other levels. For this reason, investigators interested in examining psychosocial variables at a particular level (e.g., effects of stressful life events on metabolic control) must measure or control for variables at other levels that may affect glycemic functioning, in order to adequately assess the relationships of interest. Otherwise, important relationships may be masked. Moreover, interactions among variables at the different levels would be of considerable interest to investigate, but have not been seriously attempted as yet.

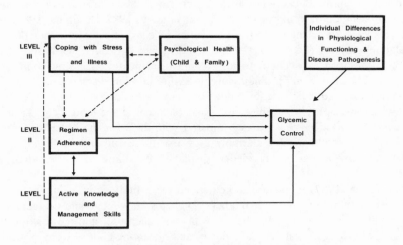

PSYCHOSOCIAL FACTORS RELATED TO DIABETIC CONTROL

FIG. 7.1. Model of psychosocial influences on metabolic control for younsters with IDDM.

In terms of strategies for improving metabolic control, this framework might suggest priorities for intervention efforts. Interventions might first begin at the lower levels of the framework, and incorporate some of the more difficult and complex upper levels, as necessary.

Each of the components in the model is reviewed briefly in turn.

Diabetes Knowledge and Management Skills.   The first factor under consideration is the youngster's and parents' active knowledge of diabetes. Numerous authors have stressed the importance of educating children with chronic illness and their families regarding regimen requirements and rationale for treatment (e.g., Dunbar & Stunkard, 1977; Rapoff & Christophersen, 1982; Varni, 1983). Given the complexities of diabetes management and the high degree of self-regulation required, it seems reasonable to assume that children and parents must have the requisite knowledge and skills to implement the regimen—as a beginning step toward good glycemic control.

Active knowledge of diabetes goes beyond basic understanding of the disease process, which may or may not be related to treatment adherence or glycemic control (Shope, 1981; Varni, 1983). It does include an accurate understanding of the tasks that constitute successful diabetes management, and the ability to accurately execute daily self-care tasks and make regimen adjustments when problems arise.

Recent studies assessing patient knowledge or skills in diabetes management suggest that children's and parents' knowledge and skills are often quite poor (Epstein, Coburn, Becker, Drash, & Siminerio, 1980; Johnson, Pollak, Silverstein, Rosenbloom, Spillar, McCallum, & Harkavy, 1982; La Greca, 1982), and that diabetes knowledge is related to better levels of treatment adherence and metabolic control (La Greca, 1982). Johnson and colleagues (Johnson et al., 1982) developed a psychometrically sound measure for assessing youngsters' diabetes knowledge and problem-solving skills. In a large sample of 6- through 18-year-olds, and their parents, a developmental progression in level of diabetes knowledge was observed. The 6- to 8-year-olds scored about 50% correct on the General Knowledge measure as compared with 75% for the older adolescents and 87% for mothers. One alarming aspect of these authors' findings was the relatively low levels of knowledge displayed by many of the children and parents.

La Greca (1982) replicated and extended these findings in a sample of 7- to 15-year-old children and their mothers. Diabetes knowledge and problem-solving skills were assessed with the Johnson et al. measure, and the relationships among knowledge, treatment adherence, and metabolic control were examined. Again, chronological age was a significant predictor of diabetes knowledge. However, knowledge was differentially related to adherence and control for the preadolescents and adolescents in the sample. For the younger children, mothers' knowledge of diabetes was significantly related to adherence and control, whereas for the adolescents, their own knowledge level, and not their parents', was related to adherence and control.

These findings are interesting from the standpoint of diabetes education efforts, which are often directed solely toward the indentified patient. In the case of preadolescents, considerable family involvement would be indicated. Moreover, because most children begin to assume greater responsibility for self-care during the early teen years, it may be particularly important to target this developmental period for renewed education efforts.

Aside from knowledge of the disease, skills, in executing daily management tasks appear to be critical for successful treatment outcome. Perhaps one of the most intriguing findings of the La Greca (1982) study was that, across the sample of children and youth, those who assumed *more* responsibility for self-care displayed poorer levels of metabolic control than those with less responsibility. Associations between responsibility and control were most pronounced for the preadolescents, particularly for the children responsible for glucose charting, glucose testing, and measuring insulin. These results could not be attributed to lower knowledge levels in these children, as the children who assumed high responsibility for self-care knew significantly more about diabetes than those with lower levels of responsibility. Treatment adherence was not a factor either, as levels of responsibility and adherence were unrelated.

These findings suggested the possibility that the children responsible for their own care may not have been executing the glucose monitoring or insulin measurement tasks *effectively,* even though they appeared to possess adequate knowledge to do so. This interpretation is consistent with the work of Len Epstein and Suzanne Johnson, and their respective colleagues (Epstein et al., 1980; Johnson et al., 1982). For instance, Epstein et al. (1980) found that children with diabetes displayed errors in over 54% of their judgments of urine glucose concentrations (i.e., they read the glucose charts incorrectly). Most of these errors were false negatives; children tended to read an absence of urine glucose, when elevated glucose levels were actually present. Inasmuch as insulin requirements are based on the glucose records, problems in disease management could easily result from inaccurate implementation of this task.

Similarly, Johnson et al. (1982) found an alarmingly high rate of errors in insulin dose calculations among children and adolescents. Moreover, childrens' skills in urine testing and insulin measurement showed low correlations with general knowledge and problem-solving levels. Clearly, even *knowledgeable* children and youth may be prone to errors in glucose testing or insulin measurement. If such errors occur on a regular basis, they would certainly affect glycemic control.

Further efforts to investigate the role of skills and knowledge in diabetes management and glycemic control would be desirable. Given the complexity of some of the psychosocial factors that may affect glycemic functioning (i.e., see Fig. 7.1), certainly improving diabetes knowledge and skills may be the easiest level for diabetes care intervention efforts. Moreover, information on children's and parents' diabetes knowledge and skills may be essential for examining other parameters of interest, such as the effects of stress on metabolic functioning or treatment adherence. Unless the child and family can adequately carry out the prescribed treatment regimen, problems in adherence and control are likely to arise, independent from other considerations. Futhermore, knowledge and skills may interact with other variables at higher levels in the hierarchy (Fig. 7.1). It is possible that the effects of stressors on metabolic functioning may be lessened in cases where the child and/or parent possess excellent knowledge and skills, and can adjust the child's regimen in response to fluctuations in glucose levels. On the other hand, stress effects may be most pronounced in individuals with little ability to cope with an unstable metabolism. Questions such as these await future investigations.

Treatment Adherence.   Although adequate knowledge and skills appear to be necessary for successful diabetes management and glycemic control, additional factors must be considered with such a complex and chronic disease. Even if one has obtained the requisite knowledge and skills, and is prescribed an adequate regimen, there is no guarantee that the regimen will be followed. Treatment adherence is a very complex issue, likely to be influenced by one's health beliefs, attitudes, and health motivation, one's ability to self-regulate behavior, as well as social and financial barriers to self-care.

With children and adolescents, treatment adherence is further complicated by the fact that they may not yet possess the cognitive skills or emotional maturity to provide adequate self-care. Thus, responsibility for disease management may be shared with the parents—and sometimes other family members as well. Several studies examining children's and parents' involvement in diabetes care (Etzwiler & Sines, 1962; La Greca, 1982; Partridge, Garner, Thompson, & Cherry, 1972) have found that many children assume responsibility for urine testing and insulin administration in the years just prior to adolescence. However, even through the adolescent years, parents often remain highly involved in the dietary aspects of diabetes management, as by ensuring that the proper foods are consumed and that meals and snacks are eaten on time. This information points to the fact that child *and* family influences on treatment adherence must be considered.

With a multicomponent regimen, as is the case for diabetes, assessing treatment adherence becomes an extremely complex issue. (See Cluss & Epstein, 1985; Epstein & Cluss, 1982, for extended discussions of measurement issues in adherence research.) To further complicate matters, several investigators have noted that the degree of adherence to one aspect of the regimen does not necessarily relate to adherence to other regimen components (La Greca, 1982; Schafer, Glasgow, McCaul, & Dreher, 1983).

In one study (La Greca, 1982), considerable variability was observed in children's and adolescents' compliance levels across several diabetes tasks (see

TABLE 7.1
Adherence to Diabetes Care Tasks for Children and Adolescents

	Rank by Level of Adherence	
	Preadolescents	Adolescents
Administering insulin	1	2
Keeping doctors appointments	2	1
Taking sugar to avoid hypoglycemic reactions	3	3
Eating snacks	4	4
Testing glucose	5	5
Charting glucose	6	6
Eating proper foods/ sticking to meal plan	7	7[a]
Carrying sugar to treat reactions	8	8[a]

[a]Indicates significantly lower adherence on these tasks for adolescents.

Table 7.1). Adherence with insulin administration and keeping doctor's appointments were clearly the easiest for most of the children and families involved, whereas carrying sugar to treat reactions, maintaining a proper diet/meal plan, and recording and testing glucose levels, were the most problematic. Adolescents tended to have more difficulty with adherence than preadolescents, especially with respect to eating the proper foods/sticking to the meal plan and carrying sugar to treat reactions, highlighting particular areas of difficulty for adolescents. Moreover, adherence to eating the proper foods and carrying sugar were significantly related to levels of metabolic control for the adolescents, as were adherence to eating regular snacks and administering insulin. Overall, average levels of compliance were related to metabolic control, as anticipated.

Schafer et al. (1983) recently obtained similar results with a group of adolescents. These authors found that adolescents' levels of adherence were significantly related to glycemic control for the following tasks: extent to which prescribed diet was followed; care in measuring insulin; and number of daily glucose tests completed.

Together these findings suggest an interrelationship between adherence and control, at least for some aspects of the diabetes regimen. However, the *reasons* for poor adherence and existing barriers to proper care have received less attention. A better understanding of factors that underlie poor adherence is important for promoting more effective diabetes coping skills and designing appropriate interventions for children, adolescents and families.

In the Schafer et al. (1983) study, self-reports of barriers to adherence were negatively related to following the diet and care in measuring insulin, however, the nature of these barriers were not delineated.

La Greca and Hanna (1983) examined children's and parents' diabetes-related health beliefs in conjunction with assessments of treatment adherence and

TABLE 7.2
Percentage Reporting that "Nothing"
Interfered with Diabetes Care

	Children	Mothers
Insulin administration	44.4	50.0
Glucose testing	3.9	9.1
Maintaining diet	32.4	20.6
Eating on time	20.0	28.6
Carrying sugar	12.8	22.6

glycemic control. In general, their results supported the utility of the Health Belief Model (e.g., Becker, Drachman, & Kirscht, 1972; Becker, Radius, Rosenstock, Drachman, Shuberth, & Teets, 1978) for examining issues in adherence to diabetes care.

Of most practical interest were the findings regarding barriers to adherence. Children and mothers were asked to describe specific barriers to adherence for 5 diabetes management tasks: insulin administration, glucose testing, eating proper foods, eating meals and snacks on time, and carrying sugar to treat reactions. These responses were later rated on their degree of seriousness, and an average seriousness score was obtained for each child and parent. Children who reported less serious barriers to self-care were found to be significantly more adherent with their diabetes regimen, and to be in better glycemic control. An identical pattern was observed for mothers' reports of barriers to care. Based on these encouraging results, the specific barriers were categorized and analyzed more closely.

Table 7.2 depicts the percentage of children and mothers who reported that *nothing* interfered with each of the 5 self-care tasks. Clearly, the task that presented the least problem was insulin administration. Fewer barriers were described for insulin administration, and many of these were rarely occurring events—such as "a spouse forgetting when the other parent is sick." By contrast, the vast majority of children and mothers reported barriers to glucose testing.

"Forgetting" was primarily a problem for *glucose testing,* and *carrying sugar to treat reactions.* Although *forgetting* was also a common barrier for insulin administration, closer examination of the responses for this management task disclosed that most reflected unusual or rarely occurring events related to a severe disruption in the family routine. In terms of coping or management strategies, these findings suggest that some children and parents may need visible cues or reminders to test glucose or carry sugar. Cues may also be important for proper insulin administration when there is a major change in the family's usual routine (e.g., posting emergency instructions when a key parent is sick or indisposed).

In examining the types of barriers more specifically, it was observed that multiple problems were reported for any given task. For example, an analysis of

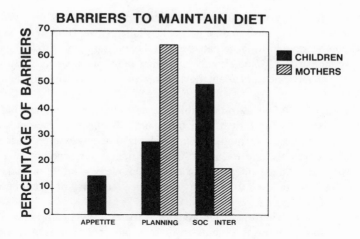

FIG. 7.2. Percentage of children with IDDM and their mothers reporting appetite, planning/problem solving, and social interference barriers to maintaining their meal plan.

the barriers reported for maintaining a diet/sticking to the meal plan (Fig. 7.2)
disclosed that appetite, planning/problem-solving, and social interference accounted for most of the difficulties in this area of diabetes management. Interestingly, social situations were reported to present considerable barriers to
meal plan adherence for children, although mothers were apparently much less
aware of these issues. Examples of social situations that children described
included: "skipping scheduled snacks when with friends," and "eating *forbidden* foods when out with friends." These data suggest that children and adolescents may need assistance in coping more effectively with social situations that
interfere with diabetes management. Training in diabetes-related coping skills or
interpersonal problem solving might prove to be very beneficial in this regard.
Yet, few investigators have attempted to intervene in a controlled manner in this
area (e.g., Follansbee, La Greca,& Citrin, 1983; Gross, Johnson, Wildman, &
Mullett, 1981).

Another common set of barriers to care involved situations that called for
planning and problem solving. Examples of situations that involve planning
barriers are: schedule conflicts, traveling away from home, not having a
place/pocket to carry sugar, or running out of supplies (e.g., clinitest tablets). An
unexpected change in plans is an example of a situation that involves problem-
solving skills related to diabetes care. Children reported many planning and
problem-solving barriers for *glucose testing, eating on time,* and *carrying sugar.*
On the other hand, mothers reported numerous problem-solving issues for *maintaining the proper diet* (see Fig. 7.2) and *eating on time.* These latter findings are

intriguing in that, as noted previously, parents are often highly involved in the dietary aspects of children's and adolescents' diabetes care (La Greca, 1982). In terms of coping strategies, these data suggest that children and parents may need more assistance in developing effective planning and problems-solving strategies, so that they can more flexibly adapt the demands of diabetes care to their changing needs and schedules.

One conclusion to be drawn from this data is that there is no one solution for improving diabetes management and treatment adherence. Different self-care tasks can present very different coping problems. For any one individual, barriers to care might include examples of forgetting, poor problem solving, or social difficulties. Unless interventions can accomodate a variety of such issues, or alternatively are tailored to the individual's needs, they will likely be limited in their effectiveness.

Although not studied directly, motivational issues are very important considerations for understanding problems in diabetic adherence. Research on compliance with medical regimens (see La Greca, 1987 for a review) suggests that treatment adherence is usually much poorer: (a) with chronic versus acute illnesses, (b) with complex versus simple disease regimens, (c) with regimens that require major life-style modifications, (d) and for illnesses that are asymptomatic or that produce few or no positive consequences for good self-care. All of these negative indicators are present for the management of IDDM, underscoring the potential for serious motivational problems. In fact, Varni and Wallander (1984) suggest that nonadherence should be expected with children's chronic illness, in the absence of strong incentives for proper self-care. Efforts to provide rewards or incentives may be necessary, in many cases, to encourage children to develop good self-care habits. Recent work by Epstein (Epstein, Beck, Figueroa, Farkas, Kazdin, Daneman, & Becker, 1981), and others (Lowe & Lutzker, 1979; Schafer, Glasgow, & McCaul, 1982) highlights the value of implementing reinforcement systems in order to improve children's adherence to diabetes care.

In summary, adherence to certain aspects of the diabetes regimen appears to be related to metabolic control in children and adolescents with IDDM. In turn, factors related to treatment adherence include certain diabetes-related health beliefs and attitudes, and the presence of various social and personal barriers to self-care. Assuming that diabetes knowledge and skills are adequate, factors related to adherence may represent the next level for potential intervention efforts. Efforts to increase motivation for successful self-care (such as through incentives for proper execution of management tasks), and to reduce treatment barriers, may serve to improve treatment adherence and glycemic control.

Stress and Psychological Functioning.   At the third level of the model (Figure 1) are factors related to stress and psychological functioning. In each of these areas, empirical evidence supports a direct link between dysfunction in these areas and disruptions of metabolic control. These disruptions appear to occur independent of management skills and level of adherence, but may be exacerbated by lapses in self-care or inadequate understanding of diabetes management. At this level in the model, interventions to improve metabolic control may be more complex and psychological in nature, but also must take into account knowledge or adherence difficulties that could be present.

A. *Ability to cope with stress and illness.* Even if a child and family possessed adequate knowledge and skills, and followed the prescribed treatment, metabolic functioning could still be out of control. Glycemic control has been demonstrated to be adversely affected by stress and illness, both of which have direct metabolic effects (Sulway, 1980). Both psychological and physical stressors (e.g., infections) are associated with the secretion of glucose counter-regulatory hormones, such as catecholamines, cortisol, growth hormone, and glucagon, which may disrupt glycemic control by increasing levels of free fatty acids or producing marked changes in plasma glucose levels (Carter, Gonder-Frederick, Cox, Clarke, & Scott, 1985; Hinkle & Wolf, 1952; Stabler, Morris, Litton, Feinglos, & Surwit, 1986; Tarnow & Silverman, 1981). Moreover, indirect influences on glycemic functioning may occur through problems with treatment adherence (Barglow, Hatcher, Edidin, & Sloan-Rossiter, 1984). Some individuals may be prone to relax or abandon standards of self-care when ill or under stress, further complicating diabetic control.

In terms of physiological responses to acute psychological stress, classic studies by Hinkle and Wolf (1952) revealed increases in plasma ketones and glycosuria (sugar in the urine) in diabetic individuals exposed to laboratory-induced stress. These physiologic changes point to a disruption in normal carbohydrate metabolism. Work by Vandenbergh and colleagues (Vandenbergh, Sussman, & Titus, 1966; Vandenbergh, Sussman, & Vaughn, 1967) similarly demonstrated changes in carbohydrate metabolism in diabetic individuals as a result of stressful laboratory conditions.

More recently, Bradley (1979) found that individuals' reports of stressful life events were associated with disruptions in metabolic control, as evidenced by increased glycosuria, changes in insulin prescription, and increased clinic visits. Similar results have been obtained by other investigators as well (e.g., Grant, Kyle, Teichman, & Mendels, 1974). These studies highlight the destabilizing metabolic effects of stress for individuals with diabetes.

However, it is of interest to note that not all individuals with diabetes demonstrate a similar physiologic response to acute stress; an observation that parallels work with nondiabetic individuals. Carter and colleagues (Carter et al., 1985) studied plasma glucose responses to several challenging laboratory tasks (e.g., mental arithmetic task) among adults with IDDM, finding that stress responses varied across individuals (some showed a plasma glucose rise, others a plasma glucose decline) but were very stable within individuals. Other work with adolescents (Stabler et al., 1986) suggests that personality variables, such as the presence of the Type A[1] behavior pattern, are associated with stress-related hyperglycemia, and may account for the idiosyncratic pattern of stress effects observed by other diabetes investigators. These data are compatible with studies of nondiabetic individuals (e.g., Dembroski, MacDougall, Shields, Petitto, & Lushene, 1978; Dembroski, MacDougall, William, Haney, & Blumenthal, 1985) that have demonstrated greater cardiovascular reactivity to acute stressors in individuals who display the Type A behavior pattern or its components.

Recent efforts to improve glycemic functioning in individuals with IDDM through stress reduction methods, such as relaxation training (RT), have been promising. Decrements in insulin requirements (Fowler, Budzynski, & Vandenbergh, 1976; Seeburg & DeBoer, 1980), and improvements in metabolic control (Lammers, Naliboff, & Straatmeyer, 1984) have been apparent in persons with IDDM who are taught relaxation procedures. However, it is interesting to note that positive changes in metabolic control as a result of RT usually are observed in some, but not all, individuals. Given the aforementioned idiosyncracies in individuals' physiologic responses to acute stressors, it is likely that stress reduction techniques may be most useful and appropriate for those who display stress-related hyperglycemia, or a pattern of heightened sympathetic reactivity to stress.

Although interesting and potentially useful, it should be noted that stress-reduction studies have not focused, as yet, on children or adolescents with IDDM. This area of diabetes research may prove to be a valuable avenue for future inquiry.

B. *Psychological Health.*   Finally, the psychological health of youngsters with IDDM and their families are important factors contributing to metabolic control. High levels of emotional distress frequently accompany severely dysfunctional family situations, or serious personal difficulties, and can have destabilizing effects on youngsters' metabolic control, much in the same manner that other physical and mental stressors affect control. In contrast, low levels of family conflict, and low levels of anxiety and depression have been commonly reported for youngsters in good metabolic control.

Baker, Minuchin and colleagues (Baker & Barcai, 1970; Baker, Minuchin, Milman, Liebman, & Todd, 1975; Minuchin, Baker, Rosman, Liebman, Milman, & Todd, 1975; Minuchin, Rosman, & Baker, 1978) conducted some of the initial and now classic studies of family dysfunction and diabetes. These investigators identified a group of youngsters with IDDM who displayed "brittle" or very labile diabetes and who came from families characterized by un-

---

[1] The Type A behavior pattern refers to those individuals who display extremes of competitiveness, hostility, and time urgency in the face of environmental stresses and challenges (Glass, 1977). This behavior pattern has been implicated as a factor in cardiovascular disease and autonomic arousal to stress.

usually high levels of conflict and emotional disturbance (also known as psycho-somatic families). Observations of interactions among members of psychosomatic families during a series of standard tasks (Baker et al, 1975; Minuchin et al., 1975) disclosed a high degree of enmeshment or overinvolvement of family members, overprotectiveness, inflexible family interactions, and the inability of family members to resolve conflicts effectively.

Moreover, in "psychosomatic diabetes," the psychological stress of the dysfunctional family appeared to directly and adversely affect youngsters' physiological functioning and glucose metabolism (Baker, Barcai, Kay, & Haque, 1969; Baker & Barcai, 1970). Typically, children with psychosomatic diabetes experienced repeated episodes of ketoacidosis, despite taking insulin as prescribed. Glycemic control restabilized in these youngsters when they were hospitalized and removed from their family setting, without any changes in their diabetes treatment regimen.

Other investigations also support a link between family functioning and glycemic control. Interventions focused on multifamily groups or parent simulation of diabetes have resulted in more positive perceptions of the family environment as well as improvements in adolescents' glycemic control (Citrin, Zigo, La Greca, & Skyler, 1982).

Aside from the destabilizing effects of severe family conflict, there is reason to believe that positive family adaptation can affect diabetes very favorably (Anderson & Auslander, 1980). Consistent with this notion, Swift et al. (Swift, Seidman, & Stein, 1967) found that youngsters with good levels of metabolic control could be characterized as having few conflicts at home, low levels of stress in their relationships with their parents, and an overall satisfactory home adjustment. Anderson, Miller, Auslander, and Santiago (1981) reported more favorable family functioning among adolescents in good diabetic control. Such youngsters perceived their families as more cohesive and less in conflict than those in poor control. Moreover, families of children in good control have been noted to be less prone to divorce than families of poorly-controlled or non-diabetic youth (Simonds, 1977).

While positive family environments appear to facilitate good glycemic control, potential mechanisms underlying this relationship have not been specified. Greater family involvement in diabetes management, better levels of treatment adherence, lower levels of emotional distress, and higher levels of psychosocial support, all may be factors that differentiate adaptive from dysfunctional families, and contribute to differences in youngsters' metabolic control. A better appreciation of the *critical* differentiating variables may enable psychologists and diabetes specialists to develop appropriate treatment strategies for improving glycemic control when the family environment is less than optimal. Long term family therapy is not a practical or possible intervention approach in most cases.

On an individual level, psychosocial research also has supported a relationship between youngsters' metabolic control and levels of anxiety and depression (Anderson et al., 1981; Mazze, Lucide, & Shamoon, 1984; Simonds, 1977), although findings in this area have been somewhat equivocal (e.g., Simonds, Goldstein, Walker, & Rawlings, 1981). In the Anderson et al. study, adolescents in good control reported less anxiety and higher self-concepts relative to poorly controlled youngsters. Similarly, Simonds (1977) found youngsters in good control to have fewer interpersonal and noninterpersonal conflicts, and were viewed by their parents as having fewer problems with anxiety and depression, than was the case for poorly controlled youth. In general these findings suggest a relationship between good mental health and successful diabetic control. However, the causal nature of this relationship is not clear. Other diabetes investigators have documented decreases in patients' reported levels of anxiety and depression as a result of intensive diabetes management and improved glycemic control (e.g., Dupuis, Jones, & Peterson, 1980; Siegler, La Greca, Citrin, Reeves, & Skyler, 1982). Most likely, psychological status and physical functioning are interdependent, with feelings of anxiety and depression both resulting from as well as contributing to poor glycemic control.

Despite apparent relationships between psychological and somatic functioning, it is critical to note that youngsters with poor glycemic control do not appear to differ from nondiabetic youth in terms of the prevalence of psychiatric disorders (Simonds, 1977) or other mental health problems (see Johnson, 1980). Furthermore, cases of brittle and psychosomatic diabetes are relatively rare (Schade, Drumm, Duckworth, & Eaton, 1985). Although severely disturbed family functioning and/or serious psychosocial difficulties undoubtedly contribute to poor metabolic control in children and adolescents with IDDM, and may require psychological intervention, these cases are more the exception than the rule.

On the other hand, the vast majority of youngsters with diabetes and their families have adequate levels of emotional functioning, and still maintain unacceptable levels of glycemic control. There is clearly a need for developing effective coping strategies for these relatively normal-functioning children and families. Perhaps interventions aimed at improving active knowledge skills and treatment adherence (i.e., the first two levels of the psychosocial model), will be sufficient for improving glycemic functioning in these cases. Future research efforts that address such issues would be desirable.

INDIVIDUAL DIFFERENCES IN PHYSIOLOGICAL FUNCTIONING AND DISEASE PATHOGENESIS

Although not an integral part of the psychosocial model, it is recognized that individual differences in physiological functioning and disease pathogenesis exist, and may exert an influence on glycemic control. For instance, Schade and colleagues (Schade, Drumm, Duckworth, & Eaton, 1984) observed evidence of abnormal insulin absorption or action in almost 50% of a sample of brittle and/or insulin resistant individuals with diabetes. Other difficulties, such as insulin allergies and immunologic insulin resistance, have been observed in some individuals with IDDM (Kreines, 1965; Ludvigsson, Safwenberg, & Heding, 1977; Schernthaner, Borkenstein, Fink et al., 1983; Schernthaner, Ludwig, Mayr et al., 1976) and may require specialized treatment regimens. Although problems such as these are relatively uncommon, they do underscore the importance of coordinating medical and psychological input to achieve a better understanding of problems with glycemic control for youngsters with IDDM. Consequently, efforts to identify coping difficulties that may contribute to youngsters' poor metabolic control, as through the parameters of the psychosocial model delineated in this chapter, require careful coordination between behavioral specialists and a knowledgeable medical/diabetes team.

CONCLUSIONS

In summary, a model for organizing psychosocial findings with respect to coping and disease management in children and adolescents with diabetes has been presented. This model represents an initial step toward integrating psychosocial research findings and may serve as a springboard for future investigative efforts.

In reviewing some of the themes addressed herein, two major trends emerge. Implicit in the discussions of psychosocial issues at the various levels of the model (i.e., active knowledge, adherence, stress and psychological functioning) has been the importance of adopting a developmental perspective and a family framework for understanding and promoting effective coping and disease management in youngsters with IDDM.

Developmental level is a critical variable for appreciating children's reactions to illness, their involvement in disease management, and the types of interventions that may be most effective. Diabetes is a disease that may differentially impact youngsters at various ages. Developmental differences in children's diabetes knowledge, active management of their diabetes, and level of treatment adherence have already been described. In particular, the adolescent years were recognized as an important period for focusing diabetes reeducation efforts and dealing with issues of treatment adherence. Moreover, the normal emotional difficulties and stresses associated with this period of development may affect and aggravate the disease (Skyler, 1980). Furthermore, there is some suggestion that the interpersonal stress associated with diabetes may be especially pronounced for adolescent females (e.g., Simonds et al., 1981). These diverse findings all highlight the importance of considering a developmental framework for understanding diabetes management and promoting more effective coping skills in youngsters with IDDM.

The importance of maintaining a family approach to diabetes care is also a common theme throughout this chapter. Family members typically assume the major responsibility for diabetes management and regimen adherence for young children. However, even for adolescents, family members often maintain considerable involvement with diabetes care, at least as far as meal-related aspects of management are concerned. Families also have a major impact on youngsters' psychological functioning and emotional adjustment, and consequently on their metabolic control. With this in mind, active efforts to engage families in the intervention process, at any level of the psychosocial model, will be an important consideration.

The issues involved in coping with diabetes are interesting, complex, and challenging. Work in this area has progressed substantially in recent years, yet there is considerably more to be accomplished. With a fresh approach, renewed vigor and greater attention to multivariate issues, future research efforts may go a long way to improve the health outlook and quality of life for children and adolescents affected by this disease.

REFERENCES

American Diabetes Association. (1984). Glycemic effects of carbohydrates. *Diabetes Care, 7,* 607–608.

Anderson, B. J., & Auslander, W. (1980). Research on diabetes management and the family: A critique. *Diabetes Care, 3,* 696–702.

Anderson, B. J., Miller, J. P., Auslander, W. F., & Santiago, J. V. (1981). Family characteristics of diabetic adolescents: Relationship to metabolic control. *Diabetes Care, 4,* 586–594.

Baker, L., & Barcai, A. (1970). Psychosomatic aspects of diabetes mellitus. In O. W. Hill (Ed.), *Modern trends in psychosomatic medicine.* (Vol. 2, pp. 105–123). New York: Appleton-Century-Crofts.

Baker, L., Barcai, A., Kay, R., & Haque, N. (1969). Beta adrenergic blockade and juvenile diabetes: Acute studies and long-term therapeutic trial. *Journal of Pediatrics, 75,* 19–29.

Baker, L., Minuchin, S., Milman, L., Liebman, R., & Todd, T. (1975). Psychosomatic aspects of juvenile diabetes mellitus: A progress report. *Modern Problems of Paediatrics, 12,* 332–343.

Barglow, P., Hatcher, R., Edidin, D. V., & Sloan-Rossiter, D. (1984). Stress and metabolic control in diabetes: Psychosomatic evidence and evaluation of methods. *Psychosomatic Medicine, 46,* 127–144.

Becker, M. H., Drachman, R. H., & Kirscht, J. P. (1972). Predicting mothers' compliance with pediatric medical regimens. *Journal of Pediatrics, 81,* 843–854.

Becker, M. H., Radius, S. M., Rosenstock, I. M., Drachman, R. H., Shuberth, K. C., & Teets, K. C. (1978). Compliance with a medical regimen for asthma: A test of the Health Belief Model. *Public Health Reports, 93,* 268–277.

Bradley, C. (1979). Life events and the control of diabetes mellitus. *Journal of Psychosomatic Research, 23,* 159–162.

Carter, W. R., Gonder-Frederick, L. A., Cox, D. J., Clarke, W. L., & Scott, D. (1985). Effect of stress on blood glucose in IDDM. *Diabetes Care, 8,* 411–412.

Citrin, W. S., Zigo, M. A., La Greca, A. M., & Skyler, J. S. (1982). Diabetes in adolescence: Effects of multifamily group therapy and parent simulation of diabetes. Abstract in: *Diabetes, 31* (Supplement 2), 49.

Cluss, P. A., & Epstein, L. H. (1985). The measurement of medical compliance in the treatment of disease. In P. Karoly (Ed.), *Measurement strategies in health psychology* (pp. 403–432). (Wiley Interscience Series, T. J. Boll, Series Ed.). New York: Wiley.

Dembroski, T. M., MacDougall, J. M., & Shields, J. L., Petitto, J., & Lushene, R. (1978). A coronary-prone behavior pattern and cardiovascular responses to psychomotor performance challenge. *Journal of Behavioral Medicine, 1,* 159–176.

Dembroski, T. M., MacDougall, J. M., William, R. B., Haney, T. L., & Blumenthal, J. A. (1985). Components of Type A, hostility, and anger-in: Relationship to angiographic findings. *Psychosomatic Medicine, 47,* 219–233.

Dunbar, J., & Stunkard, A. J. (1977). Adherence to diet and drug regimen. In R. Levy, R. Rifkind, B. Dennis, & N. Ernst (Eds.), *Nutrition, lipids, and coronary heart disease.* New York: Raven Press.

Dunn, S. M., & Turtle, J. R. (1981). The myth of the diabetic personality, *Diabetes Care, 4,* 640–646.

Dupuis, A., Jones, R. L., & Peterson, C. M. (1980). Psychological effects of blood glucose self-monitoring in diabetic patients. *Psychosomatics, 21,* 581–591.

Epstein, L. H., Beck, S., Figueroa, J., Farkas, G., Kazdin, A. E., Daneman, D., & Becker, D. (1981). The effects of targeting improvements in urine glucose on metabolic control in children with insulin dependent diabetes. *Journal of Applied Behavior Analysis, 141,* 365–375.

Epstein, L. H., & Cluss, P. A. (1982). A behavioral medicine perspective on adherence to long-term medical regimens. *Journal of Consulting and Clinical Psychology, 50,* 950–971.

Epstein, L. H., Coburn, C., Becker, D., Drash, A., & Siminerio, L. (1980). Measurement and modification of the accuracy of determinations of urine glucose concentration. *Diabetes Care, 3,* 535–536.

Etzwiler, D. D., & Sines, L. K. (1962). Juvenile diabetes and its management: Family, social, and academic implications. *Journal of the American Medical Association, 181,* 94–98.

Fisher, E. B., Jr., Delamater, A. M., Bertelson, A. D., & Kirkley, B. G. (1982). Psychological factors in diabetes and its treatment. *Journal of Consulting and Clinical Psychology, 50,* 993–1003.

Follansbee, D. J., La Greca, A. M., & Citrin, W. S. (1983). Coping skills training for adolescents with diabetes. Paper presented at the Annual Meeting of the American Diabetes Association, San Antonio, Texas. Abstract in: *Diabetes, 32* (Supplement 1), 147.

Fowler, J. E., Budzynski, T. H., & Vandenbergh, R. L. (1976). Effects of an EMG biofeedback relaxation program on the control of diabetes. *Biofeedback and Self-Regulation. 1,* 105–112.

Glass, D. C. (1977). *Behavior patterns, stress and coronary disease.* Hillsdale, NJ: Lawrence Erlbaum Associates.

Grant, I., Kyle, G. C.. Teichman, A., & Mendels, J. (1974). Recent life events and diabetes in adults. *Psychosomatic Medicine, 36,* 121–128.

Gross, A. M., Johnson, W. G., Wildman, H. E., & Mullett, M. (1981). Coping skills training with insulin dependent preadolescent diabetes. *Child Behavior Therapy, 3,* 141–153.

Hinkle, L., & Wolf, S. (1952). The effects of stressful life situations on the concentration of blood glucose in diabetic and nondiabetic humans. *Diabetes, 1,* 383–392.

Johnson, S. B. (1980). Psychosocial factors in diabetes: A review. *Journal of Behavioral Medicine, 3,* 95–116.

Johnson, S. B., Pollak, T., Silverstein, J. H., Rosenbloom, A. L., Spillar, R., McCallum, M., & Harkavy, J. (1982). Cognitive and behavioral knowledge about insulin dependent diabetes among children and parents. *Pediatrics, 69,* 708–713.

Jovanovic, L., & Peterson, C. M. (1981). The clinical utility of glycosylated hemoglobin. In J. S. Skyler & G. F. Cahill, Jr. (Eds.), *Diabetes mellitus* (pp. 165–172). New York: Yorke Medical Books.

Kreines, K. (1965). The use of various insulins in insulin allergy. *Archives of Internal Medicine, 116,* 167–71.

La Greca, A. M. (1982). Behavioral aspects of diabetes management in children and adolescents. Paper presented at the Annual Meeting of the American Diabetes Association, San Francisco, California. Abstract in: *Diabetes, 31* (Supplement 2), 47.

158   LA GRECA

La Greca, A. M. (1987). Adherence with prescribed medical regimens. In D. K. Routh (Ed.), *Handbook of pediatric psychology*. New York: Wiley.

La Greca, A. M., & Hanna, N. C. (1983). Health beliefs of children and their mothers: Implications for treatment. Paper presented at the Annual Meeting of the American Diabetes Association, San Antonio, TX. Abstract in: *Diabetes, 32*, (Supplement 1), 66.

Lammers, C. A., Naliboff, B. D., & Straatmeyer, A. J. (1984). The effects of progressive relaxation on stress and diabetic control. *Behavioral Research Therapy, 22*, 641–650.

Lowe, K., & Lutzker, J. R. (1979). Increasing compliance to a medical regimen with a juvenile diabetic. *Behavior Therapy, 10*, 57–64.

Ludvigsson, J., Safwenberg, J., & Heding, L. G. (1977). HLA-types, C-peptide and insulin antibodies in juvenile diabetes. *Diabetologia, 13*, 13.

Mazze, R. S., Lucide, D., & Shamoon, H. (1984). Psychological and social correlates of glycemic control. *Diabetes Care, 7*, 360–366.

Minuchin, S., Baker, L., Rosman, B. L., Liebman, R., Milman, L., & Todd, T. (1975). A conceptual model of psychosomatic illness in children. *Archives of General Psychiatry, 32*, 1031–1038.

Minuchin, S., Rosman, B. L., & Baker, L. (1978). *Psychosomatic families*. Cambridge, MA: Harvard University Press.

Olefsky, J. M., & Kolterman, O. G. (1981). Mechanisms of insulin resistance in obesity and noninsulin-dependent (Type II) diabetes. In J. S. Skyler & G. F. Cahill, Jr. (Eds.), *Diabetes mellitus* (pp. 73–90). New York: Yorke Medical Books.

Partridge, J. W., Garner, A. M., Thompson, C. W., & Cherry, T. (1972). Attitudes of adolescents toward their diabetes. *American Journal of Disorders of Childhood, 124*, 226–229.

Rapoff, M. A., & Christophersen, E. R. (1982). Improving compliance in pediatric practice. *Pediatric Clinics of North America, 29*, 339–357.

Schade, D. S., Drumm, D. A., Duckworth, W. C., & Eaton, R. P. (1984). Factitious brittle diabetes. *Diabetic Medicine, 1*, 143A.

Schade, D. S., Drumm, D. A., Duckworth, W. C., & Eaton, R. P. (1985). The etiology of incapacitating, brittle diabetes. *Diabetes Care, 8*, 12–20.

Schafer, L. C., Glasgow, R. E., & McCaul, K. D. (1982). Increasing the adherence of diabetic adolescents. *Journal of Behavioral Medicine, 5*, 353–362.

Schafer, L. C., Glasgow, R. E., McCaul, K. D., & Dreher, M. (1983). Adherence to IDDM regimens: Relationship to psychosocial variables and metabolic control. *Diabetes Care, 6*, 493–498.

Schernthaner, G., Borkenstein, M., Fink, M., Mayr, W. R., Menzel, J., & Schober, E. (1983). Immunogenicity of human insulin (Novo) or pork monocomponent insulin in HLA-DR-typed insulin-dependent diabetic individuals. *Diabetes Care, 6*, 43–48.

Schernthaner, G., Ludwig, H., Mayr, W. R., et al. (1976). Genetic factors on insulin antibodies in juvenile-onset diabetics. *New England Journal of Medicine, 295*, 622.

Seeburg, K. N., & DeBoer, K. F. (1980). Effects of EMG biofeedback on diabetes. *Biofeedback and Self-Regulation, 5*, 289–293.

Seigler, D. E., La Greca, A. M., Citrin, W. S., Reeves, M. L., & Skyler, J. S. (1982). Psychological effects of intensification of diabetic control. *Diabetes Care, 5* (Supplement 1), 19–23.

Shope, J. T. (1981). Medication compliance. *Pediatric Clinics of North America, 28*, 5–21.

Simonds, J. F. (1977). Psychiatric status of diabetic youth matched with a control group. *Diabetes, 26*, 921–925.

Simonds, J. F., Goldstein, D., Walker, B., & Rawlings, S. (1981). The relationship between psychological factors and blood glucose regulation in insulin-dependent diabetic adolescents. *Diabetes Care, 4*, 610–615.

Skyler, J. S. (1980). Diabetes in adolescence: The forgotten years. In S. Podolsky (Ed.), *Clinical diabetes mellitus: Modern management* (pp. 463–479). New York: Appleton-Century-Crofts.

Skyler, J. S., & Cahill, G. F., Jr. (1981). *Diabetes mellitus: Progress and directions.* In J. S. Skyler & G. F. Cahill, Jr. (Eds.), *Diabetes mellitus* (Foreword. pp. ix–xii). New York: Yorke Medical Books.

Stabler, B., Morris, M. A., Litton, J., Feinglos, M. N., & Surwit, R. S. (1986). Differential glycemic response to stress in Type A and Type B individuals with insulin dependent diabetes mellitus. *Diabetes Care, 9,* 550.

Sulway, M. (1980). New techniques for changing compliance. *Diabetes Care, 3,* 108–111.

Surwit, R. S., Scovern, A. W., & Feinglos, M. N. (1982). The role of behavior in diabetes care. *Diabetes Care, 5,* 337–342.

Swift, C. R., Seidman, F. L., & Stein, H. (1967). Adjustment problems in juvenile diabetes. *Psychosomatic Medicine, 29,* 555–571.

Tarnow, J. D., & Silverman, S. W. (1981). The psychophysiologic aspects of stress in juvenile diabetes mellitus. *International Journal of Psychiatry in Medicine, 11,* 25.

Tattersall, R. B. (1979). Home blood glucose monitoring. *Diabetalogia, 16,* 71.

Tattersall, R., & Gale, E. (1981). Patient self-monitoring of blood glucose and refinements of conventional insulin treatment. In J. S. Skyler & G. F. Cahill, Jr. (Eds.), *Diabetes mellitus* (pp. 101–106). New York: Yorke Medical Books.

Travis, L. (1969). *An instructional aid on juvenile diabetes mellitus.* Galveston, TX: University of Texas Medical Branch.

Vandenbergh, R. L., Sussman, K. E., & Titus, C. C. (1966). Effects of hypnotically induced acute emotional stress on carbohydrate and lipid metabolism in patients with diabetes mellitus. *Psychosomatic Medicine, 33,* 382–390.

Vandenbergh, R. L., Sussman, K. E., & Vaughn, G. D. (1967). Effects of combined physical-anticipatory stress on carbohydrate-lipid metabolism in patients with diabetes mellitus. *Psychosomatics, 8,* 16–19.

Varni, J. W. (1983). *Clinical behavioral pediatrics: An interdisciplinary approach.* New York: Pergamon Press.

Varni, J. W., & Wallander, J. L. (1984). Adherence to health-related regimens in pediatric chronic disorders. *Clinical Psychology Review, 4,* 585–596.

Waife, S. O. (1979). *Diabetes mellitus.* Indianapolis, IN: Eli Lilly & Co.

White, P. (1960). Childhood diabetes: Its course, and influence on the second and third generations. *Diabetes, 9,* 435.

III ADULTHOOD

8 Delay Behavior Among Women with Breast Symptoms

Elizabeth M. Singer
Walter P. Carter Center,
Department of Health and Mental Hygiene,
Baltimore, Md.

INTRODUCTION

Breast cancer is the leading cause of cancer mortality among American women (Seidman, Stellman, & Mushinski, 1982). One of every eleven women will develop a breast cancer sometime in her life (Kelsey, 1979). Delay in seeking treatment is one of the major problems in early treatment of breast cancer (Mac-Mahon, Cole, & Brown, 1973).

Delay in seeking treatment is defined in the medical literature as the time period that elapses between the patient's recognition of a symptom and the first presentation of the symptom to a physician or other health professional (Podell, 1969). Estimates of the number of women who delay vary, but the evidence indicates that between 30 and 55% of all breast cancer patients delay for over 3 months (Aitken-Swan & Paterson, 1955; Greer, 1974; Margery, Todd, & Blizard, 1977).

In this chapter the literature on delay behavior is reviewed, followed by a study on the variations in delay behavior among a sample of women who had discovered breast symptoms. The goal of the study was to identify specific characteristics of women that predict delay behavior. A sample of 90 women who had a breast symptom completed a self-administered questionnaire prior to knowing the diagnosis of their symptom. Information describing their social, historical, and psychological characteristics, as well as the length of time they delayed prior to visiting a physician, was collected. The results of the analyses of these data may help to understand which psychosocial variables influence delay behavior.

INCIDENCE OF BREAST CANCER

Cancer is the second major cause of death in the United States. In 1980 there were more than 430,000 deaths due to cancer, and its incidence is still rising (American Cancer Society, 1981). Of the almost 200 different kinds of cancer, breast cancer is the most common. Each year in the United States 112,000 cases of breast cancer are diagnosed, and over 35,000 deaths occur (Kelsey, 1979). In view of the decreasing birth rates in cohorts of women of current childbearing age, and the association of breast cancer risk with nulliparity and older age at first birth, the incidence may become even higher in the future (Blot, 1980). Breast cancer is a major killer of American women (Holleb, 1974).

Breast cancer is a particularly threatening disease not only because it is a cancer, but because standard medical practice requires removal of the breast to save the patient's life. Thus, there is not only the threat of death, but, in addition, the resulting bodily disfigurement of treatment. This disfigurement can have serious psychological implications. The discovery of a symptom, such as a lump, can thereby cause great stress and anxiety for a woman (Kushner, 1976).

There is no known cause of breast cancer, nor are there known preventive behaviors which can in themselves reduce the possibility of developing breast cancer, such as the case with smoking and lung cancer (Fox, 1976). There has been in the past some consensus about the factors linked to the risk of developing breast cancer: for example, familial history and nulliparity (MacMahon et al., 1973; Kelsey, 1979). Recently, however, it has been found that the factors previously known to raise the risk of breast cancer were in fact of little help in identifying women who actually develop the disease (Seidman et al., 1982). In the study by Seidman and his colleagues only 21% of the breast cancers detected in women 30 to 54 years old, and 29% in women 55 to 84 years old, were attributable to risk factors. The researchers state risk factors do not provide useful information for control of the disease, and that all women should be treated as having an appreciable risk for breast cancer.

THE IMPORTANCE OF EARLY DETECTION

Breast cancer is an illness in which the patient can have some control over the probability of cure. Early detection and seeking immediate treatment are the most effective means of gaining this control. There are two major strategies available to women interested in exercising this control: breast self-examination in terms of detection, and not delaying in seeking medical attention. Breast self-examination requires the individual to attend closely to her body because 95% of all breast tumors are detected by the patient. And, once a lump is found, whether a patient does or does not delay in seeking treatment can determine the success of the treatment. It would be easy to compile an impressive list of quotations testifying to the importance of decreasing the delay factor for breast cancer patients. Researchers agree that those treated almost immediately after they discover the tumor live longer than do those who delay for several months. In fact, up to a year or two, every month's delay tends to reduce the chances of survival (Shapiro, Strax, & Venet, 1968; Strax, 1976; Sutherland, 1960). Therefore, whether a patient does or does not delay in seeking treatment can determine the success of the treatment. Early, local treatment can control the spreading of the cancer to other regions of the body (Brady, 1975). Understanding the determinants of this delay behavior is important.

DELAY BEHAVIOR

The concept of delay has been defined in the medical literature as the time period that elapses between the patient's recognition of a symptom and the first presentation of the symptom to a physician or health professional (Pack & Gallo, 1938). Most often a 3-month period has been taken as the cut-off point— nondelayers (those waiting less than 3 months) are compared to delayers (those waiting more than 3 months). Delay in seeking medical care has been studied principally in relation to cancer (Antonovsky & Hartman, 1974; Goldsen, 1963; Hackett, Cassem, & Raker, 1973). Studies have usually been retrospective in design, using hospital records and usually failing to control for cancer site. Patients have been interviewed either postsurgery in hospital settings or postdiagnosis, and therefore know whether their delay in seeking treatment may have been detrimental. Knowledge of their prognosis may also influence the patient's report of their delay. However, in the literature on illness behavior, there is evidence from studies on recollection of illness episodes and visits to the doctor to indicate a considerable amount of underreporting (Shuval, 1970). It would follow, then, that delay too, is underreported (Antonovsky & Hartman, 1974).

Previous studies on delay behavior among cancer patients have usually looked at such variables as socioeconomic status, knowledge about the disease, age, education, and numerous personality measures (Antonovsky & Hartman, 1974; Kegeles, 1976; Worden & Weisman, 1975). This research on delay behavior has had a number of shortcomings. Specifically, four methodological weaknesses are most striking. First, the studies consistently rely on retrospective information. Researchers have been insensitive to the problematic character of such data, and in particular to the issue that knowledge of diagnosis may influence both a subject's report of delay, and her responses on other measures. The second methodological shortcoming is the failure of most studies to provide explicit information on the measures used, or to neglect to use instruments of known and acceptable reliability and validity. A third problem lies in the failure to control for site of the disease. As was previously mentioned, breast cancer is a unique disease in that 95% of all tumors are discovered by the women themselves.

Unlike other cancers, symptoms for breast cancer *are* detectable by the patient. Thus, comparing delay behavior among people with lung cancer versus those with breast cancer is not focusing on the importance of being able to self-detect.

Finally, a fourth methodological weakness lies in the design and data analysis of these studies. While it is difficult for any single study to examine all of the possibly relevant variables influencing delay behavior, little attention has been given to a multivariate analysis of the data, or to important statistical concerns with this type of data. Delay may prove to be a result of multiple factors, yet this concept of multiple causation is seldom considered. In this regard, the tendency to assume only linear relationships between a set of variables and delay may limit interpretation of the data. There is a possibility that a curvilinear relationship may be a more appropriate hypothesis in the study of delay behavior, especially when age is an independent variable. Finally, categorizing delay as a dichotomous variable may limit the usefulness of the data (Cohen, 1983). It may be more efficient to view delay behavior along a continuum, examining the extent to which a person delays.

The purpose of the information presented here was to gain a better understanding of delay behavior by improving upon some of the inadequacies of previous research outlined above. In an initial study of information-seeking and doctor-patient communication among breast disorder patients (Singer, Levin, & Taylor, 1979), the relationship between the personality variable locus of control (Rotter, 1966), and information seeking in a stressful medical situation was examined. Seventy-two women with both benign and malignant breast disorders were briefly interviewed and administered the Rotter Scale of Locus of Control (Rotter, 1966). Results of this study indicated that locus of control was significantly related to women's behavior. Women who scored as "internals"—those whom Rotter believes perceive themselves as having personal control over consequences of their behavior—reported that they practiced breast self-examination, and felt more knowledgeable about their breast condition. They also reported that they sought out information about breast disease. Women who scored as "externals" were less likely to practice breast self-examination and to seek out information.

As a follow-up of that study, a series of open-ended interviews with breast cancer patients was conducted (Singer, 1980). In the interviews these breast cancer patients described their actions and feelings from their initial discovery of a breast symptom to the time of their surgery. Although these interviews were based on retrospective reports, a number of common themes emerged: (1) feelings about having control over their health; (2) feelings that they didn't want to "know" or "find out" what their symptom meant; (3) feelings about their own past experience with breast symptoms if they had a prior history; (4) their thoughts about the people they knew who had cancer, and how they felt about these people and their cancer experience when they discovered their own symptoms; and (5) concerns about being ill, and the effect it would have on them-

TABLE 8.1
Independent Variables for the Study of Delay Behavior

Socio-Demographic and Historical Variables

    Age
    Occupation
    Education
    Marital Status - Marital Satisfaction Scale
    Race
    Religious Affiliation
    Past history of breast symptoms

Social Network Variables

    Know anyone with breast cancer
    Involvement with person with breast cancer
    Prognosis for person with breast cancer

Psychological Variables

    Repression-Sensitization Scale
    Marlowe-Crowne Scale of Social Desirability
    Miller Behavioral Style Scale - Monitor and Blunter
    Multidimensional Health Locus of Control Scale
        1. Internal Health Locus of Control Scale
        2. Powerful Health Locus of Control Scale
        3. Chance Health Locus of Control Scale

Health Behavior Variables

    General Health Concern Scale
    Knowledge of Breast Disease Quiz
    Practice of Breast Self-Examination

Stressful Life Event Variable

    Psychiatric Epidemiology Research Interview - Life
    Events Scale

---

selves and their families. Based on the results of this initial study, the in-depth interviews, and the observed deficiences in the literature on delay behavior for breast cancer patients, a set of measures was chosen for this study. These measures, presented in Table 8.1, are described in the following section. Included in this section is a brief review of the literature on these specific variables.

SOCIO-DEMOGRAPHIC AND HISTORICAL VARIABLES

Socio-Demographic Variables

In order to provide estimates of socioeconomic status, data were collected in this study on educational level, occupation, marital status, race, religious affiliation, and age. Previous research on the relationship between SES and delay has been contradictory. Some studies have found that low SES predicts longer delay, while others have found no association between SES and delay behavior (Antonovsky & Anson, 1976; Fisher, 1967; Hammerschlag, 1959; Safer & Tharps, 1979). Although previous research on delay behavior had found no relationship between marital status and delay, during the clinical interviews many women indicated that their relationships with their spouses had been a source of support during this stressful time. Within the literature on coping with stressful events, the quality and availability of social support has been implicated as an important factor in the facilitation of successful adaptation to stressful events (Cobb, 1976; Schaefer, Coyne, & Lazarus, 1981). In order to assess the quality of the subject's marital relationship, a measure of marital satisfaction was used. The Marital Satisfaction Scale included six items from the Psychiatric Epidemiology Research Interview (PERI) marital satisfaction scale (Dohrenwend, Krasnoff, Askenasy, & Dohrenwend, 1978) and five items from the Marital Coping Scale developed by Pearlin and Schooler (1978).

Historical Variable

There has been no research relating a woman's prior experience with breast symptoms to delay behavior. However, prior exposure to people who have had cancer has been significantly related to delay behavior (Henderson, 1966; Mc-Cullough & Gilbertson, 1969; Worden & Weisman, 1975). With that in mind, it follows that a woman's past experience with breast symptoms might influence her behavior upon the discovery of a new breast symptom.

Social Network Variable

Social network is defined in this study as the subject's previous exposure to people who have had cancer and her involvement with them. The literature reveals a lack of clarity about this variable's relationship to delay behavior. Although researchers agree that having friends or relatives who have had cancer may influence one's own delay behavior, whether this experience increases or decreases delay is unclear (Cobb, 1954; Green & Roberts, 1974). This may be due to the lack of measurement of the resultant outcome when there is prior experience with another person's cancer. The nature of the experience may be predictive of the subject's behavior. For example, in a clinical interview one woman reported that her sister had had breast cancer 14 years before she discovered her own lump, "I guess I knew that having a lump in my breast didn't mean I would die. I mean my sister is living testimony to the fact that cancer need not equal death. It helped so much to know that, I could face the situation right away." Alternatively, a negative experience or loss of a loved one through death from breast cancer might result in an increase in delay.

Psychological Variables

Research on the relationships between psychological variables and delay behavior among breast cancer patients has usually been based on open-ended interviews with patients following cancer surgery. There has been some consensus that the phenomena of *denial* and *repression* may be important variables in predicting delay (Cameron & Hinton, 1968; Grandstaff, 1975). In the clinical interviews, breast cancer patients reported that they wanted to "forget about" their symptom and didn't always want to "find out" what their symptom meant. In this study, an attempt was made to identify some of the psychological variables that might predict delay behavior in a stressful medical situation.

The coping literature is concerned with how one behaves when placed in threatening and/or stressful situations. People's responses to stressors have often been divided into two groups: (1) avoidance of a threatening stimulus in which the defense mechanisms of repression and denial are most commonly used, and (2) vigilance for the threatening stimulus where defenses such as intellectualization and rumination are called into play (Goldstein, 1973).

The Repression–Sensitization paradigm, as defined by Byrne and his colleagues (Byrne, Barry, & Nelson, 1963), uses the above conceptual approach to coping in stressful situations. Theoretically, the Repression–Sensitization (R–S) Scale represents an approach-avoidance continuum of defensive style. Individuals scoring as repressors, invoked more avoidance style defense mechanisms such as repression, denial and rationalization. Those scoring as sensitizers tended to use defense mechanisms such as intellectualization, obsessiveness, and rumination (Bell & Byrne, 1977). Epstein and Fenz (1967) modified the original R–S scale by removing items that were most highly correlated with anxiety and shortening the scale to 30 items. The Marlowe-Crowne Scale of Social Desirability was also used (Crowne & Marlowe, 1964). They have developed evidence to indicate that their scale measures "defensiveness." This scale is often highly correlated with the R–S scale; those who score as repressors are likely to score high on social desirability (Weinberger, Schwartz, & Davidson, 1979).

Another scale that investigates individual differences in coping styles was recently developed by Miller (1979) and is called the Monitor and Blunter Scale. It was devised to assess individuals' responses to threatening situations in terms of their information-seeking behavior. Blunters tended to block out additional information and deny the threatening nature of the stimulus, while monitors tend to acquire information and wait for the threatening stimulus to appear. Miller (1980; Miller & Mangan, 1983) has used this scale extensively in studies of patients prior to gynecological exams. She reports that the scale has been experimentally validated and responses are not related to income or education. This scale has the potential for enhancing the understanding of individual differences related to information-seeking behavior in medical situations.

Another psychological factor of importance in influencing a woman's delay behavior is the amount of perceived control in threatening or uncertain situations, or the individual's ability to relinquish control and take the role of a somewhat passive and helpless patient (Cohen & Lazarus, 1979; Moos, 1977; Parsons, 1961). The construct of personal control is usually measured by Rotter's (1966)

Locus of Control Scale (LOC). According to Rotter, some people, whom he calls "internals," perceive themselves as having personal control over the consequences of their behavior. Others, labeled "externals," perceive the consequences of their behaviors as being determined by factors outside their control. The research on locus of control suggests that persons reported to be internals are more likely to engage in action-oriented solutions, resulting in greater success and less anxiety for the individual (Kelley, 1967; Mandler & Watson, 1966; Vernon, 1971). Thus, it may be that internally oriented persons are less likely to delay in stressful medical situations than are externally oriented individuals.

Research on delay behavior and locus of control has been limited. Taylor and Levin (1977) hypothesized in a review of the literature on breast cancer that delayers would most likely score as externals on the LOC scale. As was previously stated, in an inital study conducted by the author, locus of control was significantly related to the practice of breast self-examination and information-seeking among breast cancer patients; internals practiced breast self-examination more regularly and sought out information about breast disease more often than externals (Singer et al., 1979). However, research has shown that it is often difficult to predict behavior in specific areas using a measure of generalized expectancy such as Rotter's LOC scale (Hersch & Scheibe, 1967; Lefcourt, 1973; Strickland, 1965). Rotter has written that it is best to use categories that are specific to the area of interest so that behavior may be predicted more accurately (Rotter, Chance, & Phares, 1972).

In 1976, Wallston, Maides, & Wallston developed the Health Locus of Control Scale, which measures specific aspects of one's perception of the extent to which people control their health status. More recently, Wallston and his colleagues developed a Multidimensional Health Locus of Control Scale that taps beliefs in three categories: (1) that the source of control of health-related behaviors is primarily internal, (2) that health status is primarily a matter of chance, or (3) that health status is under the control of powerful others (Wallston, Wallston, & DeVellis, 1978). These three scales, the Internal Health Locus of Control Scale (IHLC), the Chance Health Locus of Control Scale (CHLC), and the Powerful Health Locus of Control Scale (PHLC) were used in this study.

Health Behavior Variables

Knowledge about cancer is also considered an important factor in determining individual behavior when faced with the threat of that disease (Antonovsky & Hartman, 1974). Knowledge about breast cancer has increased considerably in the past decade (Simonds, 1970). However, the relationship between knowledge and delay behavior is not clear. In order to assess women's knowledge of breast disease, a pilot study was conducted by the author on women who were visiting a gynecologist for a regular medical check-up (Singer, 1981). The results of this pilot study were used to design the Knowledge of Breast Disease Quiz which was used in this study.

In addition to investigating the subject's general knowledge about breast disease, the subject's general concern about her health was examined. Rosenstock's (1976) health belief model suggests that individuals seek health care when they believe a disease is serious, and, most importantly, when they are concerned about their health and attempt to maintain good preventive health behaviors. To measure the subject's health behavior a General Health Concern Scale was selected (General Health Inc., 1980).

One major strategy for early detection of breast cancer is breast self-examination. Lack of knowledge about how to do a proper breast self-examination is an important deterrant to regular practice (Alagna & Reddy, 1982; Taylor & Levin, 1977). As one woman in a clinical interview said, "I tried it (BSE) once or twice, but everything felt lumpy, so I stopped." The practice of breast self-examination is important for the early detection of breast symptoms, however, whether the woman seeks medical treatment once she has discovered a symptom is clearly of great importance. Thus, questions referring to the subject's knowledge about BSE, and the proper practice of BSE were presented.

Stressful Life Event Variable

No studies have examined the relationship between stressful life events and delay behavior. However, research on response to stress does indicate that the amount of stress individuals are experiencing and the means by which they respond to that stress, are important variables that may influence an individual's behavior when faced with a stressful medical experience, such as the discovery of a breast symptom (Cobb, Kasl, Brooks, & Connelly, 1966; Cohen & Lazarus, 1973; Dohrenwend & Dohrenwend, 1974, 1978, 1981). In order to assess the number and kinds of stressors an individual experiences over a given length of time, a shortened version of the Psychiatric Epidemiology Research Interview (PERI) Life Events Scale was used in this protocol (Dohrenwend et al., 1978).

PROCEDURE

The subjects of this study were 90 women seeking health care for a breast symptom. All women had discovered their own symptom, and this was their first contact with a physician for this symptom. These women were recruited at five different sites in New York City. Two were breast screening clinics and three were private doctors' offices. Upon arrival at the clinic or doctor's office all patients informed the receptionist of their appointment. At this time each patient was asked by the receptionist the reason for her appointment; e.g. follow-up,

TABLE 8.2
Description of the Protocol

Part I	Description of study Consent form
Part II	Delay questions History of symptoms

--- completed in office (bracketing Part I and Part II)

Part III	General Health Concern Scale Attitudes towards medical care Health behavior in general Practice of breast self-examination
Part IV	Socio-demographic Marital Satisfaction Scale
Part V	Repression-Sensitization Scale (R-S) Marlowe-Crowne Scale of Social Desirability (M-C)
Part VI	Miller Behavioral Style Scale (Monitor and Blunter)

Part VII	Multidimensional Health Locus of Control (MHLC)
	    Internal Health Locus of Control (IHLC)
	    Powerful Health Locus of Control (PHLC)
	    Chance Health Locus of Control (CHLC)

Part VIII	Knowledge of Breast Disease Quiz
Part IX	Stressful Life Events - PERI Scale
Part X	Social network

Parts III-X completed at home and returned by mail.

regular check-up, or a discovery of a symptom. If the patient responded that she was there due to the discovery of a symptom, she was asked by the receptionist if she would like to participate in a study of health behavior being conducted at various doctor's offices and screening clinics in the metropolitan area. She was told that she would fill out a brief questionnaire while she waited for her appointment, and that she could take the remaining part of the questionnaire home with her and return it by mail. If the patient agreed to participate she was then given Parts I and II of the Protocol. See Table 8.2 for description of the Protocol.

After completing both parts of the Protocol, the subject returned it to the receptionist and was given Parts III-X of the Protocol, with a stamped addressed envelope. She was told she could complete the remaining questions at home and return it by mail to the clinic or doctor's office.

The total number of questionnaires distributed was 140. Eighty-five were returned completed (63%). Thirty-five were incomplete; that is, the subject completed the first part while waiting for her appointment, but did not mail the second part of the Protocol. Of the 35 incomplete Protocols, 20 subjects were contacted either by phone or mail, requesting the completed Protocol. Five of these Protocols were returned. Thus, the total sample size was 90. There was no significant difference in length of delay between those who completed the Protocol and the 35 subjects who did not complete it. It is important to remember that these women completed the questionnaire prior to knowing their prognosis.

Thus, unlike previous studies where delay behavior was assessed retrospectively, these data were collected prospectively.

SAMPLE CHARACTERISTICS

Seventy-two percent of the sample (n = 65) had discovered a lump in their breast, while 28% (n = 25) had symptoms of breast swelling or nipple discharge. Analyses to determine whether the type of symptom predicted delay produced no significant results.

Forty-three percent (n = 38) of the sample had a prior history of breast symptoms. However, all symptoms previous to the current one were benign; none of the women in the sample had a history of any prior malignancy. Of the 38 women who had a prior history, all prior symptoms occurred at least 1 year before the present symptom.

The mean age of this sample was 40.6 years ranging from age 15 to 67. The majority (55.6%) of the sample was married (n = 50) and an additional 11.1% (n = 10) of the subjects, although not married, had been living with their partner for longer than 1 year. Eleven women (12%) in the sample had never married, and the remaining 21.2% (n = 19) were divorced or widowed.

Over one-half (64.4%) of the sample had some college education, with 31.1% (n = 28) having had graduate training. The majority (71%) of the women in this sample were gainfully employed. Twenty-four (26.6%) of the women held professional occupations, while 14.4% (n = 13) held supervisory positions. A complete distribution of the sample by marital status, education, race, religious affiliation, and occupation is presented in Table 8.3. This was clearly a heterogeneous sample of women with considerable variation in age, education, and occupation.

RESULTS

The dependent variable for this study was length of delay. Delay was defined as the period of time occurring from the subject's first discovery of her symptom to her first contact with the medical profession. Length of delay was determined by subtracting the date of discovery from the date of her medical appointment. Delay time ranged from 1 week to 64 weeks (approximately 1 year, 3 months). Mean length of delay was 13.48 with a standard deviation of 17.49. In order to reduce the skew of the distribution of delay (a long, right hand tail) and to deal with extreme values, the dependent variable was transformed by using the square root of length of delay (Cohen & Cohen, 1975). The mean length of delay when transformed was 3.1, the standard deviation 1.9 (see Fig. 8.1). All statistical

TABLE 8.3
Characteristics of the Sample (N = 90)

	%	N		%	N
Marital Status:			**Location:**		
Never married	12.0%	(11)	Guttman	18.0%	(16)
Married	55.6%	(50)	Institute		
Single but			Columbia Screen-	14.0%	(13)
living with partner	11.1%	(10)	ing Clinic		
Divorce/Sep	15.6%	(14)	Dr. Strax's	33.0%	(30)
Widowed	5.6%	(5)	office		
Religious Affiliation:			Dr. Zuckerman's	14.0%	(13)
			office		
Protestant	11.1%	(10)	Dr. Gump's office	21.0%	(18)
Catholic	31.1%	(28)	**Symptom:**		
Jewish	38.9%	(35)			
Baptist	3.3%	(3)	Lump	72.0%	(65)
None	12.2%	(11)	Breast swelling	28.0%	(25)
Education:			or nipple dis-		
			charge		
Graduate degree	21.1%	(19)			
Some grad school	10.0%	(9)			
College grad	10.0%	(9)			
Some College	23.3%	(21)			
High school grad	20.0%	(18)			
Some high school	7.8%	(7)			
Grade school	7.8%	(7)			
Occupation:					
Professional	26.6%	(24)			
Supervisory	14.4%	(13)			
Office/Cleric	21.1%	(19)			
Semi-skill &					
unskilled	10.0%	(9)			
Housewife	24.4%	(22)			
Ethnic Background:					
Black	12.2%	(11)			
Hispanic	10.0%	(9)			
Oriental	5.6%	(5)			
Caucasian	72.2%	(65)			
100% - discovered their symptom					
Prior History of Breast Symptoms					
Yes	42.2%	(38)	- Of those with prior history all		
No	57.8%	(52)	previous symptoms occurred more		
			than 1 year ago.		

analyses in the results section were computed on both the transformed and nontransformed dependent variable of delay which yielded the same results.

Socio-Demographic and Historical Variables

Coefficients from correlation analyses of the relationships between the sociodemographic and historical variables and length of delay are presented in Table 8.4. There was a significant inverse relationship between age and length of

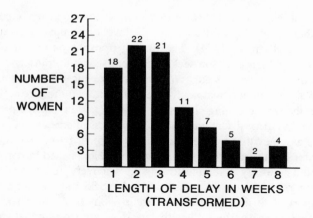

FIG. 8.1. Histogram showing distribution of length of delay among women with breast symptoms.

delay; younger women delayed longer. In addition, the location at which a subject was recruited was related to length of delay; women from the lower SES clinics delayed longer. Age and location were the only sociodemographic variables that were significantly related to length of delay. However, there were significant interrelationships among the sociodemographic variables. Age and education were related; younger women were more educated. Also, as expected, occupation and education were highly correlated; lower level of education was associated with a lower level of occupation. Also, location was significantly related to education; women seen at the lower SES clinics tended to be less educated.

As determined by a one-way analysis of variance on married versus nonmarried subjects, no significant difference was found between married and nonmar-

TABLE 8.4
Correlation Coefficients for Relationships Between Selected Variables and the Dependent Variable for the Total Sample (N = 90)

	Delay	Past History	Age	Educ	Locat	Occup
Delay	1.00	$-.20^a$	$-.22^a$	$-.14$	$-.19^a$	$-.04$
Past history		1.00	$.27^a$	$.13$	$.01$	$-.06$
Age			1.00	$-.25^a$	$-.08$	$.18$
Education				1.00	$.27^a$	$-.57^{ab}$
Location					1.00	$-.07$
Occupation						1.00

Two-tailed tests
[a] $p < .05$
[b] $p < .001$

ried women on length of delay. Contrary to most studies of delay behavior and cancer, neither the level of education nor the level of occupation predicted delay (Antonovsky & Hartman, 1974). The finding from the current study indicates that the place at which a person seeks treatment seems to transcend either their educational or occupational status. Women of low education or occupation who chose a private doctor for treatment were different than those low SES women who went to the free screening clinics. Choosing a middle income private doctor may be viewed as inconsistent with their lower levels of education or occupation. And, if one assumes that by seeking health treatment by private doctors', one receives better health care, then women who were interested in receiving better health care did not delay as long following the discovery of a symptom. It would be interesting to explore the relationship between SES and seeking health care. It may be important to understand why certain women of lower socioeconomic status place a higher priority on health care than women of equal social status.

We also see in Table 8.4 that there was a significant correlation between prior history of breast symptoms and delay; women who had a history delayed less. In addition, there was a significant relationship between age and history; older women were more likely to have a history of breast symptoms. In this sample 38 women (42%) had a prior history of breast symptoms while 52 women (58%) had no prior breast problems. Due to the significant relationships between age and length of delay, prior history and length of delay, and age and prior history, it was necessary to investigate the interactions among these variables.

Upon examination, it was found that the relationship between age and delay behavior was conditional on prior history. Older women were more likely to have a prior history of breast symptoms, and they therefore delayed less than younger women, who did not have the benefit of prior experience. These interactions were examined as described below.

Initially, an ordered (hierarchical) multiple regression analysis was computed on age, history, and, age × history with delay as the dependent variable. Both age and history were significantly related to delay; younger women delayed longer and women with a prior history delayed less ($F(1,86) = 4.28$, $p < .05$ and $F(1,86) = 3.18$, $p < .05$ respectively). In this initial regression the interaction between age and history was not significant. A subsequent hierarchical regression analysis was computed in order to determine possible curvilinear relationships among the variables. The variables were entered in the regression analysis as follows: age, age^2, history, age × history, and age^2 × history. In this analysis, history was significant at $F(1,86) = 10.03$, $p < .001$. The age × history interaction produced a significant increment, $F(1,86) = 11.36$, $p < .001$, and the age^2 × history interaction was significant at $F(1,86) = 11.35$, $p < .001$ (see Table 8.5).

These regression analyses present a number of interesting relationships. First, both age and history individually contributed significantly in the prediction of delay, although the significant history by delay relationship was not conditional

TABLE 8.5
Multiple Regression Analysis
Age, History With Delay - Linear
(N = 90)

	Mult R	R^2	R^2Change	F	df	Significance
Age	.22	.05	.05	4.28*	(1,86)	.05
History	.26	.07	.02	3.18*	(2,85)	.05
Age X History	.26	.07	.00	.07		n.s.

Multiple Regression Analysis - Curvilinear

	Mult R	R^2	R^2Change	F	df	Significance
Age_2	.22	.05	.05	.26		n.s.
Age^2	.26	.07	.02	.62		n.s.
History	.29	.08	.02	10.03**	(3,84)	.001
Age_2X History	.29	.08	.00	11.36**	(4,83)	.001
Age^2 X History	.44	.19	.11	11.53**	(5,82)	.001

on age in this first regression analysis. Second, the interaction between age and history was nonlinear. Indeed, there was a significant curvilinear interaction effect between age and history in predicting delay. That is, the relationship between prior history and delay was conditional on age. This curvilinear relationship is presented in Fig. 8.2 in the scattergram.

As can be seen in this scattergram younger women in this sample delayed longer in seeking treatment upon their discovery of a breast symptom. This finding is contradictory to what other researchers have found; that older and less educated women delay, whereas younger women who are more educated do not delay in seeking treatment (Antonovsky & Hartman, 1974). We also see in this scattergram that women with a prior history of breast symptoms delayed less than those women without any prior history of breast problems. A few outliers in this scattergram suggest that some women with prior histories of breast symptoms did delay a great deal. However, these women had experienced a large number of stressors at the time they discovered their symptom. For example, one woman who delayed 9 months reported that during that time her husband had a heart attack and her daughter had been in a serious car accident. "I knew I should get to a doctor, but I was so overwhelmed with responsibilities for my husband and daughter that I put it off."

Returning to this finding that younger women in this sample delayed longer, one can see in Fig. 8.2 that there is a curvilinear relationship between age and prior history and delay. In this sample younger women tended not to have a prior experience with a breast symptom, while middle age and older women often described previous experiences with breast symptoms in their responses. Thus, the relationship between age and delay behavior is conditional on prior history. Moving along the age axis of the scattergram, the relationship between history and length of delay varies. Older women have had more time to develop prior breast symptoms than the younger women in this sample. What is of importance

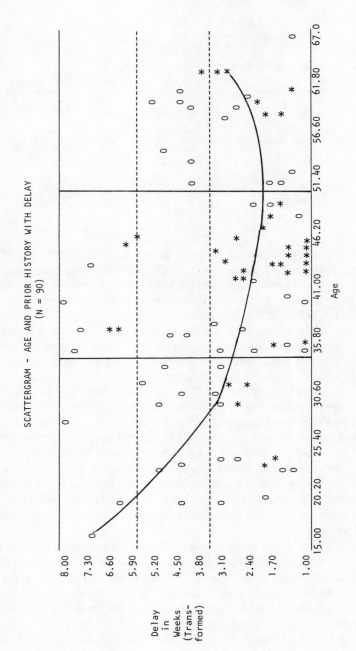

FIG. 8.2. Scattergram illustrating curvilinear relationship between age and prior history with length of delay.

0 = Subjects without prior history of breast symptoms
* = Subjects with prior history of breast symptoms

178

however, is the role that prior history plays among those women who had previous breast symptoms. For, in this sample, when even a younger woman had a prior history of breast symptoms, this experience had an impact; they did not delay in seeking treatment. Thus, the role of prior history seems important.

Prior history may be significant in predicting delay for two reasons. First, having had a prior experience with a breast symptom may decrease the psychological impact of the discovery of a new symptom. If a woman has had prior symptoms she may be familiar with her emotional response, and thus will not view the event to be as stressful as it might have been upon the discovery of her initial breast symptom.

A second reason why prior history may attenuate delay is the positive outcome associated with this experience. Specifically, the prior symptom experience resulted in a positive outcome—a benign symptom. Thus, a woman with a prior history of breast symptoms knows that her symptom need not be malignant. She may have gained, through her own prior experience, the knowledge that not all symptoms are malignant. This is an important piece of information for women with symptoms, because nine out of ten symptoms are benign (Kushner, 1976). Personal experience along with the positive outcome are important predictors of delay. An example of this type of behavior may be found in one of the protocols. One woman wrote: "I knew that since my other lump had been okay, I mean not malignant, I wasn't very worried when I noticed this one (lump). I wasn't scared about coming to the doctor because most likely it wasn't anything serious."

Although the younger women in this sample with a prior history of breast symptoms did not delay (delay meaning less than 2 months), there was still a tendency for some older women with a prior history to delay (some women above the age of 45 with prior history delayed more than 2 months, and two of them delayed 9 months). Thus, there was evidence for a curvilinear relationship between age and history. Although only a few of these women with a prior history delayed, it is interesting to examine the differences between these women and the other women with a prior history who did not delay. Age seems to be an important factor since most of the women with a prior history who delayed were over 45-years-of-age. Although their prior symptoms may have been benign, these women may have known that as they got older the likelihood of a symptom being malignant increased. Thus, these older women with a prior history who delayed, realistically may have had more to fear in seeking treatment than women 35-years-of-age who had a prior history. Therefore, understanding the role that history plays for those women who have had an instance of breast symptoms is important.

Social Network Variables

Another major finding in this study was that women who knew someone who had breast cancer delayed less ($r = -.22$, $p < .05$). In order to investigate the importance of prognosis of knowing the person with breast cancer, an ordered multiple regression was done on the 44 women in this sample who knew someone with breast cancer. First, prognosis of the person was entered into the regression, then level of involvement with that person, and then the interaction between prognosis and involvement. Within the subsample of women who knew someone with breast cancer, the prognosis for that person was significant $(F(1,42) = 4.57, p < .01)$. A good prognosis led to less delay, whereas knowing someone with a poor prognosis led to more delay. Therefore, it seems that knowing someone who had experienced breast cancer allowed an individual the opportunity to cope with the possibility of developing cancer. Conceptually, this might involve issues such as imitation and modeling as described by Bandura and Huston in their research on social learning (Bandura, 1963; Bandura & Huston, 1961, 1963). As was suggested in the findings on prior history of a breast symptom, knowing someone with breast cancer provides a different kind of experience for a woman than would be acquired from cancer literature. Though statistical information is objectively better (one in eleven women develops breast cancer) in terms of estimating one's own vulnerability, the concrete incident (a close friend, or relative has breast cancer) is vivid, real, personal, and credible (Taylor & Levin, 1977).

The impact of the personal incident makes several salient points. First, breast cancer has been a "closet" disease. Women usually do not broadcast the fact that they have had breast cancer. They are concerned about the stigma of cancer, the trauma of breast loss, the fear of being responded to as a freak or "contagious," and perhaps the expectation of discrimination (Taylor & Levin, 1977).

In addition, having a friend or relative who has a good outcome provides an example of someone who has had her disease diagnosed, and most likely, treated promptly. She has survived the threat of cancer, and serves as a role model of desirable behavior and a reminder that a diagnosis of cancer need not be equated with death.

Due to the significant relationships between having a prior history of breast symptoms and length of delay, and knowing someone with breast cancer and length of delay, it was necessary to examine the possible overlap among these two subsamples in the sample of 90 women. Are the subsample of women with a prior history (n = 38) the same subsample of women who knew someone with breast cancer (n = 44)? In order to investigate the relationships between these two variables, as well as the importance of prognosis in predicting delay, multiple regression analysis with dummy variable coding was utilized (Cohen & Cohen, 1975). Five dummy variables were created:

Group 1: women with a prior history who knew someone who had breast cancer with a good prognosis;

Group 2: women with a prior history who knew someone who had breast cancer with poor prognosis;

Group 3: women without a prior history who knew someone who had breast cancer with a good prognosis;

Group 4: women without a prior history who knew someone who had breast cancer with a poor prognosis;

Group 5: women with a prior history who did not know anyone with breast cancer.

The remaining women: those without a history and who did not know anyone with breast cancer were not included in the regression analysis.

A multiple regression was computed on these five dummy variables with length of delay as the dependent variable. The overall regression was significant at the .05 level. By testing the significance of the individual variables, the groups consisting of the variables having a history and knowing someone who had breast cancer with both good and poor prognosis produced levels of significance at the .01 and .05 level ($F(1,86) = 7.37$, $p < .01$ and $F(1,86) = 6.29$, $p < .05$). Thus, having a history of breast symptoms, and knowing someone who had breast cancer with either a good or poor prognosis, lead women to delay less upon the discovery of their own symptom (see Table 8.6).

These findings regarding prior experience with breast symptoms and knowing someone who had breast cancer illustrate an interesting conceptual approach to the understanding of delay behavior. The major thrust of these results implicate the influence of the personal experience on an individual's response in a stressful medical situation. Thus, personal experiences (prior breast symptoms) and the

TABLE 8.6
Multiple Regression Analysis - Dummy Group Variables:
Examining Prior History, Knowing Someone With Breast
Cancer, and Prognosis

	Mult R	R^2	R^2 Change	F	df	Significance
Group 1	.22	.05	.05	7.37*	(1,86)	.01
Group 2	.32	.10	.05	6.29*	(2,87)	.05
Group 3	.34	.11	.01	1.57		n.s.
Group 4	.34	.12	.01	.93		n.s.
Group 5	.35	.12	.01	.49		n.s.

Group 1: Women with a prior history, know someone with a good prognosis.

Group 2: Women with a prior history, know someone with a poor prognosis

Group 3: Women without a prior history, know someone with a good prognosis.

Group 4. Women without a prior history, know someone with a poor prognosis.

Group 5: Women with a prior history, do not know anyone with breast cancer.

people one has known (friend or relative who had breast cancer), clearly influence the person's behavior.

Psychological Variables

The present study found no relationship between the psychological variables and length of delay. The psychological measures used in this study, The Repression-Sensitization Scale, The Marlowe–Crowne Scale, The Monitor and Blunter Scale, and The Multidimensional Health Locus of Control Scale have previously been used in samples of college age students or with patients about to undergo gynecological exams or dental procedures (Byrne et al., 1963; Miller & Mangan, 1983). Although these measures have successfully predicted behavior in those types of settings, no studies have used these measures in the context of a life-threatening event, such as the discovery of a breast symptom and the possibility of having cancer.

One might speculate that the serious threat of cancer is so overwhelming a shock to the individual that typical psychological coping mechanisms are no longer adequate, such as seeking out additional information about the threatening event. In this study, it is possible that the discovery of a breast symptom and the potential threat of cancer were such powerful stimuli that normal coping behaviors were disrupted (and responses on these measures were influenced, even though these women didn't know the outcome of their symptom they were still experiencing the threat of cancer).

Susan Sontag, in her book *Illness as Metaphor* (1977) states that one of the powers of cancer lies in "the fantasy that cancer is a disease thought to be intractible and capricious . . . . it's a disease that doesn't knock before it enters, cancer fills the role of illness experienced as a ruthless, secret invasion–a role it will keep until one day, its etiology becomes as clear and its treatment as effective as those of TB (tuberculosis) have become" (p.5). It is possible, therefore, that the set of psychological measures used in this sample, while predicting behavior in less stressful medical situations, were not able to predict delay behavior in the face of a life threat.

Health Behavior Variables

Also, no relationships were found between the three health behavior variables—General Health Concern, Knowledge of Breast Disease, or practice of breast self-examination, and length of delay. Knowledge has predicted delay behavior in previous studies (Antonovsky & Hartman, 1974; Cobb, 1954; Greer, 1974). However, these studies measured knowledge level after diagnosis, whereas in this study knowledge was measured prior to diagnosis. Measuring knowledge level after diagnosis may alter the accuracy and therefore the relevance of this measure. Previously cited research finding a relationship between knowledge level and delay behavior is therefore questionable.

The reason for the absence of a significant relationship between the General Health Concern Scale and delay behavior may parallel the similar absence between the psychological variables and delay. It has been found that a high level of general health concerns predict a person's ability to take preventive health measures in usual medical situations (Alagna & Reddy, 1982; Rosenstock, 1966). However, in the context of the present study, it seems that typical health behaviors and concerns become obscured by the threat of cancer.

Stressful Life Event Variable

The present study found no relationship between stressful life events and delay behavior. This may be due to the measurement of life events. Researchers have argued that using a self-administered questionnaire for life event research is inadequate, and that more accurate reporting of events occurs when subjects are interviewed individually. The low to moderate reliability of self-administered life event scales drops even lower when subjects are asked to recall events for more than 1 year prior to the interview. (Neugebauer, 1981; Dohrenwend et al., 1978).

SUMMARY

Emphasis in this study was placed on the potential role of psychological variables in the prediction of delay behavior. However, it seems that the life threatening nature of this event, the discovery of a breast symptom, obviates the psychological processes which in the past have been related to behavior in less stressful medical situations. In future research on potentially life-threatening situations, investigators should consider those psychological variables that differentiate behavioral responses under life-threatening and non life-threatening situations. A possible area to explore would be the literature generated from the study of combat behavior; for example, identifying the various coping strategies used. Another possible area is the response of individuals to coronary bypass surgery, and subsequent changes in coping patterns after such a life-threatening event has taken place (cf. Krantz, 1980).

The major issue raised by this study is the significance of the individual's past exposure to the threat of cancer, either by having a prior history of breast symptoms, or knowing someone who had breast cancer. This past experience seems to help women make the decision to seek medical treatment more quickly upon the discovery of their own symptom. This finding is similar to what Kahneman and Tversky discuss in their work on decision making (Kahneman &

Tversky, 1972, 1973; Tversky & Kahneman, 1981). They state that people, in general, do not follow the principles of probability theory in judging the likelihood of uncertain events (i.e., that a breast symptom could indicate cancer). Rather, people tend to utilize heuristics, rather than the law of chance. One heuristic which Kahneman and Tversky describe is called "availability," that is "according to which one judges the probability of an event (e.g., snow in November) by the ease with which relevant instances (e.g., past Novembers) are recalled or imagined" (Kahneman & Tversky, 1972, p.451). As one can see, the finding in this study concerning the importance of either knowing someone who had breast cancer or having a prior experience with breast symptoms effected how women made decisions concerning their medical care. The opportunity of being previously exposed to the disease in question influenced how likely they judged the probability of such an event happening to them. Thus, future research on coping in medical situations can look at whether people use similar decision-making strategies in the presence of other life-threatening diseases. In addition, it is clearly important in future research to provide a more comprehensive exploration of a person's prior exposure to the disease being studied.

As stated early in this chapter, breast cancer remains the most common cancer and the most frequent cause of cancer death among women (Cole, 1980). When many breast cancers are brought to the attention of a physician they are already in a late stage. In an early or localized stage, breast cancer has an 85% 5-year survival rate; in a later stage, when surrounding lymph nodes and glands are involved, the 5-year survival rate is 53% (Strax, 1980).

Researchers are convinced that breast cancer can be cured if detected at an early stage (Fink, 1976; Fox, 1976). However, immediate treatment depends on the patient's readiness to make the first move toward prompt treatment. The importance of having women present themselves to a health professional at an early stage is evident. Some women, noticing a symptom that could be a danger sign of cancer, respond immediately. Others, with an equivalent symptom, delay seeking diagnosis, thus compounding the already serious problems of cancer diagnosis and treatment. Understanding both the experience of prior history and the type of exposure a woman has had to the disease, may provide important information about what influences a woman's response upon the discovery of a symptom.

These findings on prior exposure to breast cancer, although in need of replication, call for a different approach in health education. Traditionally, health education has been directed toward women considered to be at high risk for breast cancer, such as women who have a familial history of breast cancer. However, recent research indicates that all women, not just women with familial histories, should be treated as having an appreciable risk for breast cancer (Seidman et al., 1982). The present findings also suggest that women who have had no prior exposure to cancer are at most risk for delayed treatment, as opposed to women who have a familial history of breast cancer, and have had prior exposure to the disease.

ACKNOWLEDGMENT

The research in this chapter was supported in part by an NIMH predoctoral fellowship sponsored by the Psychiatric Epidemiology Training Program at Columbia University.

The author gratefully acknowledges the assistance of the late Dr. Barbara Dohrenwend and Dr. Elmer Streuning.

REFERENCES

Aitken-Swan, J., & Paterson, R. (1955). Delay and cancer. *British Medical Journal, 1,* 623–627.

Alagna, S. W., & Reddy, D. M. (1982). *Predictors of proficient technique and successful lesion detection in breast self-examination.* Unpublished manuscript, Uniformed Services University of the Health Sciences.

American Cancer Society. (1981). *Cancer facts and figures.* New York: American Cancer Society.

Antonovsky, A., & Anson, O. (1976). Factors related to preventive health behaviors. In J. W. Cullen, B. H. Fox, & R. N. Isom (Eds.), *Cancer: The behavioral dimensions.* New York: Raven Press.

Antonovsky, A., & Hartman, H. (1974). Delay in the detection of cancer: A review of the literature. *Health Education Monographs, 2*(2), 98–127.

Bandura, A. (1963, July). Behavior theory and identificatory learning. *American Journal of Orthopsychiatry, 33,* 591–601.

Bandura, A., & Huston, A. C. (1961, September). Identification as a process of incidental learning. *Journal of Abnormal Social Psychology, 63,* 311–318.

Bell, P. A., & Byrne, D. (1977). Repression-sensitization. In H. London & J. Exner (Eds.), *Dimensions of personality.* New York: Wiley.

Blot, J. (1980). Changing patterns of breast cancer among American women. *American Journal of Public Health, 70,* 833–836.

Brady, L. (1975). Cancer of the breast: Treatment today. In J. Vaeth (Ed.), *Frontiers of radiation therapy and oncology: proceedings of San Francisco Cancer Symposium.*

Byrne, D., Barry, J., & Nelson, D. (1963). Relation of revised repression-sensitization scale to measures of self-description. *Psychological Reports, 13,* 323–334.

Cameron, A., & Hinton, J. (1968). Delay in seeking treatment for mammary tumors. *Cancer, 21,* 1121–1126.

Cobb, B. (1954). Patient-responsible delay of treatment in cancer. *Cancer, 7,* 920–926.

Cobb, S. (1976). Social support as moderator of life stress. *Psychosomatic Medicine, 38*(5), 301–314.

Cobb, S., Kasl, S. V., Brooks, G. W., & Connelly, W. E. (1966). The health of people changing jobs: a description of a longitudinal study. *American Journal of Public Health, 56,* 1476–1481.

Cohen, F., & Lazarus, R. S. (1973). Active coping processes, coping dispositions, and recovery from surgery. *Psychosomatic Medicine, 35,* 375–389.

Cohen, F., & Lazarus, R. S. (1979). Coping with the stresses of illness. In G. C. Stone, F. Cohen & N. E. Adler (Eds.), *Health Psychology: A handbook*. San Francisco: Jossey-Bass.

Cohen, J. (1983). The cost of dichotomization. *Applied Psychological Measurement, 7,*(3), 245–253.

Cohen, J., & Cohen, P. (1975). *Applied multiple regression/correlation analysis for the behavioral sciences*. Hillsdale, NJ: Lawrence Erlbaum Associates.

Cole, P. (1980). Major aspects of the epidemiology of breast cancer. *Cancer, 46,* 865–867.

Crowne, D. P., & Marlowe, D. (1964). *The approval motive: Studies in evaluative dependence*. New York: Wiley.

Dohrenwend, B. S., & Dohrenwend, B. P. (1974). *Stressful life events: Their nature and effects*. New York: Wiley.

Dohrenwend, B. S., & Dohrenwend, B. P. (1978). Some issues in research on stressful life events. *Journal of Nervous and Mental Disease, 166,* 7–15.

Dohrenwend, B. P., & Dohrenwend, B. S. (1981). Socioenvironmental factors, stress, and psychopathology. *American Journal of Community Psychology, 9*(2), 128–164.

Dohrenwend, B. S., Krasnoff, L., Askenasy, A. R., & Dohrenwend, B. P. (1978). Exemplification of a method for scaling life events: the PERI life events scale. *Journal of Health and Social Behavior, 19,* 205–229.

Epstein, S., & Fenz, W. D. (1967). The detection of areas of emotional stress through variations in perceptual threshhold and physiological arousal. *Journal of Experimental Research in Personality, 2,* 191–199.

Fink, L. U. (1976). Antismoking project. In J. W. Cullen, B. H. Fox, & R. N. Isom (Eds.), *Cancer: The behavioral dimensions*. New York: Raven Press.

Fisher, S. (1967). Motivation for patient delay. *Archives of General Psychiatry, 16,* 676–678.

Fox, B. H. (1976). The psychosocial epidemiology of cancer. In J. W. Cullen, B. H. Fox, & R. N. Isom (Eds.), *Cancer: The behavioral dimensions*. New York: Raven Press.

General Health, Inc. (1980). *Personal Health Profile Questionnaire;* developed by General Health, Inc. Washington, D.C.

Goldsen, R. K. (1963). Patient delay in seeking cancer diagnosis: Behavioral aspects. *Journal of Chronic Disease, 16,* 427–436.

Goldstein, J. (1973). Individual differences in response to stress. *American Journal of Clinical Psychology, 1,* 113–137.

Grandstaff, N. W. (1975). The impact of breast cancer on the family. In J. Vaeth (Ed.), *Frontiers of radiation therapy and oncology: Proceedings of San Francisco cancer symposium*.

Green, L. W., & Roberts, B. J. (1974). The research literature on why women delay in seeking medical care for breast symptoms. *Health Education Monographs, 2*(2), 129–176.

Greer, S. (1974). Delay in treatment of breast cancer. *Proceedings of Royal Society of Medicine, 6*(1).

Hackett, T. P., Cassem, N. H., & Raker, J. W. (1973). Patient delay in cancer. *New England Journal of Medicine, 289*(1), 14–20.

Hammerschlag, C. A. (1959). Breast symptoms and patient delay: Psychological variables involved. *Cancer, 17,* 1480–1485.

Henderson, J. G. (1966). Denial and repression as factors in delay of patients with cancer presenting themselves to the physician. *Annals of New York Academy of Sciences, 125,* 856–864.

Hersch, P. D., & Scheibe, K. E. (1967). Reliability and validity of I-E control as a personality dimension. *Journal of Consulting Psychology, 31,* 609–613.

Holleb, A. I. (1974). Cancer therapy—the patient's choice? Presidential Address. *Cancer, 33,* 301–302.

Kahneman, D., & Tversky, A. (1972). Subjective probability: a judgement of representativeness. *Cognitive Psychology, 3,* 430–454.

Kahneman, D., & Tversky, A. (1973). On the psychology of prediction. *Psychological Review, 80,* 237–251.

Kegeles, S. (1976). Relationship of sociocultural factors to cancer. In J. W. Cullen, B. H. Fox, & R. N. Isom (Eds.), *Cancer: The behavioral dimensions.* New York: Raven Press.

Kelley, N. H. (1967). Attribution theory in social psychology. In D. Levine (Ed.), *Nebraska symposium on motivation.* Lincoln: University of Nebraska Press.

Kelsey, J. L. (1979). A review of the epidemiology of human breast cancer. In P. E. Startwell (Ed.), *Epidemiologic Reviews,* Volume I. Baltimore: Johns Hopkins University Press.

Krantz, D. (1980). Cognitive processes and recovery from heart attack: A review and theoretical analysis. *Journal of Human Stress, 6*(3), 27–38.

Kushner, R. (1976). *Breast cancer: A personal history and an investigative report.* New York: Harcourt, Brace, Jovanovich.

Lefcourt, M. (1973). The function of the illusions of control and freedom. *American Psychologist, 28,* 417–425.

MacMahon, B., Cole, P., & Brown, J. (1973). Etiology of human breast cancer: a review. *Journal of the National Cancer Institute, 50*(1), 21–42.

Mandler, G., & Watson, D. L. (1966). Anxiety and interruption of behavior. In C. Spielberger (Ed.), *Anxiety and behavior.* New York: Academic Press.

Margery, C. J., Todd, P. B., & Blizard, P. J. (1977). Psychosocial factors influencing delay and BSE in women with symptoms of breast cancer. *Social Science and Medicine, 11,* 229–232.

McCullough, J. J., & Gilbertson, V. A. (1969). Motivational factors in persons seeking early diagnosis of cancer: A preliminary report. *Geriatrics, 24,* 117–125.

Miller, S. M. (1979). Coping with impending stress: psychophysiological and cognitive correlates of choice. *Psychophysiology, 16,* 572–581.

Miller, S. M. (1980). When is a little knowledge a dangerous thing: coping with stressful life-events by monitoring versus blunting. In S. Levine & H. Ursin (Eds.), *Coping and health.* New York: Plenum Press.

Miller, S. M., & Mangan, C. E. (1983). The interacting effects of information and coping style in adapting to gynecologic stress: should the doctor tell all? *Journal of Personality and Social Psychology, 45*(1), 223–236.

Moos, R. (1977). *Coping with physical illness.* New York: Plenum Press.

Neugebauer, R. (1981). *The reliability of life event reports.* Unpublished manuscript, Columbia University.

Pack, G. T., & Gallo, J. S. (1938). Culpability for delay in treatment of cancer. *American Journal of Cancer, 33,* 443–462.

Parsons, T. (1961). *The social system.* New York: The Free Press.

Pearlin, L., & Schooler, C. (1978). The structure of coping. *Journal of Health and Social Behavior, 19,* 2–21.

Podell, R. N. (1969). Estimating the number of unnecessary deaths from breast cancer. *Journal of Chronic Disease, 22,* 451–462.

Rosenstock, I. M. (1966). Why people use health services. *Milbank Memorial Fund Quarterly, 44,* 94–127.

Rosenstock, I. M. (1976). Prevention of illness and maintenance of health. In J. Kosa & I. Zola (Eds.), *Poverty and health, a sociological analysis.* Cambridge, MA: Harvard University Press.

Rotter, J. B. (1966). Generalized expectancies for internal versus external control of reinforcement. *Psychological Monographs: General and Applied,* 80 (Whole No. 609).

Rotter, J. B., Chance, J., & Phares, E. J. (Eds.). (1972). *Applications of a social learning theory of personality.* New York: Holt, Rinehart and Wilson.

Safer, M. A., & Tharps, Q. J. (1979). Determinants of 3 stages of delay in seeking care at a clinic. *Medical Care, 17,* 11–29.

Schaefer, C., Coyne, J. C., & Lazarus, R. S. (1981). The health-related functions of social support. *Journal of Behavioral Medicine, 4*(4), 381–406.

Seidman, H., Stellman, S. D., & Mushinski, M. H. (1982). A different perspective on breast cancer risk factors: Some implications of the nonattributable risk. *Ca - A Cancer Journal for Clinicians, 32*(5), 301–313.

Shapiro, S., Strax, P., & Venet, L. (1968). The search for risk factors in breast cancer. *American Journal of Public Health, 58,* 820–835.

Shuval, J. T. (1970). *Social functions of medical practice*. San Francisco: Jossey-Bass.

Simonds, S. K. (1970). Public opinion surveys about cancer: an overview. *Health Education Monograph, 33,* 3–24.

Singer, E. M., Levin, S., & Taylor, S. E. (1979, September). *Doctor-patient communication and information-seeking among breast cancer patients*. Paper presented at Annual Meetings of the American Psychological Association, New York.

Singer, E. M. (1980). Coping with breast cancer: Clinical interviews. Unpublished manuscript, New York University.

Singer, E. M. (1981). Knowledge of Breast Disease Quiz. Pilot Work, New York University.

Sontag, S. (1977). *Illness as metaphor*. New York: Vintage Press, Random House.

Strax, P. (1976). Results of mass screening for breast cancer in 50,000 examinations. *Cancer, 37,* 30–35.

Strax, P. (1980, August). Strategy (motivation) for detection of early breast cancer. *Cancer, 15*(46), (4 Suppl.), 926–929.

Strickland, B. R. (1965). Prediction of social action from dimensions of internal-external control. *Journal of Social Psychology, 66,* 353–358.

Sutherland, R. (1960). *Cancer: The significance of delay*. London: Butterworth Press.

Taylor, S. E., & Levin, S. (1977). The psychological impact of breast cancer: Theory and practice. In A. J. Enelow & D. M. Donagis (Eds.), *Psychological aspects of breast cancer* (Technical Bulletin No. 1). San Francisco: West Coast Cancer Foundation.

Tversky, A., & Kahneman, D. (1981). The framing of decisions and the psychology of choice. *Science, 211,* 453–458.

Vernon, D. T. (1971). Information-seeking in natural stress situations. *Journal of Applied Psychology, 55,* 359–363.

Wallston, K. A., Maides, S., & Wallston, B. S. (1976). Health-related information seeking as a function of health-related locus of control and health value. *Journal of Research in Personality, 10,* 215–222.

Wallston, K. A., Wallston, B. S., & DeVellis, R. (1978). Development of the multidimensional health locus of control (MHLC) scales. *Health Education Monographs, 6,* 161–170.

Weinberger, D. A., Schwartz, G. E., & Davidson, R. J. (1979). Low-anxious, high-anxious, and repressive coping styles: psychometric patterns and behavioral and physiological response to stress. *Journal of Abnormal Psychology, 88*(4), 369–380.

Worden, I. W., & Weisman, A. D. (1975). Psychosocial components of lagtime in cancer diagnosis. *Journal of Psychosomatic Research, 19,* 69–79.

9 Behavioral Influences on Immune Function: Evidence for the Interplay between Stress and Health

Janice K. Kiecolt-Glaser
Ronald Glaser
*The Ohio State University College of Medicine,
Columbus, Ohio*

Within the voluminous life events literature, the objective evidence for a causal relationship between stressful events and organic disease has not been impressive. Correlations between life change scores and self-reported health are typically in the .30s or lower (Thoits, 1983). In the great majority of life events studies, researchers have found that only a minority of individuals actually show organic disease when objective assessment procedures are used.

In this chapter we discuss immunological evidence supporting a causal relationship between major and minor stressful life events and infectious disease in humans. We present data suggesting that the increased distress regularly linked with life events is also associated with poorer immune function. Based on these data, we argue that while declines in immune function are a very frequent concomitant of even certain commonplace life events, factors such as the prior health of the individual (particularly in regard to immune system function) and recent exposure to pathogens are important in determining the actual organic disease outcomes. In addition, we suggest that psychological resources which reduce distress (e.g., supportive interpersonal relationships) also concurrently attenuate adverse immunological changes.

We focus on psychoneuroimmunologic research with humans. The interested reader may wish to consult Borysenko and Borysenko (1982), Riley (1981), Monjan (1981), or Fox and Newberry (1984) for more information on related research with rodents.

BACKGROUND INFORMATION: IMMUNE SYSTEM

The immune system is the body's defense against infectious and malignant disease. In order to measure immune function, blood is obtained. and the numbers and/or functional abilities of subgroups of white blood cells (leukocytes) are assayed.

There are a number of subpopulations of leukocytes which perform specialized immunologic functions. There is no single immunological assay which provides a global measure of immune system function. However, because of the interdependence of the various componenets of the immune system, adverse changes in one subpopulation of lymphoid cells are likely to produce multiple effects. Table 9.1 provides brief definitions for the major immunological terms used in this chapter.

The time course for immunological changes should be kept in mind. Unlike hormonal changes which can occur within the course of an hour, many components of the immune system take days or even weeks to change significantly, because of the preexisting numbers and types of cells, as well as the time involved in cell replication. Although certain biochemical mediators may be rapidly synthesized in hours, significant changes in most lymphocyte subpopulations seem to take considerably longer.

There appear to be multiple pathways through which the central nervous system and the immune system can communicate. It is well known that hormones are very responsive to at least certain emotional states, and there is good evidence for endocrine and neuroendocrine mediation of immune function (Ahlqvist, 1981; Blalock, 1984). In addition, there may be direct connections as well; e.g., hypothalamic lesions can produce immunologic changes (Stein, Schleifer, & Keller 1981).

LIFE EVENTS, DISTRESS, AND IMMUNE FUNCTION

Earlier human psychoneuroimmunological research focused on the effects of very novel and very intense events on the immune response. Researchers used very small subject samples to demonstrate decrements in lymphocyte proliferation following mitogen stimulation in response to such events as the space flights of astronauts (Kimzey, 1975), bereavement following the death of a spouse (Bartrop, Luckhurst, Lazarus, Kiloh, & Penny, 1977), or exposure to 48 or 77 hours of sleep deprivation, noise, and stressful experimental tasks (Palmbald, 1981).

In contrast, the primary focus of work from our laboratory has been on the effects of relatively commonplace events on immune function. We reasoned that if stress-related immunosuppression were indeed a risk factor of any importance in the incidence of infectious disease (and perhaps malignant disease as well), then there should be significant immunological changes associated with more commonplace stressful events, as well as intense and novel events.

In our first study blood was drawn twice from 75 first-year medical students (Kiecolt-Glaser, Garner et al., 1984). The first blood draw occurred 1 month

TABLE 9.1
Immunological Terms

Antibodies	Immunoglobulins.
Blastogenesis	The proliferative response of lymphocytes to stimulation by mitogens. Blastogenesis is thought to provide an _in vitro_ model of the lymphocyte proliferative response to challenge by infectious agents.
B-lymphocytes	Lymphocytes which produce immunoglobulins, and the primary cells associated with the humoral immune system; derived from bone marrow.
Cellular immune response	Immune functions not involving antibody production, primarily T-lymphocytes. Cellular immunity is particularly important for the defense against intracellular viruses, transplanted tissue, cancer cells, fungi, and protozoans.
Helper T-lymphocytes	Cells which stimulate the production of immunoglobulins by B-lymphocytes.
Helper/Suppressor ratio	The ratio of helper and suppressor T-lymphocytes, it is sometimes used as one general index of immune function, since excessively low values are associated with immunodeficient disorders, and excessively high values with autoimmune diseases.
Humoral immune response	The arm of the immune response responsible for the production of immunoglobulins.
Hypersensitivity	Allergy, or the enhanced responsiveness of the immune system to a foreign substance which leads to pathological tissue changes. Immediate hypersensitivity reactions can occur in minutes; well-known examples are hayfever, asthma, and hives.
Immunoglobulins	Antibodies; in human, there are five major classes of antibodies, IgG, IgA, IgM, IgE, and IgD. Some antibodies can neutralize the effects of toxins, others can lyse cell membranes, while the IgE class are involved in hypersensitivity reactions.
Leukocytes	White blood cells.
Lymphocytes	The majority of leukocytes are lymphocytes, white blood cells which are important for making antibody, as well as specifically taking part in surveying for and eliminating tumor cells, and cells carrying infectious agents.
Lymphokines	Cell products which serve as chemical mediators of lymphocyte functions.
Mitogens	Substances which stimulate DNA synthesis, cell growth, and cell division for large subsets of immunological cells.
Natural killer (NK) cells	Cells which are thought to provide an important defense against cancer and virus-infected cells.
Suppressor T-lymphocytes	Act to shut off helper T-lymphocytes when sufficient antibody has been produced.
T-lymphocytes	Thymus-derived lymphocytes, critical to the functioning of the cellular immune response.

before final examinations, and the second occurred on the 1st day of final examinations. We found a significant decrease in natural killer cell (NK) activity in the examination sample. In addition, lonelier students (those who scored above the median on a loneliness scale) had significantly lower levels of NK activity. These data suggest that an important host defense may be adversely affected by a commonplace stressful event; there may be implications for health, because of the antitumor and antiviral functions of NK activity. NK cells appear to be critical in the prevention of tumor growth and metastasis in animal models (Herberman et al., 1982).

We found a similar association between higher levels of loneliness and poorer immune function using newly admitted, nonmedicated, nonpsychotic psychiatric inpatients (Kiecolt-Glaser, Ricker et al., 1984). The lonelier psychiatric patients had significantly lower levels of NK activity, as well as a poorer T-lymphocyte response to mitogen stimulation.

We found further evidence for the psychosocial modulation of NK cells in another study using 40 second-year medical student subjects. Three different NK cell assays showed significant decrements during examinations, in comparison to baseline samples taken earlier: (1) lysis of MOLT-4 cells (a different NK target cell than we had used in our previous studies), (2) percentage of NK cells as assessed by the monoclonal antibody anti-Leu-7; and (3) percentage of large granular lymphocytes, the NK cell phenotype. There was also a large change in the production of interferons by lymphocytes stimulated with a mitogen, dropping from a baseline mean of 2003.03 U/ml to 80.00 U/ml during examinations (Glaser, Rice, Speicher, Stout, & Kiecolt-Glaser, 1986b).

The large changes in interferon production may be related to the NK cell changes, since interferon is a major regulator of NK activity. Interferon can affect the growth and differentiation of NK cells from their progenitor cells. Interferon can also activate the lytic properties of target-binding cells, enhance cytolysis of target cells, and increase the number of target cells which can be killed by an effector cell (Herberman et al., 1982).

We have found reliable decrements in a number of facets of cellular immune function during examinations. We have also found significant stress-associated *increases* in plasma immunoglobulins in two different medical student classes, with all values in normal range (Glaser et al., 1986a; Kiecolt-Glaser, Garner et al., 1984). These data should be considered, however, in the context of the patterns of immune function in certain kinds of immunosuppressed patients, such as those with AIDS: In such patients, hypergammaglobulenemia (increased immunoglobulin production) is simultaneously associated with *deficits* in cellular immune function (e.g., Pitchenik, Fischl, & Spira, 1983). While AIDS patients certainly manifest much larger and more severe changes in immune function than the medical students, it is possible that there are common mechanisms underlying different types of immunosuppression which produce parallel changes in immune function.

PSYCHOSOCIAL INFLUENCES ON HERPESVIRUS LATENCY

There are convergent animal and human data which implicate stress or distress as a risk factor in the development of primary herpesvirus infections, the duration of the acute episode or primary lesion, and the frequency with which subsequent lesions (herpes simplex types 1 and 2) reappear after the primary lesion. Immunological data provide a much more sensitive way to examine changes in virus latency, in contrast to simply assessing the presence or absence of lesions or other symptoms, since the clinical symptoms are mediated through changes in cellular immune function.

There are five human herpesviruses, as listed and described in Table 9.1. Once infected with any of the herpesviruses, the host will remain latently infected with that particular herpesvirus for life; unlike other viruses such as measles, the herpesviruses are able to escape destruction by the immune system in ways which are not well understood (Glaser & Gotlieb-Stematsky, 1982). When cellular immune system function is compromised (e.g., in patients with immunosuppressive diseases such as AIDS, or in patients undergoing immunosuppressive therapies), immunological control over the latent herpesviruses is impaired, and there are characteristic *elevated* herpesvirus antibody titers. These elevated antibody titers are thought to reflect an enhanced humoral immune system response to increased virus replication. Improvements in cellular immune system function (e.g., following cessation of immunosuppressive therapy) are followed by decrements in antibody titers.

In previous research, West Point cadets who were seronegative for EBV (i.e., not previously infected) on entry into the military academy were followed for 4 years (Kasl, Evans, & Niederman, 1979). Those who had a triad of psychosocial risk factors (high levels of motivation, poorer academic performance, and having a father who was an "overachiever") appeared to have an increased risk for EBV infection. In addition, both elevated antibody titers among individuals who seroconverted without apparent clinical symptoms and the length of hospitalization among those with clinical symptoms were also significantly related to the risk factor triad.

The frequency of HSV-1 and HSV-2 lesions also appears to be related to psychological distress. Nonpsychotic psychiatric illness has been associated with a greater recurrence rate of genital herpes lesions (Goldmeier & Johnson, 1982). Among student nurses, general unhappiness was predictive of the frequency of cold sores (Luborsky, Mintz, Brightman, & Katcher, 1976).

Using a prospective design, we assessed changes in antibody titers to three latent herpesviruses (EBV, CMV, and HSV) in medical students (Glaser, Kiecolt-Glaser, Speicher, & Holliday, 1985a). Three blood samples were obtained from 49 first-year medical students, with the first sample drawn 1 month before final examinations, the second on the 1st day of final examinations, and

TABLE 9.2
The Five Human Herpesviruses

Type	Clinical Manifestations	Site of Latent Infection
Herpes Simplex Type 1 (HSV-1)	Cold sores; neonatal herpes;	Trigeminal nerve
Herpes Simplex Type 2 (HSV-2)	Genital infections; neonatal herpes	Sacral nerve
Cytomegalovirus (CMV)	Mononucleosis Syndrome; mental retardation and deafness in neonates	Not established; possible lymphocytes, endothelial cells of blood vessels
Varicella-Zoster (VZV)	Chickenpox (primary infection) Shingles (recurrence)	Neurons, multiple sites
Epstein-Barr virus (EBV)	Infectious mononucleosis; B-cell lymphoma; Burkitt's lymphoma; Nasopharyngeal carcinoma	B-lymphocytes; Epithelial cells

From Kiecolt-Glaser and Glaser (in press). Reprinted by permission of Plenum.

the third during the 1st week after their return from summer vacation. There were significant changes in the antibody titers to all three herpesviruses across the sample points, with the lowest levels found in the third sample, where students also reported the least distress. In addition, lonelier students had significantly higher antibody titers to two different EBV antigens in contrast to their class-mates who described themselves as less lonely.

The changes in antibody titers for EBV and HSV were quite large. For example, the geometric mean EBV antibody titers to virus capsid antigen were over 640 at the first two sample points, declining to 93 after summer vacation. These data are particularly noteworthy, in that seroepidemiological studies have suggested that the geometric mean titer in the adult population is about 80 (Henle & Henle, 1982). We have also found significant changes in the transformation of B-lymphocytes by EBV during examinations (Kiecolt-Glaser, Speicher, Holliday, & Glaser, 1984).

Distress-related changes in the immune system's control of latent herpesviruses may have associated risks. The herpesviruses are multipotential, having the ability to produce multiple kinds of disease (Glaser & Gotlieb-Stematsky, 1982). For example, while HSV-1 is most frequently associated with the induction of cold sores, it can also produce generalized infections, encephalitis, and death (Adam, 1982). Similarly, the mononucleosis symptoms characteristic of primary CMV infections in individuals with a normal cellular immune response are generally resolved in 3 to 6 weeks (Sullivan & Hanshaw, 1982). However, immunosup-pressed patients have high rates of morbidity and mortality associated with both the primary infection and infections resulting from reactivation of endogenous latent virus: The single major known cause of interstitial pneumonia in patients receiving immunosuppressive therapy for bone marrow transplants is CMV.

RELAXATION AND HYPNOSIS

Based on our studies with medical students and psychiatric inpatients, we rea-soned that interventions that reduced distress and/or loneliness might lead to an enhancement of immune function. We recruited subjects from local geriatric independent living facilities because previous research with institutionalized older adults indicated that increased attention reliably produced small but con-sistent positive effects (Schulz, 1980). Brief interventions (e.g., college student visits) have been associated with significant improvements in residents' moods, activity levels, memory, and self- and physician-rated health (Rodin, 1980; Schulz, 1980).

Our 45 geriatric subjects were randomly assigned to one of three protocols: progressive relaxation training, social contact, or no intervention. Subjects in the relaxation training and social contact conditions were seen individually 3 times a week for a month; they were visited by the same student each time. Blood samples and self-report data were collected at baseline before the intervention began, at the end of the 1-month intervention, and at a 1-month follow-up (Kiecolt-Glaser et al., 1985a).

At the end of the intervention, the relaxation group had significantly higher levels of NK cell activity than at baseline, and significantly lower levels of antibody to HSV and self-rated distress. While NK cell activity and self-related distress were not significantly different from baseline levels in the relaxation group at follow-up, antibody to HSV was still significantly lower than at baseline. There were not significant changes on these variables in either the social contact or no intervention groups. However, there was a general increase across groups at the end of the intervention in the T-lymphocyte response to PHA stimulation, with greater change at lower mitogen concentrations.

These data suggest that psychosocial interventions may significantly enhance immune function. These data have particular relevance for the elderly, because significant decrements in immune function are associated with aging (Braveman, in press). Poorer cellular immune function is associated with greater mortality in individuals over 80-years-of-age (Roberts-Thomson, Whittingham, Young-chaiyud, & MacKay, 1974).

These data may also have implications for possible interventions that might contribute to the control of herpesvirus latency. Consistent with the stress-related changes in our medical student herpesvirus antibody data, the geriatric relaxation subjects' decrements in HSV antibody titers suggest that common clinical stress-reduction interventions might have positive effects on immune function and herpesvirus latency.

We conducted a different kind of intervention study with first-year medical students (Kiecolt-Glaser et al., 1986). The first blood sample was obtained 1 month before the second block of examations, and the second blood sample was obtained on the last day of the 3-day examination period. We measured changes in the percentages of helper and suppressor T-lymphocytes because of their important immunological functions: helper cells stimulate the activities of a number of other immunologic cells, e.g., helper cells stimulate B-lymphocytes to produce antibody. Large reductions in the relative percentage of helper cells can produce immunodeficiency (Reinherz & Schlossman, 1980). Suppressor cells act in a feedback loop to shut off the activities of helper cells following sufficient action of the helper cells. NK activity was also assessed, as before.

In order to further examine the effects of relaxation, half of the medical students were randomly assigned to a hypnotic/relaxation group which met in the interval between blood draws. Across both groups there was a significant decrease in the percentage of helper T-lymphocytes; NK activity declined significantly as well. Frequency of relaxation practice was a significant predictor of the percentage of helper cells in the examination sample, but did not significantly predict either the percentage of suppressor cells, or NK activity.

We also assessed changes in nutritional status using three biochemical nutritional assays, transferrin, total iron binding protein, and albumin. We included these assays to explore the possibility that the changes in immune function across studies might simply reflect underlying changes in nutritional status: there are well-documented impairments in various aspects of immune function in under-nourished individuals, and moderate to severe protein-caloric malnutrition is associated with increased frequency and severity of infection (Chandra & Newberne, 1977). The three plasma protein markers were well within normal limits at both sample points.

There are also other kinds of intervention studies using immunological measures. Consistent with demonstrations by Ader and Cohen (1982) on the classical conditioning of certain aspects of immune function, recent data suggest possible conditioning of the delayed hypersensitivity (allergic) response in humans. Subjects were less reactive to a tuberculin skin test when they expected their reactions to be negative, following previous injections of saline in the test arm (Smith & McDaniel, 1983).

Hypnotic research using the "double arm" technique also suggests possible psychological mediation of delayed hypersensitivity reactions. Subjects with a known allergic response to a particular substance were injected with equal amounts in both arms, and suggestions were made that one arm would show changes, but not the other. Convergent data across different laboratories suggest that such effects are replicable, but may be a function in part of the hypnotic responsiveness of the subject (Beahrs, Harris, & Hilgard, 1970; Black, 1969; Good, 1981).

Related research with 18 asthmatic patients compared the size of skin test responses to allergens following hypnotic suggestions of no responsiveness with the skin test responses of randomly assigned control patients who were not given any suggestions (Fry, Mason, & Pearson, 1964). The patients in the hypnotic suggestion group had significantly smaller wheals than the control patients. In a second study, 29 asthmatic patients were randomly assigned to one of three conditions: (1) hypnotic suggestions that the right arm would not react to skin tests, (2) hypnotic suggestions that both arms would be nonreactive, or (3) hypnosis without suggestions for change. While there were no differences among the treatment groups, all had significantly smaller wheals compared to their baseline measures.

DEPRESSION AND IMMUNE FUNCTION

We have found reliable decrements in a number of facets of immune function in otherwise healthy medical students during examinations. Other investigators have taken a different approach, comparing immunologic data from depressed patients and nondepressed controls. Not surprisingly, the depressed patients in these studies have significantly poorer immunological function, across a number of assays. For example, depressed patients have significantly lower percentages of helper T-lymphocytes (Krueger, Levy, Cathcart, Fox, & Black, 1984), and a significantly poorer response to mitogen stimulation (Schliefer et al., 1984) than their nondepressed matched counterparts. The number of peripheral T-lymphocytes was also significantly lower among depressed patients than in matched controls (Schleifer, Keller, Siris, Davis, & Stein, 1985). The degress of immunological impairment with a psychiatric population may be related to the severity of depression (Schleifer et al., 1985).

There are also studies with psychiatric patients which have compared herpesvirus antibody titers in patients to those of controls. Certain psychiatric patient subgroups, particularly those who are more depressed, have significantly higher herpesvirus antibody titers than nonpsychiatric controls; no differences between the patient and control groups have been found when other viral antigens such as measles or rubella were used (e.g., Halonen, Rimon, Arohonka, & Jantti, 1974; Lycke Norrby, & Roos, 1974). Therefore, some of the researchers have suggested that the herpesviruses may have an etiologic role in certain psychiatric disorders. The previously discussed stress-related changes in antibody to HSV, CMV, and EBV in the medical student data (Glaser et al., 1985a) suggest that a more parsimonious explanation may be related to the higher levels of distress which are characteristic of certain psychiatric diagnoses.

CARCINOGENESIS

Exposure to environmental carcinogens occurs daily. Some carcinogens occur "naturally," e.g., aflotoxin is the carcinogenic product of a mold associated with peanuts and certain grains, while the benzopyrenes, another group of chemical carcinogens, are found in smoke and soot. There are also a growing number of carcinogens of human manufacture: Fruits and vegetables may have pesticide residues, while nitrites are found in many processed meats and some American beers.

Most carcinogens appear to induce cancer by damaging the DNA in cells (Setlow, 1978). Mutant cells formed in this way may develop and proliferate. However, most DNA changes are probably not cancerous, and most carcinogen exposure is limited.

In addition, the body has a hierarchy of mechanisms for dealing with carcinogen exposure. At the first level, there are enzymes which destroy chemical carcinogens. The second stage of defense involves the repair of damaged DNA molecules after carcinogen exposure. At the third level is the immune system's destruction of mutant cells; NK activity is thought to be of primary importance in this regard.

The second level of the hierarchy, the mechanisms for repairing damaged DNA, may be the most critical step in humans. There is excellent evidence that poorer repair of damaged DNA is associated with increased carcinogenesis; for example, individuals with xeroderma pigmentosum (XP) have a genetically based deficit in their ability to repair DNA damaged by the ultraviolet radiation in sunlight. These XP individuals also have significantly greater numbers of skin cancers than individuals without the defect. Even minor defects in the DNA repair system can result in a significantly increased incidence of cancer (Setlow, 1978).

We were interested in ascertaining whether very high levels of distress might be associated with any deficits in the DNA repair process. In order to maximize distress in our initial subject sample, we used 28 nonpsychotic, nonmedicated new psychiatric admissions. Blood samples were drawn and the MMPI was administered on the 1st week day after their admission. Subjects were divided into high- and low-distress groups using a median split on MMPI scale 2 (depression). The T-score mean of the high-distress group was 91.3, while the mean of the low-distress group was 67.5. Comparisons between the two groups on age, sex, alcohol intake, weight loss, smoking intensity and duration, number of previous admissions, psychiatric diagnosis, and presence of a sleep disturbance did not reveal even marginal differences between the groups.

We measured the repair of DNA in lymphocytes exposed to 100 rads of X-irradiation. The method used to measure DNA repair involved the assessment of changes in the three-dimensional structure of the DNA molecule by measuring the distance traveled in a gradient when centrifuged at very high speeds. This technique is particularly sensitive to alterations such as DNA strand breaks, which decrease the migration rate in the gradient. Each subject's data were computed by dividing their irradiated values by their nonirradiated values at 0, 2, and 5 hours after irradiation; using this formula, values less than 100% indicate incomplete repair.

The high-distress inpatients had significantly poorer repair than the low-distress group; most importantly, while most "normals" are fully repaired at the 5-hour endpoint using this assay, the high-distress group was only repaired to 85% of baseline values. Further comparisons between the group of psychiatric inpatients and age- and sex-matched Red Cross blood donors showed significantly poorer DNA repair in the former at the 5-hour endpoint (Kiecolt-Glaser, Stephens et al., 1985b)

These DNA data implicate distress as a possible risk factor for poorer DNA repair, and thus potentially for carcinogenesis. However, the cross-sectional nature of this study does not permit the exclusion of viable alternative hypotheses, e.g., there could be a common genetic determinant for certain kinds of affective disorders and poorer DNA repair. Therefore, we designed a second study to test the hypothesis that stress would *induce* defects in one facet of the DNA repair system.

Forty-four rats were given the carcinogen dimethylnitrosamine in their drinking water. The carcinogen induces methyltransferase, a DNA repair enzyme, in response to carcinogen damage. Half of the animals were subjected to periodic rotational stress for 16 days (Riley, 1981), and then all rats were sacrificed. We found significantly lower levels of methyltransferase in cells obtained from the spleens of the stressed animals, suggesting that stress may play a causal role in carcinogenesis (Glaser, Thorn, Tarr, Kiecolt-Glaser, & D'Ambrosio, 1985b).

The inpatient and rat DNA repair data both suggest that distress may have adverse effects on DNA repair. Coupled with the evidence that NK activity is adversely affected by stressors, these data provide evidence for both direct and indirect biochemical pathways through which distress could influence the incidence of cancer.

DISTRESS, MORBIDITY, AND MORTALITY

The significant immunologic decrements found across several medical student classes are particularly noteworthy when considered in the context of the students' previous exposure to examinations. The selection of students for medical school is based largely on their previous performance on academic examinations. Despite their repeated exposure to this very situation, they still show significant and reliable immunologic decrements.

We suggest that the distress associated with examinations is comparable to that evoked by other commonplace events. For example, the days immediately preceding departure on vacation frequently have a similar affective quality, with comparable time pressures, as work which would normally be done in the following days or weeks is compressed into a much briefer time interval. Similarly, several days spent in the company of certain of one's relatives or in-laws can evoke characteristic negative emotional responses. If the quality and intensity of emotional distress in these and similar situations is similar to that experienced by the medical students, then there may well be similar immunologic changes.

In research to date from our laboratory and others, stress-related depressions in immune function have not been clearly associated with health problems, with one exception (Cohen-Cole et al., 1983). However, there are certainly studies in the immunological literature linking impaired immune function and health (Chandra & Newberne, 1977). The absence of concurrent health impairments in the sparse human psychoimmunology literature to date may reflect the transient nature of the stressors used, the limited time periods subjects have been studied, and/or the degree to which subjects pay attention to health problems when other events such as examinations are more salient.

It is also possible that the chronicity of the stressor is an important factor. In contrast to the data showing the immunosuppressive effects of acute stress, data from one rodent study by Monjan and Collector (1977) suggest that more chronic stress may lead to an *enhancement* in immune function. Using daily high intensity intermittent noise, they showed that while the acute or short-term consequence of the auditory stressor was immunosuppression, more chronic exposure resulted in enhanced mitogen responsiveness. Similarly, Sklar and Anisman (1979) found that tumor size and survival were adversely affected by a single session of inescapable shock in mice injected with a tumor. Mice which underwent 10 daily shock sessions had tumor areas which were significantly less than that of controls, and survival times which approximated those of controls.

It should be noted, however, that Monjan and Collector (1977) operationalized "chronicity" as the changes which occurred over a 45-day period, with the enhancement in mitogen responsiveness (values above baseline levels) beginning between days 10 and 20. These rodent data should be contrasted with some of the available human data. For example, the DSM-III diagnostic criteria for major depression, the diagnostic category most frequently studied to date, specifies that the essential symptoms must have been present for a period of at least 2 weeks; in fact, most of the patients with a major depression diagnosis in our setting retrospectively report the presence of the salient depressive symptoms for weeks or months before entry into treatment. If there were simply parallel changes between rodents and humans in response to a chronic stressor, then we might reasonably expect the depressed patients to show enhanced mitogen responsiveness, rather than the previously documented decrements (Schliefer et al., 1984).

If stress-related impairments in immune function result in poorer host resistance, then epidemiological studies should show an association between distress and morbidity and mortality, particularly with respect to infectious disease. In fact, there are epidemiological data supporting the association. For example, Babigian and Odoroff (1969) found that psychiatric patients had mortality rates one and one-half to two times as high as those for the general population, even after removal of the high-risk aged, chronically ill, and alcoholic subpopulations. Divorced individuals have a significantly greater incidence of depression than married controls, and also have significantly more deaths due to pneumonia and tuberculosis, as well as a variety of nonimmunologically mediated causes such as accidents (Bloom, Asher, & White, 1978). Bereaved spouses have significantly greater rates of morbidity and mortality than their nonbereaved counterparts (Ernster, Sacks, Selvin, & Petrakis, 1979; Rees & Lutkins, 1967).

There are also epidemiological data which link distress and cancer risk. Using a sample of over 2000 nonpsychiatric men, Shekelle et al. (1981) compared those subjects whose highest scale on the MMPI was scale 2 (depression) with men who did not have scale 2 as their high point code. They found that the men with their highest elevations on scale 2 (T-score mean of 70) had twice the number of cancer deaths, across cancer sites, after correction for a number of relevant risk factors; these data are consistent with our DNA data (Kiecolt-Glaser, Stephens et al., 1985b). Furthermore, psychiatric patients have more cancer deaths than nonpsychiatric controls (Fox, 1978b). Bereaved spouses have a greater mortality rate from cancer than the general population (Ernster, Sacks, Selvin, & Petrakis, 1979).

There are several reasons why the hypothesized association between distress and cancer risk may not be obvious in prospective epidemiological research. The time period for the study is one critical factor. Fox (1978a) presents the mathematical basis for the doubling time of cells, and concludes that a solid tumor would not be visible until at least 3 years after the initial proliferation of a mutant cell; the developmental time span could cover decades, with a mutation held in check for some time. Most studies addressing psychosocial factors have used relatively short time periods.

In addition, distress is not constant, especially at the very high levels which were associated with impairments in DNA repair in our psychiatric patients. Most studies simply assess distress at a single point in time.

Finally, and most important, there are a number of other risk factors which may be much more salient. Carcinogen dosage and period of carcinogen exposure are certainly of paramount importance. Genetic vulnerabilities for certain cancers are also well-documented. There are also newer data which suggest that there may be some important genetic differences in immunocompetence as well; individuals from cancer-prone families have lower levels of NK activity (Strayer, Carter, Mayberry, Pequignot, & Brodsky, 1984).

THE FUTURE OF PSYCHONEUROIMMUNOLOGY RESEARCH

There is still relatively little human research which addresses the psychological mediation of immune function. Although such research is widely accepted by behavioral scientists, it has not achieved comparable acceptance in the basic science community among immunologists and related disciplines, and basic scientists are the essential collaborators for this interdisciplinary work. Some of this lack of acceptance may be related to earlier learning; as recently as the late 1970s, there were still immunology textbooks being published which stated there was no central nervous system mediation of immune function (Ader, 1980). Most of the newer immunology textbooks still do not explicitly address the evidence for the multiple central nervous system and immune system linkages.

In some cases it appears that the importance of the work has not been adequately evaluated. For example, the editor of *Nature* recently printed an editorial inauspiciously titled "Psychoimmunology: Before its time" (Maddox, 1984). The editorial grossly misrepresented the status of research and theory in the area, describing unreferenced psychoimmunologists "who talk as if there is no state of mind which is not faithfully reflected by a state of the immune system" (p. 400).

Despite such adverse events, there are growing numbers of biological and behavioral scientists who are initiating research in this area (Marks, 1985). Ultimately, psychoneuroimmunological research may change the ways in which biological scientists conceptualize some of the processes they are studying, as well as their data collection procedures.

REFERENCES

Adam, E. (1982). Herpes simplex virus infections. In R. Glaser & T. Gotlieb-Stematsky (Eds.), *Human herpesvirus infections: Clinical aspects* (pp. 1–567). New York: Marcel Dekker.

Ader, R. (1980). Psychosomatic and psychoimmunologic research. *Psychosomatic Medicine, 42,* 307–321.

Ader, R., & Cohen, N. (1982). Behaviorally conditioned immunosuppression and murine systemic lupus erythematosus. *Science, 215,* 1534–1536.

Ahlqvist, J. (1981). Hormonal influences on immunologic and related phenomena. In R. Ader (Ed.), *Psychoneuroimmunology* (pp. 355–403). New York: Academic Press.

Babigian, H., & Odoroff, C. L. (1969). The mortality experience of a population with psychiatric illness. *American Journal of Psychiatry, 126,* 52–62.

Bartrop, R. W., Luckhurst, E., Lazarus, L., Kiloh, L. G., & Penny, R. (1977). Depressed lymphocyte function after bereavement. *Lancet, 1,* 834–836.

Beahrs, J. O., Harris, D. R., & Hilgard, E. R. (1970). Failure to alter skin inflammation by hypnotic suggestion in five subjects with normal skin reactivity. *Psychosomatic Medicine, 32,* 627–631.

Black, S. (1969). *Mind and body.* London: William Kimber.

Blalock, J. E. (1984). The immune system as a sensory organ. *Journal of Immunology, 132,* 1067–1070.

Bloom, B. L., Asher, S. J., & White, S. W. (1978). Marital disruption as a stressor: A review and analysis. *Psychological Bulletin, 85,* 867–894.

Borysenko, M., & Borysenko, J. (1982). Stress, behavior and immunity: Animal models and mediating mechanisms. *General Hospital Psychiatry, 4,* 59–67.

Braveman, N. (in press). Immunity and aging: Immunological and behavioral perspectives. In M. Riley, J. Matarazzo, & A. Baum (Eds.), *Perspectives on behavioral medicine.* New York: Academic Press.

Chandra, R. K., & Newberne, P. M. (1977). Nutrition, immunity, and infection. In *Mechanisms of interactions.* New York: Plenum Press.

Cohen-Cole, S., Cogen, A. B., Stevens, A. W., Kirk, K., Gaitan, E., Bird, J., Cooksey, R., & Freeman, A. (1983). Psychiatric, psychosocial, and endocrine correlates of acute necrotizing ulcerative gingivitis (trenchmouth); A preliminary report. *Psychiatric Medicine, 1,* 215–225.

Ernster, V. L., Sacks, S. T., Selvin, S., & Petrakis, N. L. (1979). Cancer incidence by marital status: U.S. Third National Cancer Survey. *Journal of the National Cancer Institute, 63,* 587–585.

Fox, B. H. (1978a). Premorbid psychological factors as related to cancer incidence. *Journal of Behavioral Medicine, 1,* 45–133.

Fox, B. H. (1978b). Cancer death risk in hospitalized mental patients. Letters, *Science, 201,* 966–967.

Fox. B. H., & Newberry, B. H. (Eds.). (1984). *Impact of psychoendocrine systems in cancer and immunity.* Lewiston, NY: C. J. Hogrefe.

Fry, L., Mason, A. A., & Pearson, R. S. (1964). Effects of hypnosis on allergic skin responses in asthma and hay fever. *British Medical Journal, 5391,* 1145–1148.

Glaser, R., & Gotlieb-Stematsky, T. (Eds). (1982). *Human herpesvirus infections: Clinical aspects.* New York: Marcel Dekker.

Glaser, R., Kiecolt-Glaser, J. K., Speicher, C. E., & Holliday, J. E. (1985a). Stress, loneliness, and changes in herpesvirus latency. *Journal of Behavioral Medicine, 8,* 249–260.

Glaser, R., Mehl, V. S., Penn, G., Speicher, C. E., & Kiecolt-Glaser, J. K. (1986a). Stress-associated changes in serum immunoglobulin levels. *International Journal of Psychosomatics, 33,* 41–42.

Glaser, R., Rice, J., Speicher, C. E., Stout, J. C., & Kiecolt-Glaser, J. K. (1986b). Stress depresses interferon production concomitant with a decrease in natural killer cell activity. *Behavioral Neuroscience, 100,* 675–678.

Glaser, R., Thorn, B. E., Tarr, K. L., Kiecolt-Glaser, J. K., & D'Ambrosio, S. M. (1985b). Effects of stress on methyltransferase synthesis: An important DNA repair enzyme. *Health Psychology, 4,* 403–412.

Goldmeier, D., & Johnson, A. (1982). Does psychiatric illness affect the recurrence rate of genital herpes? *British Journal of Venereal Diseases, 58,* 40–43.

Good, R. A. (1981). Foreword: Interactions of the body's major networks. In R. Ader (Ed.), *Psychoneuroimmunology* (pp. xvii–xix). New York: Academic Press.

Halonen, P. E., Rimon, R., Arohonka, K., & Jantti, V. (1974). Antibody levels to herpes simplex type 1, measles, and rubella viruses in psychiatric patients. *British Journal of Psychiatry, 125,* 461–465.

Henle, W., & Henle, G. (1982). Epstein-Barr virus and infectious mononucleosis. In R. Glaser & T. Gotlieb-Stematsky (Eds.), *Human herpesvirus infections: Clinical Aspects.* New York: Marcel Dekker.

Herberman, R. B., Ortaldo, J. R., Riccardi, C., Timonen, T., Schmidt, A., Maluish, A., & Djeu, J. (1982). Interferon and NK cells. In T. C. Merigan & R. M. Friedman, (Eds.), *Interferons.* London: Academic Press.

Kasl, S. V., Evans, A. S., & Niederman, J. C. (1979). Psychosocial risk factors in the development of infectious mononucleosis. *Psychosomatic Medicine, 41,* 445–466.

Kiecolt-Glaser, J. K., Garner, W., Speicher, C., Penn, G. M., Holliday, J. E., & Glaser, R. (1984). Psychosocial modifiers of immunocompetence in medical students. *Psychosomatic Medicine, 46,* 7–14.

Kiecolt-Glaser, J. K., & Glaser, R. (in press). Psychosocial influences on herpesvirus latency. In E. Kurstak, Z. J. Lipowski, & P. V. Morozov (Eds.), *Viruses, immunity, and mental disorders.* New York: Plenum.

Kiecolt-Glaser, J. K., Glaser, R., Strain, E. C., Stout, J. C., Tarr, K. L., Holliday, J. E., & Speicher, C. E. (1986). Modulation of cellular immunity in medical students. *Journal of Behavioral Medicine, 9,* 5–21.

Kiecolt-Glaser, J. K., Glaser, R., Williger, D., Stout, J., Messick, G., Sheppard, S., Ricker, D., Romisher, S. C., Briner, W., Bonnell, G., & Donnerberg, R. (1985a). Psychosocial enhancement of immunocompetence in a geriatric population. *Health Psychology, 4,* 25–41.

Kiecolt-Glaser, J. K., Ricker, D., Messick, G., Speicher, C. E., Garner, W., & Glaser, R. (1984). Urinary cortisol, cellular immunocompetency and loneliness in psychiatric inpatients. *Psychosomatic Medicine, 46,* 15–24.

Kiecolt-Glaser, J. K., Speicher, C. E., Holliday, J. E., & Glaser, R. (1984). Stress and the transformation of lymphocytes by Epstein-Barr virus. *Journal of Behavioral Medicine, 7,* 1–12.

Kiecolt-Glaser, J. K., Stephens, R. E., Lipetz, P. D., Speicher, C. E., & Glaser, R. (1985b). Distress and DNA repair in human lymphocytes. *Journal of Behavioral Medicine, 8,* 311–320.

Kimzey, S. L. (1975). The effects of extended spaceflight on hematologic and immunologic systems. *Journal of American Medical Women's Association, 30,* 218–232.

Krueger, R. B., Levy, E. M., Cathcart, E. S., Fox, B. H., & Black, P. H. (1984). Lymphocyte subsets in patients with major depression: Preliminary findings. *Advances, 1,* 5–9.

Luborsky, L., Mintz, J., Brightman, U. J., & Katcher, A. H. (1976). Herpes simplex and moods, a longitudinal study. *Journal of Psychosomatic Research, 20,* 543–548.

Lycke, E., Norrby, B., & Roos, B. E. (1974). Serological study of mentally ill patients with particular reference to the prevalence of virus infections. *British Journal of Psychiatry, 124,* 273–279.

Maddox, J. (1984). Psychoimmunology: Before its time. *Nature, 309,* 400.

Marks, J. L. (1985). The immune system "belongs in the body." *Science, 227,* 1190–1192.

Monjan, A. A. (1981). Stress and immunologic competence: Studies in animals. In R. Ader (Ed.), *Psychoneuroimmunology* (pp. 185–228). New York: Academic Press.

Monjan, A. A., & Collector, M. I. (1977). Stress-induced modulation of the immune response. *Science, 196,* 307–308.

Palmbald, J. (1981). Stress and immunologic competence: Studies in man. In R. Ader (Ed.), *Psychoneuroimmunology* (pp. 229–257). New York: Academic Press.

Pitchenik, A. E., Fischl, M. A., & Spira, T. J. (1983). Acquired immune deficiency syndrome in low-risk patients. *Journal of the American Medical Journal, 250,* 1310–1312.

Rees, W. D., & Lutkins, S. G. (1967). Mortality of bereavement. *British Medical Journal, 4,* 13–16.

Reinherz, E. L., & Schlossman, S. F. (1980). Current concepts in immunology: Regulation of the immune response—Inducer and suppressor T-lymphocyte subsets in human beings. *New England Journal of Medicine, 303,* 370–373.

Riley, V. (1981). Psychoneuroendocrine influences on immunocompetence and neoplasia. *Science, 212,* 1100–1109.

Roberts-Thomson, I. C., Whittingham, S., Youngchaiyud, U., & MacKay, I. R. (1974). Aging, immune response, and mortality. *Lancet, 2,* 368–370.

Rodin, J. (1980). Managing the stress of aging: The role of control and coping. In S. Levine & H. Ursin (Eds.), *Coping and Health* (pp. 171–202). New York: Plenum Press.

Schleifer, S. J., Keller, S. E., Meyerson, A. T., Raskin, M. J., Davis, K. L., & Stein, M. (1984). Lymphocyte function in major depressive disorder. *Archives of General Psychiatry, 41,* 484–486.

Schliefer, S. J., Keller, S. E., Siris, S. G., Davis, K. L., & Stein, M. (1985). Depression and immunity. *Archives of General Psychiatry, 42,* 129–133.

Schulz, R. (1980). Aging and control. In J. Garber & M. E. P. Seligman (Eds.), *Human helplessness: Theory and applications* (pp. 261–277). New York: Academic Press.

Setlow, R. B. (1978). Repair deficient human disorders and human cancer. *Nature* (London), *271,* 713–717.

Shekelle, R. B., Raynor, W. J., Ostfeld, A. M., Garron, D. C., Bieliauskas, L. A., Liv, S. C., Maliza, C., & Paul, O. (1981). Psychological depression and the 17-year risk of cancer. *Psychosomatic Medicine, 43,* 117–125.

Sklar, L. S., & Anisman, H. (1979). Stress and coping factors influence tumor growth. *Science, 205,* 513–515.

Smith, G. R., & McDaniel, S. M. (1983). Psychologically mediated effect on the delayed hypersensitivity reaction to tuberculin in humans. *Psychosomatic Medicine, 45,* 65–70.

Stein, M., Schleifer, S. J., & Keller, S. E. (1981). Hypothalamic influences on immune responses. In R. Ader (Ed.), *Psychoneuroimmunology* (pp. 429–447). New York: Academic Press.

Strayer, D. R., Carter, W. A., Mayberry, S. D., Pequignot, E., & Brodsky, I. (1984). Low natural cytotoxicity of peripheral blood mononuclear cells in individuals with high familial incidence of cancer. *Cancer Research, 44,* 370–374.

Sullivan, J. L., & Hanshaw, J. B. (1982). Human cytomegalovirus infections. In R. Glaser & T. Gotlieb-Stematsky (Eds.), *Human herpesvirus infections: Clinical aspects* (pp. 57–84). New York, Marcel Dekker.

Thoits, P. A. (1983). Dimensions of life events that influence distress: An evaluation and synthesis of the literature. In H. B. Kaplan (Ed.), *Psychosocial stress: Trends in theory and research* (pp. 33–103). New York: Academic Press.

10 Is There Life After Type A: Recent Developments in Research on Coronary-Prone Behavior

Redford B. Williams, Jr., M.D.
Duke University Medical Center,
Durham, North Carolina

Since the conclusion that Type A behavior pattern is a risk factor for coronary heart disease was reached at the Amelia Island Conference (Review Panel on Coronary-Prone Behavior, 1981), several negative studies have raised questions about the robustness of the Type A hypothesis. In prospective studies of healthy individuals with multiple risk factors (Shekelle, Hulley et al., 1985) and survivors of a myocardial infarction (Case, Heller, Case, & Moss, 1985; Shekelle, Gale, & Norusis, 1985), both structured interview (SI) and questionnaire (JAS) measures of Type A behavior failed to predict subsequent coronary events. Following the publication of three studies, in the mid-1970s, in which Type A was found to correlate significantly with severity of coronary atherosclerosis (CAD) in patients undergoing coronary angiography, there have been ten studies of the relationship of Type A to CAD (Bass & Wade, 1982; Dimsdale et al., 1978, 1979; Kornitzer et al., 1982; Krantz, Sanmarco, Selvester, & Matthews, 1979; Krantz et al., 1981; Pearson, 1983; Scherwitz et al., 1983; Williams et al., 1980; Young, Barboriak, Anderson, & Hoffman, 1980)—only one of these studies (Williams et al., 1980) reported unequivocal evidence of a Type A-CAD association. Case et al. (1985) concluded that these negative results ". . . raise serious questions about the effect of Type A behavior on the whole spectrum of coronary disease'' (p. 740).

A comprehensive and detailed analysis of Type A and other risk factor data available on a large sample (N = 2289) of patients undergoing coronary angiography at Duke (Williams et al., 1986) provides several findings which help to place the negative angiographic studies in a better perspective. First of all, we did find that Type A behavior is significantly related to CAD severity, but only via an interaction with age. Among patients less than 45-years-of-age, Type A behavior, as assessed by the SI but *not* the JAS, was significantly (p < .01) associated with more severe CAD; among patients aged 45–55, there was no difference between the Types in CAD severity; and among patients older than 55, there was a trend (p = .02) toward more severe CAD among the Type B patients. Similar interactions with age were found for both cigarette smoking and hyperlipidemia: The strength of both as correlates of CAD severity decreased with increasing age.

This finding suggests that among the older patients the Type As represent a group of "hardy" survivors; the more biologically vulnerable individuals having died or developed chronic disease at an earlier age. Among the Type Bs, on the other hand, premature disease associated with the deleterious effects of Type A behavior did not remove the biologically vulnerable individuals from the population, and the older biologically vulnerable Type Bs continue to be present in angiographic samples.

The findings of our analyses raise serious questions about the interpretation of the negative angiographic studies. None of the negative angiographic studies systematically evaluated the Type A by age interaction. Since all of these studies included patients ranging in age up to 64–70, the crossover we found after age 50, if present in those samples, would obscure a Type A-CAD relationship that could be present in the younger patients. Of the nine negative studies cited earlier, seven had small sample sizes, of 150 or less. A power analysis based on the effect size and variances we observed in our large sample indicates that with sample sizes of 150 or less, the power to detect a significant (p < .05) Type A-CAD relationship would be less than 17%. Thus, even if they had taken the age interaction into account, those studies with sample sizes of 150 or less would have had inadequate statistical power to find a Type A-CAD relationship. Finally, of the two negative studies with larger sample sizes, 700+ and 2400+, both used questionnaires rather than the SI to assess Type A behavior. Because we also failed to find JAS scores related to CAD severity, the two negative angiographic studies with large sample sizes must also be considered seriously flawed.

The inadequacies of the negative angiographic studies—small sample sizes, use of less than the best Type A assessment tool and failure to consider the effect of age on the Type A-CAD relationship—lead to the conclusion that they cannot be accepted uncritically as supporting the null hypothesis that Type A behavior is unrelated to CAD severity. Our recent findings, in a large sample, taking age into account and using the best Type A measure, suggest that Type A behavior is indeed associated with increased *premature* CAD severity—i.e., that occurring in younger patients. The fact that such well established risk factors as smoking and hyperlipidemia also behave similarly, in both epidemiologic and angiographic studies, increases our confidence that something that is being measured by the SI is associated with increased CAD severity.

At the same time, however, it is important to note that the size of the effect in our data is small, much smaller, in fact, than the effects on CAD severity associated with both smoking and hyperlipidemia. Among the patients less than 45-years-of-age in our sample, the Type As were only 1.19 times more likely (56% vs. 47%) than the Type Bs to have a clinically significant coronary occlusion on their angiogram. Although quite reliable statistically, this is not a very large effect. Therefore, we conclude that, although it is associated with more severe CAD in younger patients, the global Type A construct may not be the best we can do in defining coronary-prone behavior.

A growing body of research suggests that not all aspects of Type A behavior—speed/impatience, ambition/job involvement, and hostility/anger—are equally related to various indices of coronary heart disease. In a recently published reanalysis of SI data on a subset of the Duke angiographic sample, Dembroski, MacDougall, Williams, Haney, and Blumenthal (1985) found that, although global Type A behavior did not correlate significantly with CAD severity—not surprising in view of the small sample size, N = 133—measures of hostility and expression of anger ("Anger-IN") did correlate with CAD severity. In addition, when hostility and anger expression were covaried, a measure of Type A speech became *significantly negatively* correlated with CAD severity. In another reanalysis of SI data, this time from an angiographic sample at Massachusetts General Hospital in which global Type A behavior had not been found associated with CAD severity, MacDougall et al. (1985) also found both hostility and anger expression measures from the SI to correlate positively with CAD severity. They also replicated the negative association of Type A speech characteristics with CAD severity when hostility and anger expression are covaried.

These findings, in two independent studies, that even when global Type A behavior is not associated with CAD severity, measures of hostility and anger expression are related significantly to CAD severity lead to the conclusion that it is the hostility/anger component of the global Type A construct which is truly coronary-prone. Indeed, the negative association of Type A speech characteristics with CAD severity following control for hostility and anger expression suggests that to the extent that Type A speech is due to factors other than hostility/anger—perhaps "enthusiasm,"—it may even be protective against development of CAD. Thus, to the extent that studies using the SI to determine Type A behavior are keying on the speech patterns to assign patients to the Type A or Type B category, they may be including a substantial number of persons in the Type A group who are not at increased, indeed, who may be at decreased risk of developing coronary disease.

Another line of research which points to the importance of hostility/anger as the toxic core of Type A behavior has used the Cook-Medley Hostility (Ho) scale from the MMPI (Cook & Medley, 1954) as an assessment tool. Williams et al.

(1980) found that Ho scores correlated more strongly than SI-determined global Type A behavior with CAD severity in a sample of 424 angiographic patients. Multivariate analysis suggested that some of the variance in CAD severity associated with the global Type A construct was due to increased Ho scores among the Type A patients, while the converse was not true.

Since the Ho scale is contained in the MMPI, it has been possible to rescore archival MMPI data from studies conducted in the past and evaluate the *prospective* relationship between high Ho scores and subsequent coronary events, as well as other health outcomes. In such a reanalysis of data on middle-aged men from the Western Electric Study, Shekelle, Gale, Ostfeld, and Paul (1983) found that coronary incidence, as well as all-cause mortality were about 1.5 times higher in men with higher Ho scores than those with lower Ho scores. The increased disease risk associated with higher Ho scores remained significant even with statistical adjustment for established risk factors. In a similar reanalysis of MMPI data, this time from physicians who had taken the MMPI at age 25 as part of a medical school course, Barefoot, Dahlstrom, and Williams (1983) found over a 25 year follow-up period that those with higher Ho scores had a 4-5 fold higher coronary rate and a 7 fold higher all-cause mortality rate than the men with lower Ho scores.

These two independent studies showing *prospective* prediction of increased coronary risk and all-cause mortality provide powerful support for the conclusion that a psychological construct measured by the Ho scale places individuals at increased risk of a wide variety of adverse health outcomes. The higher relative risk of dying among the younger men—7 vs. 1.5 for the middle-aged men— again suggests the important modulation of the effects of this construct by age. That is, by the age of 45–50, many of those most susceptible to the deleterious effects of the Ho-assessed construct will have already died, leaving a relatively hardy group of individuals in the high-Ho group. This would parsimoniously account for the weakening of Ho scores—not to mention such other established risk factors as smoking and hyperlipidemia—as a risk factor in men who enter a study later in life.

Just what is the Ho scale measuring? Whatever it is, it is extraordinarily stable. In the Western Electric Sample, the test-retest correlation in 1655 men who retook the MMPI 4 years after the first administration was .84 (Shekelle et al., 1983). In the Barefoot et al. (1983) study, test-retest stability was .85. Costa, Zonderman, McCrae, and Williams (1985) factor analyzed the MMPI data on the Duke angiographic sample and found that the Ho scale items loaded on a factor the best name for which appears to be "cynicism," reflecting a basic mistrust of human nature and motives. Support for this description of what is measured by the Ho scale has recently been provided in an extensive study of the construct validity and psychosocial correlates of the Ho scale conducted by Smith and Frohm (1985).

Thus, it appears that a cynical mistrust of others is what is being measured by the Ho scale. How could such a trait lead to such a wide variety of adverse health outcomes? One possible mechanism could be via decreased social support. There is an extensive literature, which will not be reviewed here, suggesting an association between low levels of social support and increased morbidity and mortality of all sorts. Preliminary evidence (Williams et al., 1980) has shown a negative correlation between Ho scores and the perceived adequacy of social contacts in the Duke angiographic sample. To the extent that social support leads, via at present unknown pathways, to increased risk of disease and death, the cynical mistrust of persons with high Ho scores might result in their becoming alienated from sources of social support. It is worth noting in passing that the converse hypothesis might also be true: decreased social support leads to disease and death because persons who *report* low levels of social support are higher on cynical mistrust which leads, via some as yet unclear mechanism, to increased death and disease.

Research to identify such a mechanism or mechanisms is just beginning. We have previously reported (Williams et al., 1982) that young Type A men show epinephrine and cortisol hyperresponsivity during performance of mental arithmetic, while during vigilance tasks the Type A men show testosterone hyper-resonsivity. Subsequent unpublished analyses of data from that study suggest that it is the Type A men who score high on the Ho scale who are responsible for the Type A testosterone hyperresponsivity. Muranaka et al. (1986) have recently reported that Type A men who score high on the Ho scale show more prolonged EKG T-wave attenuation in response to isoproterenol infusions than Type B men with low Ho scores. Preliminary analyses of Ho score data from samples of mono- and dizygotic twins (Richard Rose, personal communication) suggest a substantial genetic contribution to the determination of Ho scores.

The preliminary studies just cited suggest two possible mechanisms whereby high levels of cynical mistrust might lead to increased risk of disease and death. First, an individual who does not trust others to be kind and who is always concerned that others might mistreat him would be likely to go around in a state of constant vigilance, might always be "on guard." Since he expects others to behave badly, he will likely see many examples of what he concludes to be bad behavior in others, leading to increased arousals of anger. Both the increased testosterone secretion associated with vigilance and the likely increased catecholamines and cortisol associated with anger arousal could exert deleterious effects on a number of systems—e.g., cardiovascular and immune—which, over time would make the individual more susceptible to a variety of illnesses.

An alternative pathway to disease and death among persons who score high on the Ho scale could result from the possible determination of the trait of cynical mistrust itself by biological characteristics of the individual. The same catecholamine, cortisol and testosterone hyperresponsivity under appropriate conditions of environmental challenge that may be responsible for increased vulnerability to a variety of disease processes could also *cause* the individual to have the psychological trait we are calling cynical mistrust. The very preliminary evidence of a genetic determination of Ho scores is supportive of at least a partial biologic influence on cynical mistrust levels.

Clearly, much more research in both the psychosocial epidemiology and psychobiological areas will be required before definitive conclusions can be drawn regarding biobehavioral mechanisms of coronary-prone behavior. The increasing involvement of researchers from a variety of disciplines—as evidenced by numerous presentations at the recent meetings of both the Society of Behavioral Medicine and the American Psychosomatic Society—in studying all aspects of hostility and anger gives one considerable confidence that we are likely to see material progress in the next few years in our understanding of how behavior and disease are related.

ACKNOWLEDGMENTS

Preparation of this chapter was supported in part by grants, HL-18589 and HL-22740, from the National Heart, Lung and Blood Institute, by a Research Scientist Award from the National Institute of Mental Health and by a grant from the John D. and Catherine T. MacArthur Foundation

REFERENCES

Barefoot, J. C., Dahlstrom, G., & Williams, R. B. (1983). Hostility, CHD incidence, and total mortality: A 25-year follow-up study of 255 physicians. *Psychosomatic Medicine, 45,* 59–63.

Bass, C., & Wade, C. (1982). Type A behavior: Not specifically pathogenic. *Lancet 10,* 1147–1148.

Case, R. B., Heller, S. S., Case, N. B., & Moss, A. J. (1985). The Multicenter Post-Infarction Research Group: Type A behavior and survival after acute myocardial infarction. *New England Journal of Medicine, 312,* 737–741.

Costa, P. T., Zonderman, A. B., McCrae, R. R., & Williams, R. B. (1985). Cynicism and paranoid alienation in the Cook and Medley HO scale. *Psychosomatic Medicine, 48,* 283–285.

Cook, W. W., & Medley, D. M. (1954). Proposed hostility and pharisaic-virtue scales for the MMPI. *Journal of Applied Psychology, 38,* 414–418.

Dembroski, T. M., MacDougall, J. M., Williams, R. B., Haney, T. L., & Blumenthal, J. A. (1985). Components of Type A, hostility, and anger-in: Relationship to angiographic findings. *Psychosomatic Medicine, 47,* 219–233.

Dimsdale, J. E., Hackett, T. P., Hutter, A. M., Block, P. C., Catanzano, D. M., & White, P. J. (1978). Type A personality and extent of coronary atherosclerosis. *American Journal of Cardiology, 43,* 583–586.

Dimsdale, J. E., Hackett, T. P., Hutter, A. M., Block, P. C., Catanzano, D. M., & White, P. (1979). Type A behavior and angiographic findings. *Journal of Psychosomatic Research, 23,* 273–276.

Kornitzer, M., Magotteau, V., & Degre, C. et al. (1982). Angiographic findings and the Type A pattern assessed by means of the Bortner scale. *Journal of Behavioral Medicine, 5,* 313–320.

Krantz, D. S., Sanmarco, M.I., Selvester, R. H., & Matthews, K. A. (1979). Psychological correlates of progression of atherosclerosis in men. *Psychosomatic Medicine, 41,* 467–475.

Krantz, D. S., Schaeffer, M. A., Davia, J. E., Dembroski, T. M., MacDougall, J. M., & Shaffer, R. T. (1981). Extent of coronary atherosclerosis, Type A behavior and cardiovascular response to social interaction. *Psychophysiology, 18,* 654–664.

MacDougall, T. M., Dembroski, T. M., Dimsdale, J. E., Hackett, T. P. (1985). Components of Type A, hostility, and anger-in: Further relationships to angiographic findings. *Health Psychology, 4,* 137–152.

Muranaka, M., Williams, R. B., Lane, J. D. et al. (1986, March). *T-wave amplitude during catecholamine infusion study: A new approach to biological mechanisms of coronary-prone behavior.* Paper presented at Annual Meeting, Society of Behavioral Medicine, San Francisco.

Pearson, T. A. (1983). Risk factors for arteriographically defined coronary artery disease. Doctoral dissertation, Johns Hopkins University. Ann Arbor. *University Microfilms International #83-16989.*

Review Panel on Coronary-Prone Behavior and Coronary Heart Disease; Coronary-prone behavior and coronary heart disease: A critical review. (1961). *Circulation 63,* 1199–1215.

Scherwitz, L., McKelvain, R., Laman, C., Patterson, J., Dutton, L., Yusim, S., Lester, J., Kraft, I., Rochelle, D., Leachman, R. (1983). Type A behavior, self- involvement, and coronary atherosclerosis. *Psychosomatic Medicine, 45,* 47–57.

Shekelle, R. B., Gale, M., & Norusis, M. (1985). Type A behavior (Jenkins Activity Survey) and risk of recurrent coronary heart disease in the Aspirin Myocardial Infarction Study. *American Journal of Cardiology, 56,* 222–225.

Shekelle, R. B., Gale, M., Ostfeld, A. M., & Paul, O. (1983). Hostility, risk of coronary heart disease, and mortality. *Psychosomatic Medicine, 45,* 109–114.

Shekelle, R. B., Hulley, S. G., Neation, J. et al. (1985). The MRFIT behavior pattern study: II. Type A behavior and incidence of coronary heart disease. *American Journal of Epidemiology, 122,* 559–570.

Smith, T. W., & Frohm, K. D. (1985). What's so unhealthy about hostility? Construct validity and psychosocial correlates of the Cook and Medley HO scale. *Health Psychology, 4,* 503–520.

Williams, R. B., Barefoot, J. C., Haney, T. L. et al. (1986, March). *Type A behavior and angiographically documented coronary atherosclerosis in a sample of 2,289 patients.* Presented at the Annual Meeting, American Psychosomatic Society, Baltimore, MD.

Williams, R. B., Haney, T. L., Lee, K. L., Kong, Y., Blumenthal, J. A., & Whalen, R. E. (1980). Type A behavior, hostility, and coronary artherosclerosis. *Psychosomatic Medicine, 42,* 539–549.

Williams, R. B., Lane, J. D., Kuhn, C. M. et al. (1982). Type A behavior and elevated physiological and neuroendocrine responses to cognitive tasks. *Science, 218,* 483–485.

Young, L. D., Barboriak, J. J., Anderson, A. A., & Hoffman, R. G. (1980). Attitudinal and behavioral correlates of coronary heart disease. *Journal of Psychosomatic Research, 24,* 311–318.

11 The Effect of Depression on Cardiovascular Reactivity

Joel E. Dimsdale, M.D.
University of California, San Diego

INTRODUCTION

It is a paradox in science that highly relevant information may not be transferred across disciplines. Sometimes two or more research disciplines are working on similar problems but are unaware of the potential utility of combining these disparate approaches into a more sophisticated analysis. This task of inter-disciplinary communication now faces psychiatry, psychology, and cardiology in studying the effects of depression on cardiovascular reactivity.

One approach emanates from behavioral medicine and psychosomatic research and focuses on measuring cardiovascular reactivity to behavioral stressors. Another approach comes from epidemiological research on the prevalence of depression and on its possible relationship to cardiovascular disease. The final thread comes from psychiatric research on physiological alterations in depression.

BEHAVIORAL REACTIVITY

When examining any physiological signal, one has a choice between studying that signal at rest or in response to some stimulus. Unfortunately, there is a tendency to regard reactions to behavioral perturbation as noise, as opposed to an inherently interesting signal. This makes it rather difficult to examine the role of behavioral factors on pathophysiology.

Nowhere is this clearer than in the measurement of blood pressure (BP). All epidemiological and actuarial approaches rely on measuring BP while minimizing stressing the subject; they derive information about the subject's resting baseline and, from this, calculate subsequent risk. This is a major assumption that may be counterproductive. A person experiences roughly 100,000 separate blood pressures a day. First off, it is hard to accept that three casual, resting blood pressures are informing us about the individual's general blood pressure state. Second, by relying on invasive intraarterial monitors or noninvasive ambulatory blood pressure recorders, investigators have documented an extensive variability in blood pressure in ambulatory subjects. This variability remains even after controlling for changes in diet or posture. It would appear that the subject's behavioral environment accounts for most of this variability.

How well does a static resting blood pressure correlate with the subject's average overall ambulatory blood pressure? Pickering, Harshfield, Kleinert, and Laragh (1982) have demonstrated that the correlation between an office blood pressure and an ambulatory (or behaviorally responsive) blood pressure is disappointingly low, that misdiagnosis occurs in both directions—viewing a normotensive individual as hypertensive, and viewing a hypertensive individual as normotensive on the basis of casual office blood pressures. Ambulatory readings of BP as compared to clinic BPs are better correlates of increased left ventricular mass (Devereux et al., 1983) and better predictors of subsequent cardiovascular morbidity and mortality (Perloff, Sokolow, & Cowan, 1983).

Similar observations can be made about the role of reactivity measures on virtually any blood chemistry. If the compound has a rapid half-life and/or rapid response time, it is influenced by behavioral stimuli. For instance, plasma norepinephrine (NE) is exquisitely responsive to behavioral stressors (Dimsdale, Young, Strauss, & Moore, 1986). Figure 11.1 depicts the NE levels found at rest and contrasts them with the levels encountered when volunteers talked openly about the troubles they faced in their lives.

Although one can assay newly discovered hormones, the work of measuring the effects of behavioral stimuli on these new hormones has lagged. As a result, for many of the recently discovered neuropeptides, there is little information about the normal range of response of these peptides to behavioral stressors. Similarly, there is still insufficient knowledge about the neuropeptide response to stressors in patient groups, be they psychiatric or cardiac.

The situation is a bit better in terms of measuring BP reactivity. Here, a number of intriguing studies have examined the reactive components of blood pressure. One of the more influential of these studies was performed by Keys et al. (1971), who followed 279 men for 23 years in an effort to learn what risk factors predicted the subsequent cardiac morbidity and mortality from cardiovascular disease. The strongest predictor of such disease was the degree of blood pressure elevation in response to a cold pressor task. If a pressor response to cold is such a good predictor of subsequent cardiovascular disease, could the reactivity to other stimuli predict subsequent disease?

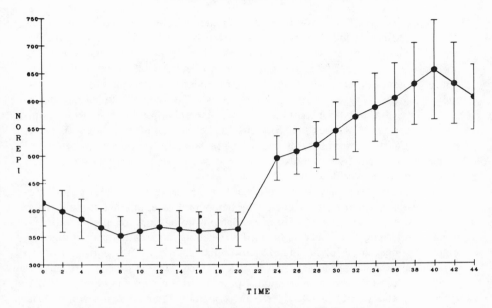

FIG. 11.1 Plasma norepinephrine levels were obtained from volunteers for 20 minutes while listening to restful music, and then for the following 20 minutes while the volunteers discussed the stressors in their lives.

The best model for this is exercise testing. The principle of dynamic exercise testing is to increase the demands upon the heart in such a fashion as to bring out ischemic changes that may be inapparent at rest. Another function of exercise testing is to reveal a *forme fruste* of subsequent hypertension. It would appear that cardiologists are comfortable with reactivity studies using dynamic exercise. Medicine has been more reluctant, however, to utilize behavioral stimuli because of an ideological opposition to accepting their importance—because of the belief that they are difficult to standardize, too time consuming, too trivial or (conversely) too aversive.

Fortunately, this view about behavioral reactivity studies is diminishing. Faulkner, Kushner, Onesti, and Angelakos (1981) examined 50 Philadelphia adolescents at high risk for developing hypertension. In a follow-up of 41 months, the youths who had a greater BP response to mental stress tasks on intake were more likely to develop fixed hypertension.

Hollenberg et al. (1981) examined blood pressure and renal blood flow in normal individuals, hypertensive individuals, and normotensive offspring of hypertensive individuals. The investigators found that the renal blood flow response to a stressful cognitive task differentiated the three groups.

Numerous investigators have examined the influence of type A behavior pattern on reactivity to behavioral stressors. It is beyond the focus of this paper to discuss whether or not type A behavior is a risk factor for coronary disease; suffice it to say that this is a matter of considerable controversy (Dimsdale, 1985). Regardless, approximately 40 studies have been performed using various indices of reactivity and various stressor tasks. The general conclusion from these studies is that type A individuals hyper-respond physiologically to stressful stimuli (Krantz & Manuck, 1985). This field is maturing by relying on more precise definitions of type A, by examining personality components within type A that are associated with increased risk, and by focusing on patient groups that may be more vulnerable to type A's effect.

In summary, there has been a productive outpouring of research examining the physiological reactivity triggered by behavioral or emotional stimuli. This work is strongly focused on cardiovascular physiology and on peripheral hormonal levels. The work has also focused on defining the normal range of physiological response and is beginning to focus on the reactivity found in patients with various cardiovascular diseases. There is a paradox here. In order for reactivity to occur, a central nervous system must process information and orchestrate the responses, and yet the reactivity studies generally ignore the possibility that patients with psychiatric illness may have an altered reactivity profile. The rest of this paper will discuss the possible links between depression, reactivity, and cardiovascular disease.

DEPRESSIVE SYNDROMES

In the preceding pages, I have outlined the developing field of stress reactivity studies as applied to cardiovascular disease. In this section, I discuss the importance of considering stress reactivity in depressed patients. The logic in favor of this argument is that: (1) depression is a common disorder; (2) that depression is felt to be related to stressors; (3) that there is an increased prevalence of cardiovascular disorder amongst depressed patients; and (4) that the physiology of depression resembles physiological changes observed during reactivity studies.

1. Depression is the most common psychiatric disorder. When defined rigorously according to the current diagnostic standards, depression occurs in 10% of men and 20% of women over the course of their lifetime (American Psychiatric Association, 1980). The entire diagnostic nomenclature for depression has changed in recent years. Current (DSM-III) criteria require the existence of a disorder that persists for at least 2 weeks and profoundly affects mood, appetite, sleep, motor behavior, energy, self-worth, and sense of pleasure. Using these criteria, one distinguishes between *depression* and *distress*. In other words, this diagnostic approach recognizes that sadness is a part of life and that only

when that sadness persists in time and severity should it be considered as bona fide depression. What is excluded from this definition of depression is a sense of distress, chronic demoralization, morale loss, or subtle depression. Such non-specific psychological distress obviously affects an additional population of individuals.

I have lingered over this question of the diagnostic ambiguity of depression because most cardiovascular epidemiological studies use depression loosely in the broad sense of *depression plus demoralization,* whereas most psychiatric studies focus on depression as a discrete, demarcated psychiatric illness. Given that the boundaries of depression are hazy, one needs both an open mind and a measure of doubt about extending the domain of depression into broader and less well defined areas, such as social isolation, helplessness, vital exhaustion, sadness, or the tendency to experience life as a struggle.

2. Given the heterogeneity of depression, it is not surprising that there are many theories regarding its etiology. There is the usual schism between researchers proposing a strictly environmental or intrapsychic origin of depression versus those who espouse a strictly biologic origin of depression. However, increasingly, investigators have suggested that the development of depression may be a biological variant of the response to a stressful environment.

Breslau and Davis (1986) studied this complex question in a unique population. They compared approximately 300 mothers of chronically disabled children with an equivalent number of mothers of healthy children, reasoning that caring for a disabled child is profoundly stressful. The authors tracked the incidence of both depressive symptoms and full-fledged depressive epidsodes in both populations. They observed a complex set of findings. The mothers of disabled children complained of more depressive symptoms but were *not* more vulnerable to major depressive disease. However, the occurrence of depression in mothers of disabled children followed a different pattern. The depression appeared at an earlier age and recurred at a higher rate. There was no evidence that the symptomatology of depression differed across the two groups. Thus, according to these researchers, a situation of chronic, profound, persisting stress, such as caring for a severely disabled child, may not cause an increased rate of depressive illness. However, the stress may well affect both the onset and the course of the illness.

3. Over the years, many studies have suggested that depressive syndromes, demoralization, or emotional drain are related to cardiovascular illness. Unfortunately, the bulk of these studies have failed to use common tools for assessment of depression and have failed to consider how these variously defined depressive symptoms relate to depression.

Depressed patients have an increased risk for various forms of cardiovascular disease, including hypertension, myocardial infarction, and sudden death. The awareness of this relationship goes back to 1898 when Maurice Craig recorded blood pressure in depressed patients during their illness and after their recovery. He found that blood pressure elevations paralleled closely the clinical course of the depression (Craig, 1898). Others (Doust, Monroe, & Christie, 1980) have observed that blood pressure varied with mood in rapid cycling manic-depressive patients, increasing during the depressed phase of the patient's illness. In a recent study of older patients with depression, hypertension was diagnosed in 40% of the population (Tresch, Folstein, Ravins, & Hazzard, 1985). The evidence linking depression to hypertension is less strong when depressive symptoms as opposed to *depression* are studied (Friedman & Bennet, 1977; Monk, 1980).

This relationship between stress, depression, and cardiovascular disease is found in many cultures. In a study from Gothenburg, Sweden, Lindegard (1982) examined all of the general hospital and psychiatric hospital admissions for a 10-year interval. Admission for depression was associated significantly with the subsequent development of myocardial infarction. Investigators in the Netherlands have described an increased cardiovascular risk in subjects who resemble mildly depressed patients. Subjects with this syndrome have an increased rate of myocardial infarction in the ensuing 12 months (Appels, 1983).

The relation between depression and cardiovascular disease may extend beyond hypertension and myocardial infarction to include death from heart disease. Kaplan (1985) followed approximately 7000 individuals for 20 years to track variables associated with CHD mortality. Depressive symptoms and helplessness were significantly related to CHD mortality. After controlling for age, sex, and initial health status, helplessness persisted as independently related.

Lebovitz et al. (1967) made a similar observation in their prospective study of CHD mortality among 2000 men followed for 5 years. In the group of men who went on to develop CHD, significant elevations on the D scale of the MMPI were twice as common in those who died of their MI as compared to those who survived. This finding was essentially replicated by Bruhn et al. (1969) in their 7-year study of 47 MI survivors.

Paffenbarger et al. (1966) extracted data from a long-term (i.e., decades) follow-up study of 40,000 male college students. Diffuse symptoms of anxiety and depression, in general, and a sense of exhaustion, in particular, predicted a significantly higher rate of CHD deaths in the follow-up interval. In a subsequent study, the investigators found that the sense of exhaustion in undergraduates was the best univariate predictor of fatal, as opposed to nonfatal, CHD events (Thorne, Wing, & Paffenbarger, 1968).

Even sudden death may be related to this interplay between stress and depression. There is a 6-fold increase in sudden cardiac death in the first 6 months of bereavement following death of a spouse (Talbott, Kuller, Detre, & Perper, 1977). Many carefully designed studies of behavioral factors and sudden death find that the sudden death occurred in a setting of acute and unusual emotional arousal in roughly 20% of sudden death victims (Dimsdale & Ruberman, 1987).

For many years researchers in psychosomatic medicine have suggested a link between a subtle form of depression and myocardial infarction or sudden death (Bruhn, Chandler, & Wolf, 1969). Wolf (1969) characterized this depression as "joyless striving" or the "Sisyphus complex." Researchers in behavioral cardiology are considering this pattern anew and hypothesizing that a subtly depressed subset of type A individuals are at higher risk for subsequent development of cardiovascular illness (Dimsdale, 1985).

This postulated link between depressed mood and cardiovascular illness is far from established. An important criticism is that the subtle, depressed mood is not so much a formal affective disorder but a prodrome of the underlying cardiovascular disease. Considerable additional research is necessary before we will have a firm sense for the contours of this relationship. The major point, however, is that depressive syndromes and cardiovascular disorders are major sources of morbidity and mortality and MAY NOT be operating independently of each other. Consideration of the physiological response to emotional stressors and the physiology of depression itself reinforces the likelihood that depression may be related to cardiovascular disease.

PHYSIOLOGICAL ALTERATIONS OF DEPRESSION

In the preceding paragraphs I have argued for a linkage between depressed mood and cardiovascular disorders. The possibility of such a linkage is made more likely by the probable dysregulation of the noradrenergic neurotransmitter system in depressed patients (Siever & Davis, 1985). Numerous studies have reported increased plasma norepinephrine (NE) levels in depressed patients (Lake, Pickar, Ziegler, Lipper, Slater, & Murphy, 1982; Wyatt, Portnoy, Kupfer, Snyder, & Engelman, 1971); many studies also report elevations in plasma epinephrine levels, although this is less well established.

Recently, some investigators have scrutinized subpopulations of depressed patients to learn if particular subgroups have a noradrenergic dysregulation. There is some evidence that the NE elevation is particularly pronounced in patients with a current or previous bout of major depressive episode with melancholia. In this patient group NE levels were related to dexamethasone suppressability, such that nonsuppressors had higher NE levels (Roy, Pickar, Linnoila, & Potter, 1985). Patients with current or past melancholia have elevated NE levels at rest and while standing. Furthermore, the increase in NE provoked by standing (standing–rest) is greater than that found in normals or patients with other depressive disorders (Fig. 11.2). In a related study, Rudorfer, Ross, Linnoila, Sherer, & Potter (1985) found that, although the resting levels of NE were not elevated in depressed patients, the increase in NE in response to orthostatic challenge was significantly more pronounced in this group.

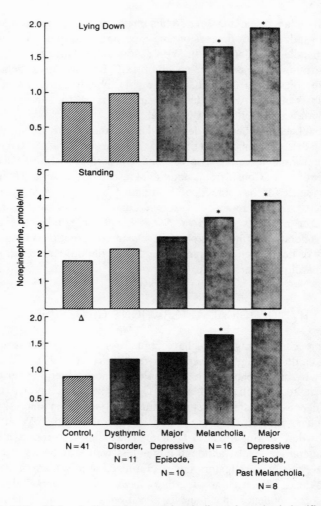

FIG. 11.2. Melancholic and past melancholic patients had significant elevations of plasma norepinephrine (NE) compared with control subjects in lying (F=7.03, P<.0001) and standing (F=7.40, p<.0001) positions and in change (delta) in plasma NE level from lying to standing (F=3.49, P<.01). Past melancholic patients also had significant NE elevations compared with dysthymic disorder patients in lying and standing positions (P<.05 for each comparison). Asterisks indicate groups with significant elevations on analysis of variance. Reprinted from Roy et al., 1985, *Archives of General Psychiatry*, Vol. 42, No. 12, 1181–1185.

Because of the complex physiology of NE, efforts have extended beyond measuring peripheral plasma levels. Norepinephrine spill-over from the synapse is elevated in about half of patients with primary depressive illness (Esler, Turbott, Schwarz, Leonard, Bobik, Skews, & Jackman, 1982). Some have suggested that depressed patients have supersensitive, presynaptic, alpha-2-adrenergic receptors and a resulting decrease in NE release; although others have failed to observe this finding (Kafka & Paul, 1986). Such studies have used radioligand binding to quantify the number and affinity of receptors both centrally and in the periphery. These approaches have also measured receptor function via agonist infusions. It is striking that these sorts of refined characterizations of noradrenergic functioning have, for the most part, not been used in behavioral cardiology studies.

There are many other physiological changes in depression. I have highlighted alterations in the sympathetic nervous system because of the clear involvement of sympathetic functioning in stress response and also because of the clear cardiovascular ramifications of alterations in sympathetic functioning. Just as alterations in sympathetic nervous system functioning have been reported in depressed patients, similar types of alterations have been suggested in cardiovascular disease patients.

CONCLUSION

Research in behavioral cardiology has focused on characterizing the individual's sympathetic nervous system functioning during static or resting conditions and during dynamic or stress conditions. Investigators are increasingly focusing on these dynamic measures of reactivity to stressors (Matthews et al., 1986). This approach has not been applied in recent studies of depressed patients. Indeed, most studies of sympathetic nervous system functioning in depressed patients explore the physiology of the patients at rest. Little is known about, for instance, the excursions of plasma catecholamines or even the blood pressure response of depressed patients when they are under stress. This is a remarkable area of ignorance given the probably elevated cardiovascular risk of depressed patients. It is also remarkable given that we already know that depressed patients have a subtly different sympathetic nervous system under basal circumstances and that depression may be viewed as a type of stress response. One hopes that psychiatry, psychology, and cardiology can join forces in explaining this important area.

ACKNOWLEDGMENT

This work was supported in part by grant HL-36005 from the NIH.

REFERENCES

American Psychiatric Association. (1980). *DSM-III,* American Psychiatric Association.

Appels, A. (1983). The year before myocardial infarction. In T. Dembroski (Ed.), *Biobehavioral bases of coronary heart disease* (pp. 18–38). Basel: Karger.

Breslau, N., & Davis, G. (1986). Chronic stress and major depression. *Archives of General Psychiatry, 43,* 309–314.

Bruhn, J., Chandler, B., & Wolf, S. (1969). A psychological study of survivors and nonsurvivors of myocardial infarction. *Psychosomatic Medicine, 31,* 8–19.

Craig, M. (1898). Blood pressure in the insane. *Lancet, 1,* 1742–1747.

Devereux, R., Pickering, T., Harshfield, G., Kleinert, H., Denby, L., Clark, L., Pregibon, D., Jason, M., Kleiner, B., Borer, J., & Laragh, J. (1983). Left ventricular hypertrophy in patients with hypertension: Importance of blood pressure response to regularly recurring stress. *Circulation, 68,* 470–476.

Dimsdale, J. (1985). Controversies regarding type A behavior and coronary heart disease. *Cardiology Clinics, 3*(2), 259–267.

Dimsdale, J., & Ruberman, W. (1987). Stress and cardiac arrhythmias/sudden cardiac death. *Circulation, 76,* (Supplement I), 198–201.

Dimsdale, J., Young, D., Strauss, W., & Moore, R. (1986). Do plasma norepinephrine levels reflect behavioral stress? *Psychosomatic Medicine, 48,*296.

Doust, J., Munro, A., & Christie, H. (1980). Vascular correlates of circular type manic-depressive disorder, *Biological Psychiatry, 15,* 741–748.

Esler, M., Turbott J., Schwarz, R., Leonard, P., Bobik, A., Skews, H., Jackman, G. (1982). The peripheral kinetics of norepinephrine in depressive illness. *Archives of General Psychiatry, 39,* 295–300.

Falkner, B., Kushner, H., Onesti, G., & Angelakos, E. (1981). Cardiovascular characteristics in adolescents who develop essential hypertension. *Hypertension, 3,* 521–527.

Friedman, M., & Bennet, P. L. (1977). Depression and hypertension, *Psychosomatic Medicine, 39,* 134–142.

Hollenberg, N., Williams, G., & Adams, D. (1981). Essential hypertension: Abnormal renal vascular and endocrine responses to a mild psychological stimulus. *Hypertension, 3,* 11–17.

Kafka, M., & Paul, S. (1986). Platelet alpha-2-adrenergic receptors in depression. *Archives of General Psychiatry, 43,* 91–95.

Kaplan, G. (1985). Psychosocial aspects of chronic illness: Direct and indirect associations with ischemic heart disease mortality. In R. Kaplan & M. Criqui (Eds.), *Behavioral epidemiology and disease prevention* (pp. 237–269). New York: Plenum.

Keys, A., Taylor, H., Blackburn, H., Brozek, J., Anderson, J., & Simmson, E. (1971). Mortality and coronary heart disease among men studied for 23 years, *Archives of Internal Med. 128,* 201–214.

Krantz, D., & Manuck, S., (1985). Measures of acute physiologic reactivity to behavioral stimuli: Assessment and critique, In A. Ostfeld & E. Eaker (Eds.), *Measuring psychosocial variables in epidemiologic studies of cardiovascular disease* (pp. 407–452). NIH publication, 85–2270.

Lake, C., Picker, D., Ziegler, M., Lipper, S., Slater, S., & Murphy, D. (1982). High plasma norepinephrine levels in patients with affective disorder. *American Journal of Psychiatry, 139,* 1315–1318.

Lebovits, B., Shekelle, R., Ostfeld, A., & Paul, O. (1967). Prospective and retrospective psychological studies of coronary heart disease. *Psychosomatic Medicine, 29,* 265–272.

Lindegard, B. (1982). Physical illness in severe depressives and psychiatric alcoholics in Gothenburg, Sweden. *Journal of Affective Disorders 4,* 383–393.

Matthews, K., Weiss, S., Detre, T., Dembroski, T., Falkner, B., Manuck, S., & Williams, R. (1986). *Handbook of stress reactivity and cardiovascular disease.* New York: Wiley.

Monk, M. (1980). Psychologic states and hypertension. *American Journal of Epidemiology, 112,* 200–208.

Paffenberger, R., Wolf, P., Notkin, J., & Thorne, N. (1966). Chronic disease in former college students. *American Journal of Epidemiology, 83,* 314–328.

Perloff, D., Sokolow, M., & Cowan, R. (1983). The prognostic value of ambulatory blood pressure. *Journal of the American Medical Association, 249,* 2792–2798.

Pickering, T., Harshfield, G., Kleinert, H., & Laragh, J. (1982). Ambulatory monitoring in the evaluation of blood pressure in patients with borderline hypertension and the role of the defense reflex. *Journal of Clinical and Experimental Hypertension, A4*(495), 675–693.

Roy, A., Pickar, D., Linnoila, M., & Potter, W. (1985). Plasma norepinephrine levels in affective disorders. *Archives of General Psychiatry, 42,* 1181–1185.

Rudorfer, M., Ross, R., Linnoila, M., Sherer, M., & Potter, W. (1985). Exaggerated orthostatic responsivity of plasma norepinephrine in depression. *Archives of General Psychiatry, 42,* 1186–1192.

Siever, L., & Davis, K. (1985). Overview: Toward a dysregulation hypothesis of depression. *American Journal of Psychiatry, 142,* 1017–1031.

Talbott, E., Kuller, L., Detre, K., & Perper, J. (1977). Biologic and psychosocial risk factors of sudden death from coronary disease in white women. *American Journal of Cardiology, 39,* 858–864.

Thorne, M., Wing, A., & Paffenbarger, R. (1968). Chronic diseases in former college students: VII. Early precursors of nonfatal coronary heart disease. *American Journal of Epidemiology, 87,* 520–529.

Tresch, D., Folstein, M., Ravins, P., & Hazzard, W. (1985). Prevalence and significance of cardiovascular disease and hypertension in elderly patients with dementia and depression. *Journal of the American Geratric Society, 33,* 530–537.

Wolf, S. (1969). Psychosocial forces in myocardial infarction and sudden death. *Circulation, 40* (suppl. IV), 74–83.

Wyatt, R., Portnoy, B., Kupfer, D., Snyder, F., & Engelman, K. (1971). Resting plasma catecholamine concentrations in patients with depression and anxiety. *Archives of General Psychiatry, 24,* 65–70.

12 Preventing Relapse Following Treatment for Depression: The Cognitive Pharmacotherapy Project

Steven D. Hollon
Vanderbilt University

Mark D. Evans
University of Minnesota

Robert J. DeRubeis
University of Pennsylvania

In this chapter, we examine the nature of the changes occurring as a consequence of cognitive therapy that may account for the prophylactic effect associated with that approach. In particular, three models of cognitive change during treatment are evaluated; deactivation, accomodation, and compensation, any or all of which may describe the process of change during cognitive therapy. Each of these models should be associated with different patterns of consequences and each should have different implications for the nature and stability of the changes produced. These three models are examined in light of the recently completed cognitive-pharmacotherapy (CPT) project, which found clear evidence of relapse prevention following treatment with cognitive therapy.

NATURE OF DEPRESSION

Clinical depression is one of the most prevalent of the major psychatric disorders. Epidemiological studies estimate that the disorder occurs in anywhere from 10% to 20% of all adults, with milder, nondiagnosable mood swings occurring in an even broader cross-section of the population (American Psychiatric Association, 1980). Depression can range in severity to include episodes severe enough to necessitate hospitalization and appears to be a major concommitant of suicidal ideation and behavior. Although good economic impact studies are still lacking, there can be little doubt that the disorder has a major impact in terms of undermining job performance and productivity (Miller, 1975), family and interpersonal relations (Coyne, 1976a, 1976b; Weissman & Paykel, 1974), and physical health (Avery & Winokur, 1976).

In the majority of instances, depression is a self-limiting disorder marked by an episodic course. This means that any given epidsode is likely to pass with time, even in the absence of intervention, but that subsequent episodes are likely to occur in the future (Zis & Goodwin, 1979). On the average, a moderate to severe episode of the type likely to necessitate some form of outpatient intervention can be expected to last about 3 to 6 months, with episodes reoccurring on the average of every 3 years (Beck, 1967). Although many patients evidence a full recovery and appear symptom-free between episodes, a significant minority evidence a more nearly chronic course, with continuing symptoms of dysphoria present on an ongoing basis (Akiskal, 1983; Akiskal, Rosenthal, Haykal, Lemmi, Rosenthal, & Scott-Strauss, 1980).

INTERVENTIONS FOR DEPRESSION

Major breakthroughs in intervention technology over the past 3 decades have greatly advanced our ability to intervene in the acute episode. A variety of pharmacological agents, the various antidepressant medications, have been clearly established as effective interventions, producing symptomatic relief in about 60–70% of the treated population (Klein & Davis, 1969; Morris & Beck, 1974). Electroconvulsive therapy has similarly proven effective, although its use is typically restricted to the most severely depressed, frequently psychotic, inpatients who have proven nonresponsive to antidepressant medications (Turek & Hanlon, 1977). Various psychosocial interventions, including cognitive therapy (Beck, Hollon, Young, Bedrosian, & Budenz, 1985; Blackburn, Bishop, Glen, Whalley, & Christie, 1981; Murphy, Simons, Wetzel, & Lustman, 1984; Rush, Beck, Kovacs, & Hollon, 1977), interpersonal therapy (Weissman, Prusoff, DiMascio, Neu, Goklaney, & Klerman, 1979), and various other approaches (Bellack, Hersen, & Himmelhoch, 1981; Fuchs, & Rehm, 1977; McLean & Hakstian, 1979; Roth, Bielski, Jones, Parker, & Osborn, 1982) have similarly proven effective. In general, the best of the psychosocial approaches also appear to generate a response rate of about 70%, with no clear contraindication, and perhaps some slight advatage accruing to the combination of drugs and psychotherapy (cf. Hollon & Beck, 1978; Klerman, 1986; Rounsaville, Klerman, & Weissman, 1981)

However, while proving at least comparable to the antidepressants in terms of average efficacy, the various psychosocial interventions are typically far more expensive to provide. A representative course of antidepressant therapy will typically involve weekly or bimonthly meetings with a physician averaging about 20 to 30 minutes in length over a 2-to-3-month period. A psychosocial intervention for depression will typically involve 15 to 20 hour long sessions over the same interval, a threefold increase in professional time and resultant expense. Clearly, a cost-benefit analysis, limited only to considering the acute epidsode, would appear to suggest that medications alone may be the treatment-of-choice, given their lower cost to produce the same general outcome.

Prophylaxis Following Treatment

Recent studies, however, have suggested a prophylactic effect for cognitive therapy relative to pharmacotherapy, given that both treatments are terminated shortly after symptomatic relief is achieved. Rush et al. (1977) reported differential relapse favoring cognitive therapy over imipramine pharmacotherapy through 6 months posttreatment. In a subsequent report, Kovacs, Rush, Beck, and Hollon (1981) found a continuation of this phenomenon, although differences were no longer statistically significant at 1 year posttreatment. Blackburn and colleagues have similarly reported a reduced relapse rate for patients treated with cognitive therapy relative to patients treated with pharmacotherapy (Blackburn, Eunson, & Bishop, in press). Thirty percent of the cognitively treated patients evidenced a full clinical relapse during the 1 year follow-up versus 70% for the pharmacologically treated patients. Simons, Murphy, Levine, Wetzel (1986) reported similar findings in a 1-year follow-up of the Murphy et al. (1984) sample. Although not conclusive, these findings suggest the presence of a prophylactic effect for the cognitive approach.

The Cognitive-pharmacotherapy (CPT) Project

Our own group has recently contrasted cognitive therapy, combined cognitive-pharmacotherapy, pharmacotherapy alone, and pharmacotherapy plus continued maintenance in the treatment of nonbipolar, nonpsychotic depressed outpatients (Hollon, DeRubeis, Evans, Tuason, Wiemer, & Garvey, 1986). Patients in the pharmacotherapy plus continued maintenance condition were kept on study medications (imipramine) for the first year of the 2-year period. The maintenance medication levels for each patient was not less than half of the maximum dosage received by that patient during the earlier 3 month acute treatment phase, generally between 125 and 300 mg per day. Patients in the remaining three conditions received no scheduled treatment during the 2 year follow-up. Differential relapse rates as a function of active treatment condition are presented in detail in Evans, Hollon, DeRubeis, Piasecki, Tuason, and Vye (1985). Relapse was defined as an exacerbation of depressive symptomatology as indexed by patient self-report. Protocol originally called for scores on the self-report Beck Depression Inventory (BDI: Beck, Ward, Mendelson, Mock, & Erbaugh, 1961) of 16 or above covering a 2 week interval, with a clinician rated 17-item Hamilton Rating Scale for Depression (HRD: Hamilton, 1960) of 14 or above at some point during that 2

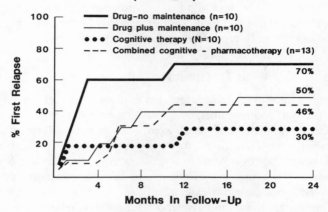

FIG. 12.1.   Time to first relapse/recurrence as a function of differential treatment: Liberal criteria.

week interval. While this protocol could be followed in many cases, a sizable minority of the patients in the follow-up were sufficiently noncompliant that a modification in protocol was required. Under a more liberal criterion, whenever a self-report BDI exceeded 16, the patient was designated a "relapse." Figure 12.1 presents a cumulative "time to first relapse" curve for the four treatment cells. Cumulative rates for each treatment cell are given as percentages of patients entering the follow-up phase. Sixteen patients completed treatment in each of the four treatment conditions. Four patients in each of the single modality cells and two of the patients in the combined treatment cell failed to respond to treatment during the acute treatment phase, leaving 12 patients in each single modality and 14 patients in the combined modality at risk for relapse during the follow-up period.

As can be seen, the cumulative relapse rate was much greater for the pharmacologically treated patients not continued on study medication after the 3 month acute treatment period. Seventy percent of these patients (7 of 10, with 2 lost to follow-up by virtue of noncompliance with ongoing assessments) had one or more relapses over the 2 year follow-up period, with six of the seven "first" relapses occurring during the first 6 months posttreatment. In contrast, the other three cells each evidenced a marked reduction in relapses; cognitive therapy at 30% of (3 of 10, with 2 patients lost to follow-up), combined cognitive-pharmacotherapy at 46% (6 of 13, with 1 patient lost to follow-up), and pharmacotherapy plus extended maintenance at 50% (5 of 10, with 2 patients lost to follow-up). Further, relapses in these other three cells, when they occurred, were more likely to be distributed later in the follow-up period (although few patients had a "first" relapse during the second year of the follow-up). Survivorship analyses, which take into account not only discrete events (e.g., relapse versus no relapse), but also time "survived" prior to relapse, indicated that the differences between the groups was significant, $X^2_{(1)} = 4.01$, $P < .05$, with the pharmacotherapy no maintenance group differing from the other three.

As shown in Fig. 12.2, this pattern was maintained even when a more conservative criterion for relapse was adopted. In that more conservative criterion, two consecutive BDI's of 16 or above over a 2 week period were required to designate a patient as having relapsed.

These data would be consistent with an interpretation that suggests that cognitive therapy, whether provided with or without medication during the acute treatment phase, appears to protect the patient against relapse following treatment termination. Continuing study medication also appears to be prophylactic, a finding consistent with a growing body of studies in the pharmacotherapy literature (e.g., Glen, Johnson, & Shepherd, 1984; Prien, Kupfer, Mansky, Small, Tuason, Voss, & Johnson, 1984). It might be argued, however, that the observed differences in relapse were the function not of any active prophylaxis provided by the psychosocial intervention or the continued medication, but rather the result of a malignant reaction to the withdrawal of medication in the no maintenance group. If that were the active mechanism operating, however, then we would have expected to see a comparable elevation in relapses for the combined cognitive-pharmacotherapy cell at the beginning of the follow-up phase or for the pharmacotherapy plus maintenance cell at the 1-year point in the follow-up phase when patients in these cells were withdrawn from medications. No such elevations were evident.

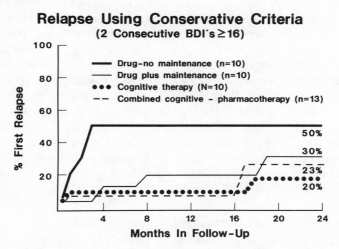

FIG. 12.2.   Time to first relapse/recurrence as a function of differential treatment: Conservative criteria.

Similarly, it might have been that unscheduled returns to treatment confounded the experimental comparisons, since a patient may well have suppressed the emergence of a clinical episode by seeking additional treatment before becoming depressed enought to trigger our relapse criterion. Several such unscheduled returns did occur in our uncontrolled follow-up. However, return to treatment rates were not differential across the four cells, with the greatest number (three) occurring in the same cell (drugs—no maintenance) that had the highest relapse rate.

IMPLICATIONS OF DIFFERENTIAL PROPHYLAXIS

Although the sample sizes involved are too small to draw definitive conclusions, it would appear that cognitive therapy may well have a prophylactic impact on subsequent episodes. The remainder of this paper focuses on speculations as to exactly what goes on in cognitive therapy that might provide such protection, assuming that such an effect is confirmed by subsequent research. Before turning to that topic, however, there are two additional (but related) points about the nature and timing of the relapses observed that merit comment.

Relapse versus Recurrence

First, as noted above, it is evident from Figs. 12.1 and 12.2 that the bulk of the relapses occurred early in the follow-up period. This suggests that the return of symptomaticity noted might be more accurately described as a relapse into the target episode rather than the recurrence of a wholly new episode. This distinction between *relapse* within an ongoing episode and *recurrence,* in which a new episode emerges following a symptom-free interval, has become important since the advent of symptomatic treatments for depression (Prien & Caffey, 1977). Prior to the advent of the antidepressant pharmacological agents (and, more recently, the psychosocial interventions), the typical episode of outpatient depression had an expected course of from 3 to 6 months, with an average of 3 years between episodes (Beck, 1967). If we were observing the advent of new episodes (recurrences), we would expect an increasing incidence in the later stages of year 2 of the follow-up, rather than a peaking of renewed symptomaticity early in year 1. Subsequent symptomatic episodes later during follow-up may well have represented recurrences (new episodes), but the initial episodes charted in Fig. 12.1 appear to have largely been symptomatic relapses into the original episode.

Pharmacotherapy as Symptomatic Treatment

This brings us to the second point, which is that if the above logic is accurate, it is quite likely that at least one of the treatments, tricyclic pharmacotherapy, is largely symptomatic in nature; that is, it suppresses symptomatology *without* directly influencing the most distal processes in the initial and/or maintaining causal chain. In other words, whatever mechanisms drive the episode of depression, they are not directly influenced by the antidepressant medications. Rather, those pharmacological agents must have their influence further along in the causal chain. Otherwise, there is no way to explain the reemergence of the index episodes (relapses). *The episodes must still have been going on in some very real way, in order to reassert themselves when treatment was terminated.*

The implications of the above statement (if, indeed, it is valid) are quite important. First, it suggests that clinical practice regarding pharmacological treatment needs to shift in the direction of maintaining active medications beyond the end of symptomaticity through the length of the *expected* episode. In all likelihood, pharmacotherapy should probably involve at least 12 months of medication from the time drugs are initiated. Such a strategy would approximate what was done in the medication plus maintenance condition of the CPT trial.

Second, if the depressive episode "lives on" during successful pharmacotherapy until it has run some natural course, then those basic causal mechanisms should be available for empirical scrutiny by identifying variables elevated in symptomatic depressives that have not normalized in the asymptomatic depressives still on medication.

A Research Design for Discerning Mechanisms of Change

It would appear that a productive research strategy for use in searching for the causally active mechanisms of depression would involve a four-cell design contrasting symptomatic depressives, asymptomatic depressives who have been treatment free and episode free for over a year, asymptomatic depressives who are still in pharmacotherapy and still within a limited period of time (i.e., 3 months) from the beginning of their current episode, and normal controls who have never been depressed, as shown in Table 12.1. Three logical classes of variables are presented; symptoms (and other state-dependent variables), causally active mechanisms (or their correlates), and stable traits (variables which might be causal in the larger sense of being predisposing variables, Brown & Harris, 1978, but which cannot account for the emergence of specific epidsodes). As depicted, only the currently depressed group should exhibit state-dependent symptoms, whereas all three groups of current and former depressives should exhibit abnormal values on the noncausal traits. Only two groups, those who are currently depressed and those who are asymptomatic as a result of treatment but are still within the expected period of their current episode, should exhibit elevations in the causal mechanisms or their correlates.

The advantage of this design over the traditional depressed versus nondepressed comparison is that it allows for a deconfounding of state-dependent symptoms, mechanisms (or their correlates) causally active in initiating or maintaining the given episode, and noncausal traits. Note that a traditional design, contrasting only currently symptomatic depressives with nondepressed controls

TABLE 12.1
Logical Status of Symptoms (States), Causally Active Mechanisms
(or Mechanism Correlates), and Stable Traits in Four Depressed
and Nondepressed Groups

	Currently Symptomatically Depressed		Successfully Treated Depressives Within Expected Period of Episode		Formerly Depressed Not Currently Within Expected Period of Episode or in Treatment		Non-Depressed
Symptoms (state variables)	abnormal	>	normal	=	normal	=	normal
Mechanisms (or mechanism correlates)	abnormal	=	abnormal	>	normal	=	normal
Stable Traits	abnormal	=	abnormal	=	abnormal	>	normal

would yield comparable differences between the groups across all the relevant variables. Likely candidates for further study as potential mechanisms in such designs would include those variables already shown not to normalize with the assumption of asymptomaticity, such as REM sleep abnormalities (Kupfer & Reynolds, 1983; Kupfer, Spiker, Coble, Neil, Ulrich, & Shaw, 1980), marital and other intimate interpersonal relationships (Weissman, Klerman, Prusoff, Sholomskas, & Padian, 1981; Weissman, Klerman, Paykel, Prusoff, & Hanson, 1974), cortisol regulation as indexed by dexamethasone suppression (Carroll et al., 1981), and attributional styles (DeRubeis, Evans, Hollon, & Tuason, 1986).

Finally, any treatment which provides a prophylactic effect after termination may help further highlight those mechanisms by virtue of normalizing their values before such normalization occurs in patients being successfully treated with drugs. That need not be the case, for reasons we return to in the following paragraph, but, if the intervention works by virtue of affecting basic causal mechanisms, then these processes should normalize in cognitive therapy before they normalize in pharmacotherapy.

It is possible that a treatment which has a prophylactic effect produces this effect not by directly affecting causal mechanisms, but by virtue of compensating for them by blocking the emergence of their symptomatic consequences. This possibility is discussed in greater detail in the subsequent section.

THREE MODELS OF CHANGE IN COGNITIVE THERAPY FOR DEPRESSION

A cognitive theory of depression holds that dysfunctional beliefs and maladaptive information processing contributes to the etiology and maintenance of depression (Beck, 1967, 1970). The model, as originally proposed, is actually a diathesis-stress model, in which the dysfunctional cognitive processes provide the diathesis, and various negative (and significant) life events provide the stress (Beck, 1984). According to this formulation, an individual with a predisposition to hold certain beliefs and/or process information in a depressotypic fashion is at particular risk for developing an episode of depression in the face of distressing life events.

A cognitive theory of change in the treatment of depression would hold that interventions which focus on changing those dysfunctional beliefs and maladaptive information processing heuristics should result in a concomitant reduction in symptomatic depression (Beck, 1970; Beck, Rush, Shaw, & Emery, 1979; Hollon & Beck, 1979). Attention has focused on several components of thinking: *automatic thoughts,* the relatively accessible thoughts and beliefs which can be reported by the individual; *underlying assumptions,* the relatively inaccessible attitudes and beliefs seen by Beck (1967, 1970) as underlying and unifying the individual's belief systems; *cognitive errors,* such as overgeneralization, magnification, and selective abstraction, among others, which may well correspond to the logical *heuristics* noted by Kahneman and Tversky to operate in normal populations (Kahneman, Slovic, & Tversky, 1982), and *schemata,* the integrated clusters of beliefs and processes which organize thinking, particularly in the absence of certainty (Markus, 1977; Neisser, 1967, 1976; Nisbett & Ross, 1980). Depressotypic schemata refer to both existing negative content and systematic biases in the selection and processing of novel content. When a depressive schema is operating, the individual has difficulty recalling positive life events (Clark & Teasdale, 1982) or more positive self-descriptions (Derry & Kuiper, 1981), generating benign attributions for negative events (Seligman, Abramson, Semmel, & Von Baeyer, 1979), generating positive expectations for coming events, or perceiving his or her own impact on the world (Garber & Hollon, 1980).

Although the precise role and operation of cognitive processes in the etiology and maintenance of depression remains controversial (Coyne & Gotlib, 1983), numerous authors have argued for the utility of the constructs (Goldfried & Robins, 1982, 1983; Hollon & Kriss, 1984; Turk & Salovey, 1985a, 1985b; Turk & Speers, 1983). The following discussion assumes some validity for the cognitive model.

Activation—Deactivation

Starting from that assumption, we can ask how cognitive therapy influences depressive schemata. At last three models can be identified, as presented in Table 12.2 and as articulated elsewhere (Ingram & Hollon, 1986). The first model, *activation–deactivation* refers to a situation in which cognitive therapy (and perhaps other therapies) exert their impact on depression by virtue of deactivating an operating depressive schema. Basic schema theory holds that any individual may possess a number of different schemata, only one or some of

TABLE 12.2
Models of Change in Cognitive Therapy for Depression

Model	Description
Activation-Deactivation:	Operative depressive schema is deactivated, with nondepressive schema activated. No change in causal mechanisms (schema) and no reduction in likelihood of recurrence (although possible decrements in likelihood of relapse).
Accommodation:	Operative depressive schema is modified in a profound way. Basic changes in causal mechanisms (schema) and reduced likelihood of relapse/recurrence.
Compensatory skills:	Operative depressive schema is left unchanged, but development of compensatory skills (script) compensates for or offsets pernicious influence of schema. No change in causal mechanisms (schema), but reduced likelihood of relapse/recurrence.

which are active at any given moment. For example, the senior author of this manuscript is both a clinical researcher and a parent. At work, his scientist/academician schema is generally operating, but, given the appropriate cues (e.g., a telephone call from home or a coworker's comment, etc.), he can readily begin thinking like a parent. The reverse happens at home, when the "parent" schema is dominant, but the academician schema can readily be triggered by an appropriate stimulus. It is logically possible that cognitive therapy works, when it works, by deactivating depressive schemata *but not altering their basic nature.*

The implication of this process would be that while treatment may be successful, the risk of recurrence should remain relatively unaffected. Relapse may be rendered less probable, if the diathesis-stress model is valid, since some new precipitating life event would need to occur to trigger the emergence of renewed symptomaticity.

Two sets of clinical observations, neither supported, as yet, by controlled studies, tend to support this activation–deactivation model. First, it is striking how similar the attitudes and beliefs are of individuals experiencing a subsequent episode to the attitudes and beliefs that they evidenced at the beginning of the original episode. This observation suggests that the same beliefs simply resurface, even though they may not have been evident when the patient was euthymic. Second, an examination of the individual response curves for the patients treated with cognitive therapy in the CPT project suggestes that, for many, that process was more nearly discontinuous than smooth. While the group response curve was negatively decelerated, the individual response curves were often discontinuous. Of the three models, activation–deactivation is the process most likely to be discontinuous, since it need not involve the gradual accumulation of learning processes.

Working against the activation–deactivation model is the already noted evidence of relapse prophylaxis. If no basic change in underlying structures was going on, why would a pattern be obtained in which pharmacotherapy termination, but not cognitive therapy termination, was followed by rapid relapse? Even though relapse would be rendered *less* probable by a deactivation process, there should be no difference in the *relative* likelihood of relapse between two or more interventions that both stimulated deactivation. It may, of course, be the case that the activation–deactivation model best describes the change process for some patients, but not all, within either modality. Clearly, detailed ideographic studies of the consistency of themes across episodes would be desirable.

Accommodation

The second major model, *accommodation,* is the process most often invoked by cognitive theorists to explain change in treatment (Beck, 1967, 1970; Evans & Hollon, in press; Hollon & Garber, in press; Hollon & Kriss, 1984). Accommodation refers to the process of change in the basic cognitive schemata, either content or process or both. One of the major findings of the last 2 decades is just how difficult accommodation is to achieve (Nisbett & Ross, 1980, Ross, 1977). It appears that the presence of existing beliefs tends to color the recognition of and search for new information (Snyder, 1981), and influences behaviors in the direction of producing outcomes consistent with those beliefs, the self-fulfilling prophecy phenomenon (Darley & Fazio, 1980). Nonetheless, it is apparent that cognitive change can and does occur, particularly in the face of empirical disconfirmation of existing beliefs, exposure to alternative conceptualizations, and insight into the processes followed to arrive at those judgments (Ross, 1977).

With regard to depression, those who adhere to an accommodation model would argue that basic change in depressive schemata does occur during various therapies (e.g., cognitive therapy). Evans and Hollon (in press) have suggested that the basic process of change may not be one of getting depressed patients to think like nondepressives. Rather, the process is seen as one of encouraging the client to utilize relatively atypical, deliberate information-processing strategies, as opposed to automatic processes, as defined in Schneider and Shiffrin's distinction (Schneider & Shiffrin, 1977; Shiffrin & Schneider, 1977). Thus, nonnormative strategies are used to shift the content of cognition in the direction of greater realism.

The optimal way to detect the presence of accommodation should be by contrasting interventions producing a prophylactic effect (e.g., cognitive therapy) versus those producing no such effect (e.g., pharmacotherapy). Within the context of a larger design such as presented in Table 12.1, accommodation should appear as greater differential change in the appropriate cognitive "causal mechanisms" for cognitively treated patients relative to pharmacologically treated patients. To date, no such studies have actually been executed, but the measurement technologies now exist to make such an effort feasible.

Compensatory Skills

The third and final model involves the development of *compensatory skills* which block or suppress the emergence of symptomaticity without affecting the underlying causal or maintaining mechanisms. Such compensatory skills might involve behavioral or cognitive self-management skills that do not affect basic inference generation but which do modify its consequences. The analogy here would be to a disorder like diabetes in which insulin self-management ameliorates many of the negative consequences of the disease without affecting its basic nature.

The operation of such a model would be detected by first establishing a differential relapse/recurrence phenomenon, then finding an absence of accommodation in the type of design just described, but the presence of certain acquired performance skills. Note further that the test for accommodation would suggest that recently treated patients with a reduced risk of relapse/recurrence should be more similar to the "never depressed" controls in terms of potential causal mechanisms. In the compensatory skills model, recently treated patients would still possess these depressive schemata, but they would be unlike those in any of the other groups in that they would possess and demonstrate the relevant compensatory behaviors. As for designs capable of detecting accommodation, we know of no current studies which have examined these processes. Perhaps the closest approximations have been Rippere's studies of coping strategies in normal populations (Rippere, 1977a, 1977b, 1977c). Measurement technologies for the assessment of acquired coping skills are not as well developed as for the detection of psychopathologic schemata. Work adapting Abelson's (1981) concept of *scripts*, knowledge structures guiding goal-directed action sequences, may prove of use in this regard. Clearly, work in the area of measurement technology development needs to be done before these hypotheses can be explored.

SUMMARY

The preceding comments have been largely speculative in nature. Nonetheless, they may facilitate the development of research strategies that can better answer important questions of etiology and maintenance in depression, with the ultimate goal of both refining treatment strategies and developing preventative programs. We began with the growing body of literature suggesting a differential prophylactic effect for cognitive therapy in the treatment of depression. Such a phenomenon would be important in its own right for pragmatic clinical purposes, but its theoretical implications could prove even more important. Basically, such a phenomenon, if replicated, may provide a means of identifying the key processes maintaining, if not causing, episodes of depression. Suggestions are given for novel research comparisons that may facilitate such identification.

Within the context of cognitive therapy, three models of change are presented and evaluated in light of this purported differential prophylactic effect. Activation–deactivation, which predicts symptomatic relief but no major change in underlying mechanisms, may hold for some patients, but cannot account for differential prophylaxis. Accommodation, the preferred explanatory mechanism for most cognitive intervention theorists, would predict both symptom relief and change in underlying mechanisms for therapies producing a prophylactic effect. Compensation, the third model, would predict symptom relief and specific skills acquisition, but no change in causal mechanisms for those same prophylactic therapies.

Ultimately, it is hoped that such speculations as the preceding can help both solidify our understanding of depression and of the change process. If so, we should be able to enhance the efficacy of our existing interventions and, perhaps, develop new prophylactic and preventative strategies as well. It has long been known that theoretically relevant treatment outcome work can enhance our understanding of the psychopathologies of interest. It may well prove that differential prophylaxis can play the same role.

ACKNOWLEDGMENT

Preparation of this chapter was supported, in part, by a grant from the National Institutes of Mental Health (RO1-MH33209) to the Department of Psychology, University of Minnesota, and the Department of Psychiatry at the St. Paul-Ramsey Medical Center, St. Paul, Minnesota. We would like to express our appreciation to Judy Garber for her comments on an earlier version of this chapter and to Bonnie Arant Ertelt and Barbara Ann Hendricks for their secretarial assistance in the preparation of this manuscript. Requests for reprints should be sent to Steven D. Hollon, Department of Psychology, Vanderbilt University, 134 Wesley Hall, Nashville, TN 37240.

REFERENCES

Abelson, R. P. (1981). Psychological status of the script concept. *American Psychologist, 36*, 715–729.

Akiskal, H.S. (1983). Dysthymic disorder: Psychopathology of proposed chronic depressive subtypes. *American Journal of Psychiatry, 140*, 11–20.

Akiskal, H. S., Rosenthal, T. L., Haykal, R. F., Lemmi, H., Rosenthal, R. H., & Scott-Strauss, A. (1980). Characteriological depressions: Clinical and sleep EEG findings separating 'subaffective dysthymias' from 'character spectrum disorders'. *Archives of General Psychiatry, 37,* 777–783.

American Psychiatric Association (1980). *Diagnostic and statistical manual of mental disorders* (3rd ed.). Washington, D.C.: American Psychiatric Association.

Avery, D., & Winokur, G. (1976). Mortality in depressed patients treated with electroconvulsive therapy. *Archives of General Psychiatry, 33,* 1029–1037.

Beck, A. T. (1967). *Depression: Clinical, experimental and theoretical aspects.* New York: Harper & Row.

Beck, A. T. (1970). Cognitive therapy: Nature and relation to behavior therapy. *Behavior Therapy, 1,* 184–200.

Beck, A. T. (1984). Cognition and therapy. *Archives of General Psychiatry, 41,* 1112–1114.

Beck, A. T., Hollon, S. D., Young, J., Bedrosian, R. C., & Budenz, D. (1985). Treatment of depression with cognitive therapy and amitriptyline. *Archives of General Psychiatry, 42,* 142–148.

Beck, A. T., Rush, A. J., Shaw, B. F., & Emery, G. (1979). *Cognitive therapy of depression: A treatment manual.* New York: Guilford Press.

Beck, A. T., Ward, C. H., Mendelson, M., Mock, J. E., & Erbaugh, J. K. (1961). An inventory for measuring depression. *Archives of General Psychiatry, 4,* 561–571.

Bellack, A. S., Hersen, M., & Himmelhoch, J. (1981). Social skills training compared with pharmacotherapy and psychotherapy in the treatment of unipolar depression. *American Journal of Psychiatry, 138,* 1562–1567.

Blackburn, I. M., Bishop, S., Glen, A. I. M., Whalley, L. J., & Christie, J. E. (1981). The efficacy of cognitive therapy in depression: A treatment trial using cognitive therapy and pharmacotherapy, each alone and in combination. *British Journal of Psychiatry, 139,* 181–189.

Blackburn, I. M., Eunson, K. M., & Bishop, S. (in press). A two-year naturalistic follow-up of depressed patients treated with cognitive therapy, pharmacotherapy and a combination of both. *British Journal of Psychiatry.*

Brown, G. W., & Harris, T. (1978). *Social origins of depression.* New York: The Free Press.

Carroll, B. J., Feinberg, M., Greden, J. F., Tarika, J., Albala, A. A., Hackett, R. F., James, N. McI., Kronfol, Z., Lohr, N., Steiner, M., de Vigne, J. P., & Young, E. (1981). A specific laboratory test for the diagnosis of melancholia. *Archives of General Psychiatry, 38,* 15–22.

Clark, D. M., & Teasdale, J. D. (1982). Diurnal variation in clinical depression and accessibility of memories of positive and negative experiences. *Journal of Abnormal Psychology, 91,* 87–95.

Coyne, J. C. (1976a). Depressions and the response of others. *Journal of Abnormal Psychology, 85,* 186–193.

Coyne, J. C. (1976b). Toward an interactional description of depression. *Psychiatry, 38,* 28–40.

Coyne, J. C., & Gotlib, I. H. (1983). The role of cognition in depression: A critical appraisal. *Psychological Bulletin, 94,* 472–505.

Darley, J. M., & Fazio, R. (1980). Expectancy confirmation processes arising in the social interaction sequence. *American Psychologist, 35,* 867–881.

Derry, P. A., & Kuiper, N. A. (1981). Schematic processing and self-reference in clinical depression. *Journal of Abnormal Psychology, 90,* 286–297.

DeRubeis, R. J., Evans, M. D., Hollon, S. D., & Tuason, V. B. (1986). *Components and mechanisms in cognitive therapy and pharmacotherapy for depression: III. Processes of change.* Unpublished manuscript, University of Minnesota and the St. Paul-Ramsey Medical Center, Minneapolis-St. Paul, Minnesota.

Evans, M. D., & Hollon, S. D. (in press). Patterns of personal and causal inference: Implications for a cognitive therapy of depression. In L. B. Alloy (Ed.), *Cognitive processes in depression.* New York: Guilford Press.

Evans, M. D., Hollon, S. D., DeRubeis, R. J., Piasecki, J., Tuason, V. B., & Vye, C. (1985). *Accounting for relapse in a treatment outline study of depression.* Paper presented at the annual meeting of te Association for the Advancement of Behaviar Therapy, Houston, TX.

Fuchs, C. Z., & Rehm, L. P. (1977). A self-control behavior therapy program for depression. *Journal of Consulting and Clinical Psychology, 45,* 206–215.

Garber, J., & Hollon, S. D. (1980). Universal versus personal helplessness in depression: Belief in uncontrollability or incompetence? *Journal of Abnormal Psychology, 89,* 56–66.

Glen, A. I. M., Johnson, A. L., & Shepherd, M. (1984). Continuation therapy with lithium and amitriptyline in unipolar depressive illness: A randomized, double-blind controlled trial. *Psychological Medicine, 14,* 37–50.

Goldfried, M. R., & Robins, C. (1982). On the facilitation of self-efficacy. *Cognitive Therapy and Research, 6,* 361–380.

Goldfried, M. R., & Robins, C. (1983). Self-schema, cognitive bias, and the processing of therapeutic experiences. In P. C. Kendall (Ed.), *Advances in cognitive-behavioral research and therapy* (Vol. II, pp. 33–80). New York: Academic Press.

Hamilton, M. (1960). A rating scale for depression. *Journal of Neurology, Neurosurgery, and Psychiatry, 23,* 56–62.

Hollon, S. D., & Beck, A. T. (1978). Psychotherapy and drug therapy: Comparison and combinations. In S. L. Garfield & A. E. Bergin (Eds.), *The handbook of psychotherapy and behavior change: An empirical analysis* (2nd ed. pp. 437–490). New York: Wiley.

Hollon, S. D., & Beck, A. T. (1979). Cognitive therapy of depression. In P. C. Kendall & S. D. Hollon (Eds.), *Cognitive-behavioral interventions: Theory, research, and procedures* (pp. 153–203). New York: Academic Press.

Hollon, S. D., DeRubeis, R. J., Evans, M. D., Tuason, V. B., Wiemer, M. J., & Garvey, M. J. (1986). *Cognitive therapy, pharmacotherapy and combined cognitive-pharmacotherapy, in the treatment of depression: I. Differential outcome.* Unpublished manuscript, University of Minnesota and the St. Paul-Ramsey Medical Center, Minneapolis-St. Paul, Minnesota.

Hollon, S. D., & Garber, J. (in press). Cognitive therapy: A social-cognitive perspective. In L. Y. Abramson (Ed.), *Social-personal inferences in clinical psychology.* New York: Guilford Press.

Hollon, S. D., & Kriss, M. R. (1984). Cognitive factors in clinical research and practice. *Clinical Psychology Review, 4,* 38–78.

Ingram, R. E., & Hollon, S. D. (1986). Cognitive therapy of depression from an information processing perspective. In R. E. Ingram (Ed.), *Information processing approaches to psychopathology and clinical psychology* (pp. 259–281). New York: Academic Press.

Kahneman, D., Slovic, P., & Tversky, A. (Eds.), (1982). *Judgment under uncertainty: Heuristics and biases.* Cambridge, England: Cambridge University Press.

Klein, D. F., & Davis, J. M. (1969). *Diagnosis and drug treatment of psychiatric disorders.* Baltimore, MD: Williams & Wilkins.

Klerman, G. L. (1986). Psychotherapy and drug therapy. In S. L. Garfield & A. E. Bergin (Eds.). *Handbook of psychotherapy and behavior change* (3rd Ed., pp. 777–818). New York: Wiley.

Kovacs, M., Rush, A. T., Beck, A. T., & Hollon, S. D. (1981). Depressed outpatients treated with cognitive therapy or pharmacotherapy: A one-year follow-up. *Archives of General Psychiatry, 38,* 33–39.

Kupfer, D. J., & Reynolds, C. F. (1983). Neurophysiological studies of depression: State of the art. In J. Angst (Ed.), *The origins of depression: Current concepts and approaches* (pp. 235–252). New York: Springer-Verlag.

Kupfer, D. J., Spiker, D. G., Coble, P. A., Neil, J. F., Ulrich, R., & Shaw, D. H. (1980). Depression, EEG sleep and clinical response. *Comprehensive Psychiatry, 21,* 212–220.

Markus, H. (1977). Self schemas and processing information about the self. *Journal of Personality and Social Psychology, 35,* 63–78.

McLean, P. D., & Hakstian, A. R. (1979). Clinical depression: Comparative efficacy of outpatient treatments. *Journal of Consulting and Clinical Psychology, 47,* 818–836.

Miller, W. R. (1975). Psychological deficit in depression. *Psychological Bulletin, 82,* 238–260.

Morris, J. B., & Beck, A. T. (1974). The efficacy of anti-depressant drugs: A review of research (1958–1972). *Archives of General Psychiatry, 30,* 667–674.

Murphy, G. E., Simons, A. D., Wetzel, R. D., & Lustman, P. J. (1984). Cognitive therapy and pharmacotherapy, singly and together in the treatment of depression. *Archives of General Psychiatry, 41*, 33–41

Neisser, U. (1967).*Cognitive psychology*. New York: Appleton-Century-Croft.

Neisser, U. (1976). *Cognition and reality: Principles and implications of cognitive psychology*. San Francisco: Freeman.

Nisbett, R. E., & Ross, L. (1980). *Human inference: Strategies and shortcomings of social judgment*. Englewood Cliffs, NJ: Prentice-Hall.

Prien, R. F., & Caffey, E. M. (1977). Long-term maintenance drug therapy in recurrent affective illness: Current status and issues. *Diseases of the Nervous System, 164*, 981–992.

Prien, R. F., Kupfer, D. J., Mansky, P. A., Small, J. G., Tuason, V. B., Voss, C. B., & Johnson, W. E. (1984). Drug therapy in the prevention of recurrences in unipolar and bipolar affective disorder. *Archives of General Psychiatry, 41*, 1096–1104.

Rippere, V. (1977a). Commonsense beliefs about depression and anti-depressive behavior: A study of social consensus. *Behavior Research and Therapy, 15*, 465–473.

Rippere, V. (1977b). Some cognitive dimensions of antidepressive behavior. *Behavior Research and Therapy, 15*, 57–63.

Rippere, V. (1977c). "What's the thing to do when you're feeling depressed?"—A pilot study. *Behavior Research and Therapy, 15*, 185–191.

Ross, L. (1977). The intuitive psychologist and his shortcomings. In L. Berkowitz (Ed.), *Advances in experimental social psychology* (Vol. 10, pp. 173–220). New York: Academic Press.

Roth, D., Bielski, R., Jones, M., Parker, W. G., & Osborn, G. (1982). A comparison of self-control therapy and combined self-control therapy and antidepressant medication in the treatment of depression. *Behavior Therapy, 13*, 133–144.

Rounsaville, B. J., Klerman, G. L., & Weissman, M. M. (1981). Do psychotherapy and pharmacotherapy for depression conflict? *Archives of General Psychiatry, 38*, 24–29.

Rush, A. J., Beck, A. T., Kovacs, M., & Hollon, S. D. (1977). Comparative efficacy of cognitive therapy in the treatment of depressed outpatients. *Cognitive Therapy and Research, 1*, 17–38.

Schneider, R. M. & Shiffrin, W. (1977). Controlled and automatic human information processing: 1. Detection, search, and attention. *Psychological Review, 84*, 1–66.

Seligman, M. E. P., Abramson, L. Y., Semmel, A., & Von Baeyer, C. (1979). Depressive attributional style. *Journal of Abnormal Psychology, 88*, 242–247.

Shiffrin, R. M., & Schneider, W. (1977). Controlled and automatic human information processing: II. Perceptual learning, automatic attending, and a general theory. *Psychological Review, 84*, 127–190.

Simons, A. D., Murphy, G. E., Levine, J. E., & Wetzel, R. D. (1986). Cognitive therapy and pharmacotherapy for depression: Sustained improvement over one year. *Archives of General Psychiatry, 43*, 43–49.

Snyder, M. (1981). Seek, and ye shall find: Testing hypotheses and theories about other people. In E. T. Higgins, C. P. Herman, & M. P. Zanna (Eds.). *Social cognition: The Ontario symposium* (Vol. 1, pp. 277–303). Hillsdale, NJ: Lawrence Erlbaum Associates.

Turek, I. S., & Hanlon, T. E. (1977). The effectiveness and safety of electroconvulsive therapy (ECT). *Journal of Nervous and Mental Disease, 164*, 419–431.

Turk, D. C., & Salovey, P. (1985a). Cognitive structures, cognitive processes, and cognitive-behavior modification: I. Client issues. *Cognitive Therapy and Research, 9*, 1–18.

Turk, D. C., & Salovey, P. (1985b). Cognitive structures, cognitive processes, and cognitive-behavior modification: II. Judgments and inferences of the clinician. *Cognitive Therapy and Research, 9*, 19–34.

Turk, D. C., & Speers, M. A. (1983). Cognitive schemata and cognitive processes in cognitive-behavioral interventions: Going beyond the information given. In P. C. Kendall (Ed.), *Advances in cognitive-behavioral research and therapy* (Vol. II, pp. 1–32). New York: Academic Press.

Weissman, M. M., & Klerman, G. L., Paykel, E. S., Prusoff, B., & Hanson, B. (1974). Treatment effects on the social adjustment of depressed patients. *Archives of General Psychiatry. 30,* 771–778.

Weissman, M. M., Klerman, G. L., Prusoff, B. A., Sholomskas, D., & Padian, N. (1981). Depressed outpatients: Results one year after treatment with drugs and/or interpersonal psychotherapy. *Archives of General Psychiatry, 38,* 51–55.

Weissman, M. M., & Paykel, E. S. (1974). *The depressed woman: A study of social relationships.* Chicago, IL: University of Chicago Press.

Weissman, M. M., Prusoff, B. A., DiMascio, A., Neu, C., Goklaney, M. & Klerman, G. L. (1979). The efficacy of drugs and psychotherapy in the treatment of acute depressive episodes. *American Journal of Psychiatry, 136,* 555–558.

Zis, A. P., & Goodwin, F. K. (1979). Major affective disorder as a recurrent illness: A critical review. *Archives of General Psychiatry, 36,* 835–839.

Author Index

Numbers in italics indicate pages with complete bibliographic information.

Subject Index

261